FOUR THERAPIES INTEGRATED

FOUR THERAPIES INTEGRATED
A Behavioral Analysis of Gestalt, T.A. and Ego Psychology

Arthur J. Frankel
University of Louisville

Prentice-Hall, Inc., Englewood Cliffs, New Jersey 07632

Library of Congress Cataloging in Publication Data

Frankel, Arthur J., (date)
    Four therapies integrated.

    Bibliography: p.
    Includes Index.
    1. Psychotherapy. I. Title. II. Title: 4 therapies
integrated. [DNLM: 1. Behavior therapy. 2. Psycho-
therapy. 3. Transactional analysis. 4. Ego. WM 425
F829f]
RC480.5.F69 1984   616.89'14   83-13875
ISBN 0-13-330464-7

Cover design: Ben Santora
Manufacturing buyer: John Hall

Printed in the United States of America

10 9 8 7 6 5 4 3 2 1

ISBN 0-13-330464-7

Prentice-Hall International, Inc., *London*
Prentice-Hall of Australia Pty. Limited, *Sydney*
Editora Prentice-Hall do Brasil, Ltda., *Rio de Janeiro*
Prentice-Hall Canada Inc., *Toronto*
Prentice-Hall of India Private Limited, *New Delhi*
Prentice-Hall of Japan, Inc., *Tokyo*
Prentice-Hall of Southeast Asia Pte. Ltd., *Singapore*
Whitehall Books Limited, *Wellington, New Zealand*

To **Shannon**

my daughter, whose coming first
inspired this book

and

To **Marilyn**

my wife, who supported my work
in many, many ways.

CONTENTS

PREFACE

This book was borne out of frustration, the frustration many clinicians feel in trying to help people in the midst of so many competing theories of human behavior. Because of life's unpredictable pathways, I ended up with intensive training in four of the major therapies of the twentieth century: Ego Psychology, Behavior Therapy, Transactional Analysis, and Gestalt—in that order. As I progressed through the practicing and teaching each of them, I successively came to believe that each represented THE TRUTH, and I tried to convert colleagues, students, and clients to my way of thinking with an almost missionary zeal. However, one thread of continuity followed me throughout this process: I had a strong foundation in the scientific method, and I always attempted to develop scientific rationales for what I was doing. This was not always easy, given that the art of treatment often outweighs its scientific bases.

I ultimately realized that not all of these apparently incompatible theories could be accurately describing what controls human behavior. Yet there seemed to be glimmerings of THE TRUTH in each of them. Through teaching and research, consulting, clinical work, and observing fellow practitioners, I saw that it is in the *practice* of therapy—what clinicians do, rather than what they think—that a common ground could be found.

Most professionals practice eclectically. While their clinical work is usually founded on one of the major psychological theories, they adopt intervention strategies from other therapies that seem reasonable and effective, and that generally fall within their basic belief systems. What is needed is an orderly method of viewing the techniques and procedures across therapies, and a more scientific way of assessing what makes sense to use. This, then, is the major purpose of the book.

What makes such a monumental task surmountable is that I have identified the major techniques and procedures of each therapy and emphasized their integration on a *practice* level, rather than trying to integrate the underlying theories. The theoretical foundations of each therapy have not been ignored—just de-emphasized in the context of integrating practice. In addition, I have developed what I consider to be a series of scientifically-based rationales for assessing the efficacy of different intervention strategies: a therapeutic Rosetta Stone, if you will. It is clearly not the only means for accomplishing this task; but it is, I believe, a significant contribution to developing models for the integration of treatment methodologies.

Although my graduate degrees are in Social Work and Psychology, this book is geared towards all professionals in the helping professions. The problem of how to choose and integrate techniques from a wide variety of therapeutic models is shared by many professionals and students, no matter what their professional label.

I wish to thank a number of people for their support in making this book possible. In the behavioral area, Martin Sundel, M.S.W., Ph.D., and Edwin J. Thomas, Ph.D. gave me professional support and encouragement over the years while the manuscript was in preparation. My wife, Marilyn L. Frankel, M.S.W., helped me particularly with the Gestalt chapters. William S. Warner, Ph.D., who died in 1979, formerly of the Gestalt Institute of Cleveland, modeled important aspects of Gestalt therapy as well. David A. Steere, Ph.D., helped to critique the descriptive chapter on Transactional Analysis and was also one of the people who trained me in TA. John W. Ray, Jr., M.S.S.W., A.C.S.W., gave me invaluable support in the descriptive Ego Psychology chapter; Professor Howard W. Borsuk, M.S.S.W., also helped critique that chapter, and both spent many long hours discussing Ego Psychology with me. Finally, I'd like to acknowledge the contribution of the reviewers—Ronald Rooney, Department of Social Work, the University of Wisconsin at Madison; Eleanor Tolson, School of Social Work, the University of Washington; and Lonnie Snowden, Department of Social Welfare, University of California at Berkeley—whose comments and suggestions proved to be most helpful during the final drafting of the manuscript.

Arthur J. Frankel

INTRODUCTION

The integration of clinical practice, or the combining of techniques and procedures from different theory bases, is the theme of this book. It is first an attempt to define in terms of measurable behavior the labels professionals use when they try to help people cope with problems. Once these labels from Behavior Therapy, Gestalt, TA, and Ego Psychology are behaviorally defined, I conduct a behavioral analysis of them, ultimately judging their efficacy in treatment. What I learned from this complex and sometimes impossible task was that each of the four major therapies contained a practice technology that could be reasonably compatible with the others, even when their respective theoretical foundations were not.

Before beginning on our integrative journey, a few issues need to be addressed. First, since I have Ph.D.s in both Social Work and Psychology, I am aware of the problem in using labels to describe what professionals do when they try to help people resolve problems. Social workers talk about *casework, social treatment,* or *clinical social work*; psychologists generally label the process *psychotherapy*. Other professionals use the term counseling. I will not address myself to the traditional issues generated by the differential use of these terms, important as they may be. Judging by the way I have seen professionals actually practice, I cannot often discriminate their degree as easily as the psychological theory base under which they were trained. Be that as it may, the theories of psychotherapy I discuss in this book are not owned by any profession and are used by all. The extent to which they are intrapsychic, interpsychic, or include broader environmental systems in their scope are also independent of professional labels. However, you may be able to identify how these issues are differentially emphasized in each therapy, based on the kind of training you received or are now receiving.

It is my intent to use the terms *therapist, psychotherapist, clinician,* and *practitioner* to mean everyone who professionally does therapeutic work with clients, regardless of their professional label, including social workers, psychologists, psychiatrists, and counselors. In addition, I will use the terms *therapy* and *psychotherapy* to define the process of what happens when a professional attempts to help another person change his or her own behavior, which always includes, as you will see from my analysis, the environment in which a problematic behavior occurs.

Finally, let us enter into this attempt to integrate the practice of psychotherapy with a sense of comradery. It is not my wish that you should always agree with my assumptions, hypotheses, or conclusions. Psychotherapy is barely past the stage of placebo and magic, so in an attempt to bring some order to the process we must recognize our essential infancy; to be too certain of our ideas is simply not founded in fact—only in bias. As certain as I appear to be sure of myself—and I want you to believe I am—my purpose is to stimulate you, to challenge you, into facing the problem of how to make sense of so many competing theories in the therapeutic marketplace. How do we choose which techniques and procedures spawned from these different approaches are the best for us and our clients? In the final analysis, it is what therapists do with clients and not so much what they think that ultimately binds them together as brothers and sisters. In that light, we can learn much from what practitioners do, regardless of their theoretical persuasions. The foundations I have developed here for attempting to integrate psychotherapy provide what I consider to be a good beginning for choosing effective techniques and procedures from apparently incompatible therapies.

This book is divided into three sections: a description of the four therapies under consideration; a behaviorial analysis of them; and a final integration chapter where I summarize and make conclusions. The first section will be useful for quickly reviewing those therapies with which you are familiar, and for learning the basic foundations of the therapies about which you know less. I have summarized the important philosophies, concepts, and intervention strategies for each of the therapies. It is important to have some understanding of the individual approaches so that the later analysis and integration will make sense.

I encountered two challenges in describing the therapies and the practices associated with them. First, it was of course very difficult to encompass the scope of such comprehensive psychological theories in four chapters. Yet, there is something to be said for synthesizing and reducing huge volumes of information into more palatable amounts. Each chapter is structured similarly to assist in the comparisons and contrasts that are made later in the book. In addition to general theory and treatment processes, the important therapeutic issues of motivation, assessment, resistance, transference, the role of the therapist, and termination criteria are covered in each chapter. I expect, though, that if you discover an interest in one or more of the therapies after reading these descriptive chapters, it will only whet your appetite for more. Therefore, all chapters in the first section end with a reference list to guide your further inquiries.

This first section is not meant to be an empirical analysis of the four therapies presented. That task has been attempted, and will continue to be attempted, by many others. Rather, it is a general summary of what has been written about these therapies. For those of you who have interest in the empirical foundations of the four therapies and would also like to look at comparative outcome studies, I have included some major research journals in each area at the end of their respective chapters.

The second challenge I faced was in describing the therapies as if each were a singular entity. The fact is that Gestalt, Transactional Analysis, and Ego Psychology are practiced in diverse ways. Even Behavior Therapy, which is often viewed as more systematic and replicable than most approaches, is laced with differences represented by polarities between the "pure" operant Skinnerians and the Cognitive Behavior Therapists. In the face of sometimes diverse treatment procedures and theoretical crosscurrents, I sought a common ground. There are therapists who generally think and practice according to the way each therapy is described here. However, a review of the literature, including the references cited at the end of the chapters, will give the reader a broader view of the different approaches within the same theory base.

The next section, the behavioral analyses, represents what I believe to be a significant contribution to understanding why each therapy works, to the extent that it does, and develops the rationales for integrating techniques and procedures from different therapies into your present or future practice. This analysis will be most helpful if you have some practice or theoretical foundation in the behavioral approach and at least one or more of the other three therapies. The descriptive first section of the book will be helpful in this regard.

Therapists without a firm foundation in at least the behavioral area will probably need to approach the behavioral analyses section slowly and with some care. This section is essentially an exercise in logic where behavioral principles are applied to describe treatment theory and practice in Gestalt, Transactional Analysis, and Ego Psychology. The process is inherently complex and without some background in the behavioral approach, you might have difficulty with unfamiliar nomenclature and concepts.

Mine is not the first attempt to integrate psychotherapy, although perhaps it is the most comprehensive attempt to do so with an emphasis on practice rather than theory. In any case, at the end of chapter 5, there is a reference list of books in which authors have dealt with the integration of psychological theories.

The final section, the integration, flows right out of the analysis, summarizing what was discussed. In addition, I make specific recommendations about what I believe to be the most effective techniques and procedures from each therapy. I make judgments about the strengths and weaknesses of Behavior Therapy, Gestalt, Transactional Analysis, and Ego Psychology, especially concerning their assessment and intervention strategies.

It is my hope this book will assist you in facing the challenge of integrating your clinical practice, using more systematic and scientifically based rationales. I wish you the same intellectual stimulation and excitement I have enjoyed.

Now let us proceed.

CHAPTER ONE
BEHAVIOR THERAPY
The Behavioral Approach

BASIC PHILOSOPHY

The generally accepted founder of Behavior Therapy as it is known today is B. F. Skinner. From its inception the behavioral approach has been controversial in traditional psychotherapeutic circles because of its insistence in following scientific methodology, and its philosophy of human behavior. The scientific method gives Behavior Therapy some credibility among scientists, but there have always been therapists who believe the practice of psychotherapy is more an art than a science. Indeed, they argue it is not possible to apply the psychology of rats and monkeys to humans. In addition, because of the research constraints, Behavior Therapy cannot be as serendipitous and spontaneous as some other therapies—it is a very structured approach to problem solving.

On the other hand, because of its adherence to the scientific method, therapeutic techniques are reported in relatively clear terms that can be better replicated by researchers and therapists alike. Behavior Therapy is critically concerned with how therapists behave. No matter from where a technique emanates, if it can be empirically demonstrated to be effective, then behaviorists must take it seriously. There is certainly some advantage for a therapy to systematically describe procedures, and in turn, for clients to receive specific instructions. Additionally, because the roots of the behavioral approach are in animal research, many of the techniques do not need a verbal clientele. This is of tremendous advantage when working with retarded citizens or the severely emotionally disturbed.

Where Behavior Therapy has been most controversial involves its belief systems. Some behaviorists maintain that humans are born essentially as empty blackboards on which the environment writes behavior patterns. Free will or determinism is a myth and not based on the reality of how we are conditioned. Our choices are determined by our conditioning history and not by a process of free will exercised at a given moment. This idea cuts at the very quick of hundreds of years of philosophy on human existence and does not sit well with a number of psychotherapists.

The behavioral approach has additionally been attacked as a controlling means to behavior change, disregarding personal freedom. It is seen by some as so powerful that its usage should be closely monitored. It *is* possible to control behavior, and by understanding the laws that control human behavior authorities of all kinds could then be in a better position to control people. However, it is not the knowledge or the theory that controls human behavior—it is people who try to oppress other people. If Behavior Therapy is used to support personal growth, it is no different from any other therapy. Indeed, if people can be taught how to keep themselves from being overly controlled, it would be a boon to the human race. It is absurd that we should curtail Behavior Therapy because a few abuse it, any more than we should cut off electricity because it is sometimes used to kill people. In fact, as we learn more about what controls human behavior, we will be in more powerful positions to help—and to hurt. The issue of whether the behavioral approach is good or evil has nothing to do with the theory. It has to do with the people who acquire the knowledge and what they do with it. For that reason, we need to be vigilant.

Regardless of the philosophical dialogues surrounding this approach to psychotherapy, it is the effectiveness of the techniques and procedures that has established Behavior Therapy as one of the major treatment methodologies. Whether you like or dislike it may be an important value judgment to make—but you cannot afford to ignore it.

THEORY

Defining Behavior

Behavior is defined in four ways: overt, verbal, covert, and physiological. Overt behavior we can see; verbal behavior we can hear; covert behavior includes thoughts, dreams, imagery, and feelings; and physiological behavior includes heart rate, blood pressure, and muscular contractions.

DEFINITIONS OF BEHAVIOR

Overt	Verbal	Covert	Physiological
behavior we can see	behavior we can hear	thoughts, dreams, imagery, feelings	heart rate, blood pressure, muscle tension, and so on
Overt and verbal are often lumped together and called overt behavior.		Covert and physiological are often lumped together and called covert behavior.	

In addition to describing behavior in the overt and covert domains, there is also a discrimination based on what controls a response. Behaviors that are elicited or whose occurrence is ultimately controlled by antecedent stimuli are called *respondent behavior*; behaviors that are ultimately under the control of what happens after the behavior occurs, its consequence, are called *operant behaviors*. This distinction is much more than just a semantic difference. As we shall see, an assessment suggesting a problem is under the control of antecedents or consequences will dictate the directions of therapy.

Respondent Behavior

Classical conditioning. Ivan Pavlov in the 1920s and B. F. Skinner in the 1940s laid the foundation of contemporary Behavior Therapy. One might view them as the paternal grandparents of the field. Pavlov demonstrated the Classical Conditioning phenomena where certain circumstances, called *unconditioned stimuli*, could elicit unconditioned behavior from animals and people. The behavior, called an *unconditioned response*, is apparently genetically determined—the behavior appears after an appropriate stimulus is presented without any prior learning experiences. Some of the more common responses or reflexes that follow Pavlov's S-R reflex phenomena are: air puff to eye—eye blink; hammer to knee (gently, please)—knee jerk; food near mouth—salivation; fire to hand—pain and hand jerks away.

Pavlov discovered that new stimuli could be paired with the original S-R pairing to produce a new S-R connection. For example:
An unconditioned stimulus elicits an unconditioned response

```
food              salivation
         elicits
  UCS ───────── UCR
```

By pairing a bell, the conditioned stimulus, concurrently with the presentation of food:

```
    UCS               UCR
    food ───────── salivation
     |
     |
    bell ───────── salivation
     CS                CR
```

you can produce a conditioned response which looks like, but surprisingly enough, is not exactly like the original one. In this case when you ring a bell the dog will start salivating without the presentation of food.

Similarly, if a dog barks loudly (UCS) and scares a child (a UCR startle response), a new pairing might develop where the sight of large dogs (CS) would elicit an anxiety response (CR). Diagrammed it would look like this:

```
      UCS               UCR
   dog bark ───────── startle response
      |
      |
 sight of dog ───────── anxiety
      CS                CR
```

Once the new CR is conditioned, a dog bark will automatically elicit anxiety. Notice that the new CR, anxiety, is not exactly the same as the original startle response, the UCR.

While all this might be interesting, you might wonder how Classical Conditioning became associated with therapy. The last example offers a clue. UCS-CS pairings such as the one above were seen as instrumental in the development of anxiety-related problems, including phobias.

Systematic desensitization.   In the 1950s Joseph Wolpe pioneered a behavioral treatment strategy for phobias and other anxiety-related disorders using the principles of Pavlovian Classical Conditioning. He, and other behaviorists after him, hypothesized that anxiety, and probably *all* feelings, for that matter, ultimately occur as physiological responses such as heart rate, blood pressure, and most important, muscle tension. True, when people are anxious they think about it. But I defy you to completely relax your muscles and tell me you feel anxious, or for that matter, scared, hurt, or angry. You may think about being anxious, but your body won't feel it unless you start tensing muscles somewhere. Using this hypothesis and the Laws of Classical Conditioning, an effective treatment for anxiety and phobias was developed called *systematic desensitization*. People who are anxious are taught to deeply relax their muscles while imagining fearful scenes. They are literally conditioned to respond to fear with relaxation, instead of muscle tension.

Systematic desensitization puts two parallel procedures together in order to "cure" a phobia. First, the client is taught deep muscle relaxation. This is not hypnosis. When we are anxious we rarely know all of the muscle groupings that are tensed. Usually we are aware of some major tension, but not the specific muscles. Over a period of three or four sessions, clients learn to identify *every* major muscle in their bodies and practice controlling tensing and relaxing. After a short period of consistent practice, clients not only command tight muscles to relax but also can go into a state of deep muscle relaxation whenever they wish.

Teaching relaxation can take a number of forms. Learning to control alpha waves, galvanic skin responses, and body temperature also lead to relaxation. These methods are popular but require instrumentation. Muscle-relaxation training requires only relatively simple instruction, a few therapeutic sessions, and practice. Remember, you cannot be anxious and relax at the same time. Since your anxiety-related muscle tension results from conditioning, you can recondition yourself to react with relaxation instead of muscle tension when a frightening stimulus is presented.

Concurrent with relaxation training, the therapist discusses scenes with the client where the phobic stimulus has been present. These scenes are made as graphic as possible. You can even use pictures or the actual phobic stimulus if available. But it is critical to put the scenes, no matter what kind they are, in *rank order*, starting with the least threatening scene and going to the most anxiety-producing scene. As a simple example, the scenes for a snake phobia could range from seeing a picture of a snake to holding a snake. Between twenty and fifty scenes are developed, depending on the complexity of the phobia.

When the relaxation training is completed and the phobic scenes are developed, clients put themselves into a state of deep muscle relaxation and the therapist begins describing the scenes, least anxiety producing first. If the client feels any tension developing, the scene presentation immediately stops until the client is completely relaxed again. This process continues until the last scene is presented, with the client still in a state of deep relaxation.

What is remarkable about systematic desensitization is how well it works. Simple phobias can usually be dealt with in between ten and twelve sessions. Others may take up to one or two years. But the procedure has been demonstrated to have an effect on many phobias. Learning how to relax on command has enormous therapeutic value, whether you are working on a phobia or not. Regardless of why people get anxious, if they can learn to relax in the face of adversity, not only will they feel better but they will probably problem solve better, too. Anxiety is such a pervasive therapeutic issue that you will find relaxation training associated with a wide variety of client problems, such as smoking, weight loss, alcoholism, insomnia, drugs, and sexual nonperformance.

There have been a number of other behavioral techniques developed using the Laws of Classical Conditioning besides systematic desensitization. These procedures may seem quite unrelated, such as Implosion Therapy and Flooding Techniques for phobias, or habituation for nervous tics, but they all have one important factor in common: they all are working to recondition *respondent behavior*, that which is ultimately controlled by its antecedent stimuli. Operant behavior, which is controlled by its consequences, is not amenable to respondent techniques alone. Nor do operant techniques work well on respondent behaviors. However, we shall see that it is often the case that there is a connection between the two. Therefore, it is frequently possible to use both respondent and operant procedures in tandem to help people achieve significant changes in their behavior.

Operant Behavior

Most behavior that we see and hear, and many feeling and thinking responses, are under the control of what happens after the behavior has occurred. It is the consequence to that behavior, what comes just after it, that will determine whether we will perform it again. The phenomenon is the simple logic of survival. Nature has a way of providing processes that help insure a species endures. An animal performs a behavior; if the consequence is functional, that behavior will likely be performed again.

Actually there are three basic consequences that can occur affecting the probability of a behavior's future occurrence. Your behavior may receive a consequence that tells you to perform it again, called a *reinforcer*. Conversely, you may receive a consequence that gives the message that the behavior should *not* be performed again. This consequence is called a *punisher*. The third major consequence is really nothing at all—literally. It is called *extinction* and is associated with the withdrawal and absence of any important stimulus consequence after a response.

These three consequence events are the basic building blocks of operant conditioning. While we will discuss many very complex procedures, they all will owe their lives to the Laws of Reinforcement, Punishment, and Extinction (*see* Figure 1-1).

Reinforcement. The technical definition of a *positive reinforcer* is that it is a stimulus consequence that increases the probability a response will occur again. It is a probability statement. If the consequence does indeed increase the chances that the behavior will occur, it is defined as a reinforcer. We only know what to label a stimulus consequence after we have seen it in action over a period of time. If over time the probability of the behavior occurring does not increase, then that consequence cannot be called a reinforcer no matter how much you might think it should be one. Praise or M & M's for one person may be poison for another.

Primary reinforcers are necessary for life, so we are willing to work hard to receive them: air, water, food, nurturing, attention, and novel events (curiosity). We learn to work for secondary reinforcers by their early association with the primary ones. Those include material goods, money, particular kinds of attention, prestige, and power. Nobody is born with the wish to earn money. We learn to work for it initially because it gets us candy and toys. Primary reinforcers such as nurturing and attention get associated with secondary consequences such as praise and facial expressions, which then perform as reinforcers for the rest of our lives.

The phenomenon is even more subtle when you see positive reinforcers in action. For example, there are children who are constantly getting into trouble, getting yelled at or spanked. Even with all this "punishment" day after day for years, they are still "naughty." Why? In the simplest analysis, they are working for reinforcers, what most parents call *punishment*. We are rarely "punishing" our children if we consistenly spank or yell at them. These consequences are usually reinforcing the very behavior we would wish to eradicate. The key to assessing whether a consequence is a reinforcer or a punisher lies in the pattern of the contingencies. If a consequence is consistently delivered, a spanking, for example, and the probability of the prior behavior does not decrease, then it is likely a reinforcer. No matter that the child cries or promises to do better. By definition, the spanking is a positive reinforcer.

Seem strange? Let's look at an example: Jimmy, age six, is referred for therapy for serious acting out and oppositional behavior. Jimmy likes attention. It's really more than a "like." As a baby he had to have attention to survive. He gets attention from his mother and father, but some of it seems more intense than others. Positive attention feels good. He has learned that he gets it for some behavior and not for

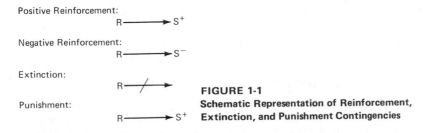

FIGURE 1-1
Schematic Representation of Reinforcement,
Extinction, and Punishment Contingencies

others. Sometimes his parents get angry and yell at him. It doesn't feel as good as positive attention, but this *negative attention* is intense, often more intense than positive attention. Both kinds of attention have value to Jimmy. Perhaps Mom and Dad are busy elsewhere, or as is true in many homes, they just don't give sufficient praise and warmth. Jimmy learns that he can perform certain behaviors that get attention; some get praise and some get anger. If he can't get praise frequently enough, anger will suffice as a viable alternative. It may be negative attention but it's better than no attention at all. Jimmy is not "sick" or "abnormal." He simply has learned how to get attention when he feels lonely, as all children do. All of us have learned to work for some negative attention. But based on our parenting, some of us work for it more often than others. If nobody teaches a child how to effectively get positive attention, nature will take its course, which is to turn negative attention into a potent positive reinforcer.

There is another phenomenon that makes negative attention even more powerful. Jimmy has feelings like the rest of us. He gets particularly angry when he doesn't get his way, which is often, as is the case with most children. Now little Jimmy doesn't know how to constructively ventilate his anger, negotiate, and compromise. Many adults don't know how to do this either. Sometimes he cries, yells, and screams. Unfortunately, this tactic rarely works. But Jimmy does learn a functional way to "get back" or effectively ventilate his anger at his parents. He notices that when they are angry at him they also get frustrated and don't seem to be enjoying themselves.

This experience with his parents leads to a very common contingency in families: a "goat getting" pattern where children learn to effectively get their parents' goats when they are angry. The negative attention that is part of getting an adult's goat is certainly not pleasant, but the "goat" becomes a functional reinforcing consequence for a child. Some children are experts at this dynamic. Thankfully, as they get older they learn to more constructively channel their anger into problem solving. But many adults have never forgotten the childhood skill, and perhaps the secret pleasure, of getting someone's goat in lieu of directly communicating anger.

Thus Jimmy's parents, who have been trying their best to punish his acting-out behavior, have actually been efficiently reinforcing the very behaviors that brought Jimmy to therapy in the first place. They have as a family developed the two major contingencies to turn negative attention into potent reinforcers: first, a consistent deficit of positive attention; second, anger, with no sufficient vehicle to communicate and resolve it. Both of these contingencies may be unwittingly developed and are probably pervasive.

The concept of reinforcement is used not only to assess what is maintaining a particular behavior pattern, as with the case of Jimmy, but just as importantly to teach new skills and more appropriate means of coping. There are a number of principles that are important in the reinforcement of new behaviors.

PRINCIPLES AFFECTING REINFORCER EFFECTIVENESS

1. *You must have a viable reinforcer.* This is not as simple as it may sound and in fact is often the greatest challenge to a behavior therapist. The first rule of thumb is to try to find a reinforcer that is already in the client's environment.

While praise is usually a good reinforcer to use, it is all too often just not effective, especially in the beginning stages of treatment. If an existing reinforcer cannot be found, then the therapist will try to develop an "artificial" one that is not normally part of the client's life. For example, M & M's, the stereotypic reinforcer widely associated with behavior therapy, are not normally used in families, schools, or work settings to systematically reinforce behavior. If another more natural reinforcer cannot be found, such as praise, then we could bring in the M & M'S as a functional stimulus consequence, assuming it worked, of course. By doing this we are taking certain risks. While the M & M's may do an effective job in reinforcing the desired new behaviors, we must face the reality that life just does not present M & M's for performance. Therefore, after the new behaviors have been learned a plan must be devised to transfer control of the behavior to more natural environmental reinforcers. The ultimate success of any treatment strategy using artificial reinforcers depends in part on the therapist's ability to help clients do this.

2.   *Reinforcers must be delivered immediately after a new behavior to be the most effective.* The longer you wait to deliver a viable reinforcer the less impact it will have. This is especially true with children but also holds for adults too. Many people have learned to "delay gratification." But in general, new behaviors need immediate reinforcing feedback to be efficiently learned.

3.   *The bigger the reinforcer the more effective it will be.* This is really a rule of thumb since it is often difficult to measure the size of a reinforcer. But in general, hearty praise works better than grudging acceptance and a dollar works better than ten cents.

4.   *Too much of a reinforcer will result in a loss of its effectiveness.* This process is called *satiation*. It is simply the result of too much of a good thing.

5.   *In order for behavior to be learned, it is most effective to present a reinforcer after every response.* But for a behavior to be maintained after it is learned, it is most effective for the reinforcer to be delivered infrequently. This very interesting phenomenon is called *schedules of reinforcement* and will be discussed later in the chapter.

6.   *In order for any reinforcer to work, the person must be in a state of deprivation for it.* This is the behavioral definition of *motivation*.

As you can see, reinforcing a behavior is more complicated than might be assumed at first glance. And to complicate life even further, the therapist and client must be perfectly clear about what behavior they are trying to reinforce. Much of the early training in behavior therapy concentrates on a therapist's ability to help clients clearly specify behavior.

There is one more important reinforcement contingency that is most often confused by clients and therapists alike, and that is negative reinforcement. Negative reinforcement is not the same as punishment. It is a stimulus consequence that increases the probability a response will occur in the future, just like a positive reinforcer. But the big difference is that a negative reinforcer reinforces a response by the withdrawal of a stimulus (*see* Figure 1-1). For example, threats are the most common example of negative reinforcers at work. If parents wish to increase the chances that their adolescent does the dishes, they can use two basic reinforcement strategies: first, they can offer praise or maybe the car for a job well done; or second, they can threaten to ground the kid if the dishes aren't done. The first case is a positive reinforcement contingency—the adolescent would supposedly be motivated to work for either the car or praise. The second case is a negative reinforcement contingency—he or she will be motivated to work to avoid an aversive consequence. The performance of the response will result in the withdrawal of the possibility of grounding.

In reality, much behavior is maintained by both positive and negative reinforcement contingencies working in concert with each other. It is true that students attend class to satisfy their curiosity and thirst for knowledge—positive reinforcement. It is also true students attend class to keep from flunking—a negative reinforcement contingency. In the same vein, many drivers keep to the speed limit to avoid getting a ticket. This is evidenced by the dramatic slowdown on the highway when a state

work for either the car or praise. The second case is a negative reinforcement contingency—he or she will be motivated to work to avoid an aversive consequence. The performance of the response will result in the withdrawal of the possibility of grounding.

In reality, much behavior is maintained by both positive and negative reinforcement contingencies working in concert with each other. It is true that students attend class to satisfy their curiosity and thirst for knowledge—positive reinforcement. It is also true students attend class to keep from flunking—a negative reinforcement contingency. In the same vein, many drivers keep to the speed limit to avoid getting a ticket. This is evidenced by the dramatic slowdown on the highway when a state trooper comes into view. And as we shall see later, negative reinforcement contingencies are very important when it comes to dealing with feelings. People will work very hard to avoid feeling anxiety—therefore, those behaviors that tend to remove anxiety, the withdrawal of an aversive stimulus, will be strongly negatively reinforced by the decrease in anxiety.

Motivation. Of all the factors that affect how effective a reinforcer will be, the most critical of these is *motivation*. Traditionally it has been assumed that some internal personality characteristic lies behind motivation, even a dark and sometimes sinister force, such as the aggressive or sexual drives in the Freudian Id. In the behavioral approach, motivation is a relatively simple yet powerful idea. Motivation is defined by a person's *state of deprivation*. If you are deprived of an important reinforcer, you will be motivated to work for it, as a hungry person will work to get food. Although this definition of motivation may seem simplistic at first, it does describe the phenomenon as it is presently used in our experience. For instance, a child's teacher tells her parents that she is just not appropriately motivated. We observe through a one-way mirror the child doing arithmetic, and sure enough, she daydreams, dawdles, and talks with her neighbors. From a behavioral point of view, this means that there is no reinforcer in her environment for which she is willing to work by doing arithmetic. Doing arithmetic doesn't get her anything meaningful. But she *is* getting reinforced for daydreaming, by teacher attention and avoidance of math. Therefore, she is motivated to daydream.

Unbeknown to her parents, I contract with the child to give her ten dollars if tomorrow she'll do her arithmetic. The next day we watch again, and behold, she appears "motivated." The secret? Obvious! Suddenly she can see that there is something in it for her if she does arithmetic. So she "motivates" herself.

Our schoolgirl is not an unusual person. *Nobody* works unless the consequence is worth achieving. Many of us go through school doing math, science, or English hating every minute of it, yet we do it because a consequence becomes important to us—good grades, praise from parents, or because if we don't do it, we get privileges withdrawn. Some parents even give money for school work. So if a child is not motivated for doing math, we need to make him or her an offer he can't refuse.

One tactic in getting a child started would be to set up an artificial reinforcement system. This means that we offer children a consequence that the normal school and home environment doesn't usually provide for doing math, such as money, food, or special privileges. We expect—perhaps hope is better—that something in the home and school environment will naturally take over motivating her arithmetic, such as praise, or the intrinsic value of learning math. Most of the time, artificial reinforcement systems such as money or food need to be of short-term duration or we end up with more trouble than we started with. However, for many of us, there was never anything intrinsically valuable about math, science, or English, and the only way we plodded through was to avoid flunking and the wrath of our parents, two very normal negative reinforcers for school behavior. The moral to this story is that in any situation you can assume we will not perform a behavior unless there is something in it for us—either to achieve or to avoid something.

It is the principle of deprivation that makes the concept of motivation so intriguing. It would be nice if everything we wanted to learn or should learn provided consequences that were intrinsically reinforcing. Such is not the case. States of deprivation define what reinforcers will be effective, and nothing is learned unless it is reinforced. Therefore, if there is a skill that must be mastered, be it academic, physical, social, or emotional, then we must first assess our present states of deprivation and offer ourselves the most appropriate reinforcer so that there will be motivation to perform.

When motivation is put in this context, it becomes possible in every situation to understand why people are not motivated to achieve the goals they or others set for them. It becomes a non sequitur to suggest that people should want to do something or that there is something wrong with them because of nonperformance. Rather let us discuss how there are apparently no functional reinforcers in the present environment for which they are in a state of deprivation. And further, if there is still a desire on their part to change their behavior, let us discuss what reinforcers could be implemented that would work, rather than what should work.

Additionally, analyzing motivation in these terms allows a behavior therapist to motivate those clients who are not usually amenable to what is called the *verbal therapies*, those that require verbal skills. As long as the context for motivation is an interaction between a person's deprivation states and what reinforcers can be made available in the environment, then nonverbal clients such as seriously retarded and autistic people, and psychotic or seriously withdrawn clients can be motivated to learn new behaviors.

Extinction and differential reinforcement.   The second major consequence that controls human behavior is really not a direct consequence at all. It is the lack of a functional consequence and is called *extinction*. The extinction phenomenon is a fascinating example of how nature takes care of animals in order that they may survive.

Remember that the ultimate reason operant behaviors occur is that they are reinforced. If a reinforcing consequence is withdrawn from a behavior, a series of predictable events will ensue. First, the behavior under extinction will increase in frequency and strength, and you will usually see more emotional responses as well, such as depression, crying, or anger. Then, if the reinforcer still hasn't returned, the behavior will decrease to whatever level is normal for that person, called *operant level behavior*.

An example is in order. Nancy, a ten-year-old, has been referred to a therapist for throwing temper tantrums. Her behavior, though obnoxious, was minimally tolerable up to this point, but now that she is ten years old, her parents say enough is enough. They have a sense of what has been reinforcing Nancy's tantrums, as do most parents. They get very frustrated with her and sometimes punish her with a lot of negative attention, otherwise known as positive reinforcement. For her part, Nancy is probably using her tantrums to get her parents' goats when she is angry. Over the years she has become a childhood expert at goat getting.

Having a sense of all this, Nancy's parents decide that they are going to try to ignore her when she throws a tantrum; in other words, withdraw their reinforcers for the tantrum behavior. Ignoring is a standard extinction technique. They begin. However, Nancy is an old hand at this. She is number two, so she tries harder. When she realizes their goats are being kept hidden, so to speak, she goes about trying to find them. Her tantrums get worse, longer, louder, all over the house, and even outside. She embarrasses her parents in public. Even though they have gritted their teeth, they eventually give in and let Nancy have it—more severe punishment and spanking than she has ever known. Her parents have unwittingly made the tantrums worse by giving in. She received her much sought after negative attention only after being worse than usual, and she learned to throw tantrums for a longer time before she finally got reinforced.

Nancy's experience demonstrates the initial extinction effect. The behavior under extinction initially increases in strength and frequency. This can be an important survival phenomenon. If an animal's food supply disappears, it will work much harder, look in new places, and try new food-gathering tactics in order to retrieve this important reinforcer. Food-gathering behavior would increase along with a lot of emotional behavior that would add impetus to the search.

In order for an ignoring procedure to decrease a behavior to operant or normal levels, two things must happen: first, the family, school, work, or even societal system must be able to tolerate a possible increase in the very behavior it is trying to get rid of. Second, it must be able to consistently withhold the reinforcers over a long period of time. If both of these conditions cannot be met, an ignoring technique should not be instituted. It would be absurd, for instance, to ignore suicide attempts just because we know they are attention getting. If we did, suicide attempts would likely decrease considerably! On the other hand, you would be surprised how many behaviors can be sucessfully ignored, even fighting and severe tantrums.

If ignoring cannot be realistically done, then there are two other major options: first, if you can't move the mountain from Mohammed, you can often move Mohammed from the mountain. When there are too many reinforcers for a behavior, it is often not possible to remove them all, such as in a classroom. If Mohammed were acting out there, he should be neutrally removed by someone who can remain calm, contingent on when he misbehaved. This procedure is called *time out from reinforcement*. It works if it can be consistently used, *and* if the time-out periods are of rather short duration, such as fifteen to thirty minutes. If you remove a child or an adult from a situation for long periods, you are probably not helping him or her learn to decrease their problem behavior. You are getting the person out of your hair, which may be very reinforcing for you. As in the ignoring procedure, the behavior under extinction in time-out will probably initially increase and a person may need to be "timed out" frequently. Again, if a family, school, work, or societal system can't effectively follow the necessary steps in a time-out procedure, then there is one more major option: differential reinforcement.

When our behavior does change, as it often does throughout life, the procedure supporting this normal process is probably differential reinforcement. You reinforce one behavior while extinguishing another. For instance, if someone is continuously interrupting during dinner table conservation, you could give him or her attention after a few minutes of silence, respond only when conversation was initiated at a desirable time, and ignore interruptions. In this way you would be reinforcing behaviors which are actually incompatible with the one you wanted to extinguish. A person can't interrupt when he or she is silent or initiating appropriate conversation. In essence, people learn a new behavior while they "unlearn" another. Additionally, they get an important consequence for the new behavior concurrent with the removal of the reinforcer for the behavior under extinction. Most of us find it easier to change old behaviors if we have a viable alternative at hand, and if we experience that an important reinforcing consequence will be delivered for the new behavior.

Another differential reinforcement option is called a *DRO contingency*, differential reinforcement of other behavior, which is also a normal way old behaviors are replaced with new ones. In this contingency people are told—either directly or indirectly—that they will be reinforced only when a behavior is not performed. For example, a couple who are having too many fights might make a deal to have a "snuggle time" if they didn't fight for twenty-four hours. It is not clearly specified what they should do instead, but they know what they shouldn't do. There are many real-life situations where it is clear what we shouldn't do, but no one tells us exactly what is expected. In those cases we often figure out what are our best alternatives and replace the old behavior patterns with no further instruction.

What is essential to remember about extinction is that in order for any behavior to stop, the reinforcer for that behavior will have to be somehow removed. Excepting the punishment phenomenon which will be discussed next, no behavior will decrease over time unless the reinforcer for it is withdrawn. How that reinforcer removal occurs is a challenge. Whether the reinforcer is actually removed from the environment or the person now refuses to accept it when offered is an open question. People can impact on both their external and internal consequences. But the phenomenon remains. Behavior will occur only if it is reinforced. A behavior will not decrease over time unless the reinforcer for that behavior is removed.

Punishment. There is one exception to the phenomenon that a behavior must lose its reinforcer before it decreases, and it is not a pleasant exception. It is called *punishment*. It *is* possible to stop a behavior through the use of a punishing consequence. Possible, but not always easy. The definition of a *punisher* is completely functional. If a consequence decreases the probability that a behavior will occur again, it is a punisher. Like reinforcement, the only way you can know if a consequence is indeed a punisher is to watch the behavior in the future. If the probability of the behavior decreases you can call the consequence a punisher. If a behavior does not decrease, but is maintained or even increases, then your punisher is really a reinforcer. As we have seen, most forms of negative attention which people call punishment are really acting as positive reinforcers. Just because a consequence is unpleasant or painful does not mean that it is a punishment.

Yet, a behavior can be permanently stopped with just one real punisher. Fortunately, few of us are willing to do what is necessary to effectively punish a person. In order for a punishing consequence to work, there are a few guidelines to follow.

1. *It should be a strong and very unpleasant experience, usually painful.* A person who sticks a finger in a light socket will never do that again. Most people aren't willing to deliver the kind of pain that would make for effective punishment—thank goodness.

2. *A punishment should not be delivered often in order for it to be effective.* In general, the more the punishing consequence is delivered, the less effect it will have. The more parents yell at or spank their children, the less effective the yelling and spanking will be as a punisher.

3. *In order for a punishment to be effective it needs to be used not only sparingly but also immediately after the behavior.* "Wait till your father or mother comes home" just won't be so effective.

4. *Punishment also needs to be delivered most intensively when it is first used.* Be tough initially, then ease up instead of the other way around. Many of us remember teachers who set strict limits and controls the first few days of class. Later they were nicer. Their children usually behaved very well. Then there were the teachers who tried to be so nice at first: "Please return to your seat, students, I would appreciate it." When some students didn't, teacher would get more and more stern until he or she was really yelling. What these teachers taught children was to habituate to negative attention. They slowly but surely dished it out in increasing doses until their frustration was evident to all—a reinforcement contingency for out-of-seat behavior was developed. What might have been a punishing consequence was lost because of the way the teachers presented the negative attention. Instead of initial intensive yelling and then becoming softer, they did the reverse.

5. *For a punisher to work effectively, it should be delivered without strong emotion.* All too often emotional behavior becomes a positive reinforcer and actually acts to increase the response you are trying to get rid of.

Regardless of how well you manage to make punishment work for you, it is probably better to use other strategies for behavior change. Punishment rarely works as we envision it should; people don't like it and it tends to hinder forming good relationships; there is even a tendency to increase the aggressive behavior of those who experience the brunt of punishment.

Yet people keep trying to punish behavior—across cultures and generations—even though it doesn't work well. Why? Basically because the "punisher" gets reinforced for using it on the "punishee." First, punishing consequences have what is called an *immediate or temporary suppression effect on behavior*. If your goal is to stop kids from fighting, you yell, and they stop, that consequence certainly reinforces your yelling behavior. Unfortunately, the fighting behavior will not be permanently punished by a yell—only for the moment—a temporary suppression effect. But, oh, the peace of that moment.

The second way the punisher gets reinforced is through the effects of anger. It doesn't do much for the future, but it sometimes "feels" good and reduces anxiety at the time to get really angry. More important, when a person displays anger, other people usually react in a dramatically different way than usual. They may get angry back, be afraid, or back off. At the least they will likely stop whatever they were doing and give attention to whoever is angry, all of which can act as the reinforcer of an anger response. Hopefully, by understanding the tremendous difficulties enountered in making punishment work as it is supposed to, especially the aversive consequences that people are so prone to use, we will as a species use better methods to help people change their behavior. But given the powerful reinforcing contingencies that control people's use of aversive stimuli, both in personal relationships and between nations, I do not believe that a change in these contingencies will come easily.

We have now covered the entire foundation of the behavioral approach: how antecedents control respondent behavior, and the kinds of consequences that increase or decrease the probability of operant behavior. All that we learn from this point on is built on these foundations. It is even reasonable to speak of these phenomena as the Laws of Behavior.

Schedules of reinforcement.   While we were discussing positive reinforcement, you will remember that in order for a behavior to be learned it has to be quickly followed by some reinforcing consequence. This is called *continuous reinforcement (CRF)*. However, after the behavior is learned, if the reinforcer continues to be delivered too frequently, the behavior could be easily unlearned. While this may sound paradoxical, it's just another way evolution has insured the survival of animals. In actuality, those responses that are really a part of your normal ongoing behavior are maintained on what is called an *intermittent reinforcement schedule*—the major reinforcers are delivered infrequently. So you actually perform many established behaviors with little or no important reinforcer immediately available.

For example, reinforcement contingencies where reinforcers are delivered after every ten responses, or every few weeks or so, better maintain behavior than CRF contingencies after the behavior has been learned. Look at the child learning how to make a bed. There is nothing intrinsically valuable about making a bed, so children need some continuous reinforcer, such as praise, to get the behavior established. It is unreasonable to praise a child each time he or she makes the bed for the rest of their lives. What naturally happens is that children learn how to do it without much reinforcing feedback. The praise levels off until they receive it infrequently. Occasionally, someone may mention how nice the room looks, the child may also give him or herself covert reinforcement, self-praise, and sometimes parents will threaten aversive consequences if the bed is not made up—negative reinforcement. But the behavior is maintained over a lifetime on a very low level of reinforcement.

In fact, unless a behavior goes naturally onto some type of intermittent reinforcement schedule, it is more vulnerable to extinction. If for some reason a behavior being maintained under a CRF schedule loses its reinforcer, the behavior will quickly follow the extinction curve and return to operant level. On the other hand, if a behavior maintained on an intermittent schedule loses its reinforcer, it will take much longer to extinguish, perhaps because it takes longer for an organism to realize that the reinforcer is no longer available.

This phenomenon is a mixed blessing. While it is helpful that we don't have to go around delivering reinforcers for every behavior, it also means that behaviors we wish to extinguish are under the control of intermittent reinforcement schedules, which means they will be harder to extinguish. It also means that it may be quite difficult to find out what these powerful infrequent reinforcers are.

There are many examples that demonstrate the power of schedules of reinforcement. Many of you have been to Las Vegas or have gambled. If you've worked a one-armed bandit (the slot machine) you know how seductive it is and how hard it is to quit. Yes, there are probably some deep psychological reasons that some people can't quit, but there are some obvious reasons, too. The schedule of reinforcement that maintains slot machine behavior is called a *variable ratio schedule* (VR). A reinforcer on a VR schedule is delivered after a variable number of responses. You don't know exactly when it's coming, but you know it will. *Any* behavior maintained on a VR schedule will occur at a high rate with very little rest. A one-armed bandit does indeed deliver money occasionally, but you never know when. So it is to your advantage to play as fast and often as possible to get as much money as possible. Unfortunately, the reinforcers are so intermittent that your chances of making money are not very good. But the VR schedule of reinforcement itself dictates the rate at which you will play, without your even realizing it.

Study behavior is generally under what is called a *fixed interval intermittent schedule* (FI schedule). In this schedule the reinforcer comes based on a time interval. As a rule, college students know their study behavior will be reinforced after two months at the mid-term and after four months at the final. Of course you get some reinforcement for acquiring knowledge, but a lot of it occurs after you perform on the exam. *Any* behavior on an FI schedule occurs on what is called a *fixed interval scallop*. Just after receiving a reinforcer on this schedule there is a very low rate of behavior. As the time for reinforcement comes closer, the rate of behavior increases dramatically until it reaches a frenzied peak just before the time the reinforcer is available for delivery. Then afterward it goes back to a very low level and starts the scallop over again. This powerful schedule encourages cramming. The FI schedule is strongest when you clearly see what the time intervals are. But even if you can't, it still works. After all, a rat doesn't carry a calendar or a watch to know when the next feeding will be. But even lower animals must have some kind of internal clock and perform the FI scallop on a schedule.

It is possible to design an educational program that reinforces consistent study behavior. A *variable interval* schedule would be used. Reinforcers on a VI schedule are delivered over various seemingly random time intervals. It takes more work and more knowledge to put into effect. But teachers, like the rest of us, follow a behavior principle that cuts across the animal kingdom—the law of least effort. An organism will normally do the least amount of work possible to achieve a desired reinforcer. One unpopular way a VI schedule is used to reinforce consistent studying is called a *pop quiz*.

At this point, most schedules are laboratory phenomena and therapists need not worry unduly about what schedule or combination of them is maintaining a behavior in the environment. Suffice it to say you should be aware that behavior is maintained on intermittent schedules. New behaviors that are being learned need to be on CRF until they are established, then they need to be put on an intermittent schedule if they are to be maintained. Most of the time this happens naturally. When it doesn't you must attend to it more systematically until nature takes it course.

Remember, though, don't expect a person to maintain new patterns of behavior unless the people in the natural environment are going to reinforce it. Under all too frequent circumstances, nothing is more predictable than a person who has just come out of an institution reverting back to old behavior patterns. The behaviors that get reinforced in institutions, no matter how wonderful, are all too often not generalized and supported in the environment. Unless the person's new behaviors were put on a very powerful intermittent schedule—which most often they are not—they are easily extinguished when they get back home.

This is why behaviorists are so concerned with involving as many people as possible in the behavior-change plans of an individual. Generally, they are not in favor of long term institutionalization unless linkages to the normal environment can be strongly integrated. If you look closely at behavior theory and practice, it is one of the major systems approaches to therapy.

In summary, for behavior to be ultimately maintained, one of two things will have to happen: either the people in the environment are going to naturally reinforce behavior on an intermittent schedule, or a person is going to have to find other people who will. The first approach is passive; the second is active, and can be learned through assertive training. While it is possible to covertly reinforce oneself when others cannot or will not, there always needs to be some intermittent environmental support for one's behavior or it will be extinguished.

Shaping. We are now ready to look at a phenomenon that is, I believe, one of the greatest contributions behavioral research has made to understanding human behavior: shaping, the art of successive approximations. Much of what we learn is by_ steps, often slowly. Shaping has always been going on, but it is only relatively recently that we have understood how it works—and how the process fails. Shaping is one essential process by which we learn new complex behaviors. Starting with a behavior we are able to perform, we go slowly, step, by step, until a new, much more complex behavior is learned. Most of what children learn academically is done through shaping. One day they learn $1 + 1 = 2$ and slowly work up to more complicated math skills. Emotional skills are also learned more effectively by breaking them down into progressive component parts. While shaping is essentially intuitive and fairly obvious, it does not always work as nature intended.

There are two major skills to be learned to master shaping: developing the art of successive approximations, and then reinforcing each step correctly. The first is called an art because it is as difficult and creative as poetry, painting, and music. There are an infinite number and variety of steps one can take in learning. For example a client comes to see us because a lack of assertive skills is getting him into trouble. He has trouble saying no when people ask him to do something at work. He is getting so overwhelmed with work that his level of performance is suffering and he is becoming very anxious. Thus the beginning of his shaping plan will be his present response to requests from co-workers: the final step will be utilizing a new skill—saying no with an intonation that lets people know he means it and hopefully in a way that does not alienate them. How do we get from the first approximation to the final one? There is no correct answer. It depends on the creativity of the client and the therapist. One series of possible sequential steps could be:

1. Learn to put people off a day or two before he tells them yes.
2. Learn to agree to do only part of the request.
3. Practice saying no with different inflections.
4. Since many people don't say no because they fear loss of acceptance, learn to ask if people will still accept him if he doesn't agree to their request (there may be five or six steps in just learning this skill).
5. Saying no to strangers.
6. Saying no to friends.
7. Saying no to co-workers.

The art is not only figuring out what the possible steps could be but also the way they are presented. Remember the old primary reading books we used to have in grade school: "See Spot. See Spot run. Run, Spot, run!" They were set up in approximations. Somebody spent much time in figuring out what the next best step in the learning sequence was. But it was the teacher, who hopefully made it fun and creative, who really made Spot come alive. Creativity is the real skill in developing and presenting successive approximations.

The second major skill to be learned is how the successive steps are reinforced. The process is often a natural one. For example, a therapist is working with a client on a series of successive approximations for the expression of anger.

(1)	(2)	(3)	(4)	(5)	(6)...(10)
Can't express anger—remains quiet, meek (this is present client behavior).	Expresses mild negative statements.	Yells at pillow.	Hits pillow.	Reports feelings of anger directed at therapist.	Tells friends she is angry.

The therapist has developed a potential shaping plan with her client. As in any road map, the route closest to the beginning is more certain than the one nearer to the end. The client needs to go from step one to step two. She may do it just because the therapist suggests it, but remember, no behavior occurs unless it is reinforced. Therefore, if she is going to start expressing any negative feelings, she will need some reinforcement. Reinforcers can initially come from herself, her therapist, or others. Chances are, present relationships will not provide the necessary reinforcers, nor is she able to adequately reinforce herself. So it usually falls on the therapist to provide the structure for the necessary initial reinforcement contingencies. Normal therapist reinforcers are praise and support.

Let us suppose that the client has begun to receive adequate reinforcement for step two and begins experimenting with the expression of mild negative feelings. If this were where she stopped, her final goal would not be achieved. Indeed, she would be stuck at step two. Once the expression of mild negative feelings has been demonstrated *and* established, the reinforcer for this step must be withdrawn—extinguished—and offered for the next step—in this case yelling at a pillow. In the same way, if she begins raising her voice sufficiently to sound angry (even at a pillow), she will only continue this behavior if she is reinforced for it. Yet, if she keeps getting support for yelling at pillows, she may never get to her friends at the end of the process. Therefore, again, the reinforcement for pillow yelling (step 3) needs to be extinguished, and a reinforcer offered for step 4—hitting pillows. The process of reinforcing a new approximation just long enough to get it established, and then extinguishing it by withdrawing the reinforcer for that step and offering it for the next, is an extremely skilled and delicate process.

(1)	(2)	(3)	(4)
Silence.	Expresses mild negative feelings [S^+ (praise), then $R\!\!\not\to$ (withdraw praise)].	Yells at pillow [S^+ (praise), then $R\!\!\not\to$ (withdraw praise)].	Hits pillow S^+ (offer praise), and so on.

When shaping is going smoothly, it seems obvious and easy. Your first-grade teacher probably did it quite naturally and skillfully when you first learned to read "cat." You were praised, and perhaps received a check or gold star on your paper. You brought it home and hopefully Mom or Dad got excited. You were pleased and proud, too. However, if one month later you were still reading "cat" and nothing else, teacher would not be so pleased. Praise would not be forthcoming for that response. Instead the teacher would probably encourage you to try the next word. Instinctively, praise for "cat" was being withdrawn, but all the time the teacher was letting you know that when the next lesson was completed you would receive praise again. Most teachers naturally use this differential reinforcement process as part of an overall broad-based shaping plan for reading. It is likely that some of your teachers did not know technically how shaping worked. They did it by intuition, as most of us do. So if the shaping plan failed for a student or two, they may not have known how to structure a more detailed and carefully delivered shaping plan.

It is important to know the technology of shaping if one is going to be a teacher or therapist. The way reinforcers are delivered and extinguished for any given step is crucial for success. There are five basic ways to sabotage the shaping process (assume praise is the reinforcer being used, as it often is).

The Goof	The Result
1. Person receives too much reinforcement (praise) at a given step.	The person gets stuck at that step (goes no further, may figure that since he or she is getting so much praise for this step, why should he or she try to perform even harder tasks).
2. Person receives too little reinforcement (praise) at a given step.	Person regresses and goes back to where he or she was (figures that if he's not getting any support for the new behavior, he might as well go back to the old behav-where he got some praise before).
3. Reinforcer is delivered inconsistently: sometimes given and sometimes not.	Person acts erratically, sometimes performs new behavior, sometimes not. Often acts confused, depressed, and/or angry, blaming him or herself for being so stupid (they can't figure out what is really expected of him. He or she is asked to perform, but doesn't get consistent support for it).
4. The reinforcer is given too late, too long after the new behavior is performed.	Person may behave erratically, the new behavior learned may be nothing like what is expected, since the reinforcer is being delivered so long after the new behavior occurred.
5. The approximations are too difficult.	Person may get angry, depressed, and/or blame self for stupidity. Will usually give up, perhaps feel helpless.

What is really fascinating about these five ways to impede a shaping plan is how easily many parents, therapists, supervisors, and teachers refuse to accept any responsibility for the failure of the learner. How many times do you hear in a therapeutic setting that a patient has "regressed," as if the "regression" is only the responsibility of the patient. If we looked at the people around the patient, what we would likely see is that this patient was receiving good, consistent reinforcement for new behavior; but then the reinforcers started coming in too infrequently and inconsistently—thus came a "regression." Not only did the client "regress" but the people around the client did, too! Or we often say a person is "stuck" as if no one else had any responsibility for the stuckness. Rather, if we took a careful look, we would see that the environment of that "stuck" person is giving him or her a goodly amount of reinforcement for the stuck behaviors. Regardless of his or her wish to move on, he is probably getting enough support where he is.

One advantage to knowing our role in the shaping process is that we can look at our own behavior to see where breakdowns occur. If the shaping process is not working, we should not infer that clients are not responsible for their own behavior. They are. But the people around them *do* impact on their behavior, and with insight into *how* that happens, we can help a person take responsibility better. Remember, while a client is responsible for his or her behavior, we are responsible for ours. It is possible for us to make it harder for a person to learn.

When you see resistant people in a learning role, be it in a classroom, therapy session, or family, instead of attributing resistance to unobservable intrapsychic quirks, look at *how* people are reinforcing them. Since you are likely a significant part of their environment as well, look at how you are reinforcing too much, too little, expecting too much or too little, or being inconsistent. By analyzing your own behavior and thus taking responsibility for your own role in a system, you will be helping others take better responsibility for their behavior as well. Understanding and developing the skills of shaping—the art of successive approximation—has many gifts to bring to a learning environment for parents, teachers, supervisors, and therapist.

Behavior chains. It is generally easier to learn a new behavior if another does not have to be unlearned at the same time. And while old dogs can certainly learn new tricks, the older the trick, the harder to get rid of it. In general, the age of the dog is probably less important than the age of the trick. Thus, while it may not be difficult to learn a new skill, the task is often made more difficult because old behavior patterns are strongly ingrained and competing for reinforcement. As you will recall, we humans follow the law of least effort. It takes less work to get reinforcement for an old behavior pattern. It's riskier and more work to learn new behaviors when the likelihood of reinforcement is far less certain.

Intermittent reinforcement is one powerful way that behavior is maintained after it is learned. That phenomenon, however, is only a part of the picture. The other very powerful process that maintains our current behavior patterns is called *chaining*. A behavior chain is synonymous with a behavior pattern. After a sequence of behaviors is learned, it becomes part of our daily pattern of living. Speaking, walking, brushing our teeth, eating, and swimming are all performed without having to concentrate on each of them. And thank goodness. Can you imagine how little people could accomplish if they had to concentrate on each step as they walked? Instead, walking is a patterned behavior, chained, so that we do it naturally without having to think about it.

Most psychotherapists see patterns of problem behavior as significant. It is true that no two incidents are exactly alike, but where there are enough similarities between a number of situations, the behaviorist will consider the behavior as "chained." For instance, when people feel hurt, they probably have a characteristic way of dealing with it. Some of us get angry, some withdraw, some cry. Usually there are a series of behaviors we go through before the incident is finished. Chains of behavioral interactions can be of varying lengths of time. Some are finished quickly, within a few minutes. Others can go on for months before they are completed. Take a look at the following examples:

EXAMPLE I

Step 1.   Charlie is "bad" at 1:00 P.M. (hits sister, throws toys, and so on).

Step 2.   Mother yells at Charlie—tells him to stop.

Step 3.   He yells back—refuses to stop.

Step 4.   Mommy hits him.

Step 5.   He throws tantrum.

Step 6.   Father comes home at 6:00 P.M.—Mother tells Father how bad Charlie has been.

Step 7.   Father "punishes" and/or has long talk with Charlie (time lapse: an afternoon).

This type of chain obviously never happens exactly the same way twice. But by discussing the problem interactions with the family, the therapist begins to see that a general pattern emerges where Mother's "goat gets got" consistently and Father usually ends up having to deal with Charlie. We might assume that whenever Charlie begins feeling in a state of deprivation for some attention from his father, he has found a patterned way of getting it.

EXAMPLE II

Step 1.   Husband and wife start arguing (about wide variety of topics).

Step 2.   They yell and scream at each other.

Step 3.   Wife walks out of room, husband leaves house.

Step 4.   Both pout for about two days, sleep in separate beds, speak very little to each other.

Step 5.   At the end of second day or so they slowly begin to speak more to each other.

Step 6.   Eventually they sit down and solve their differences.

This not uncommon marital chain took three days to complete. One might assume here that what they are working for is to problem solve, but since they don't have the skills to make the transition from anger to discussion, they use time instead. Unfortunately, the problem-solving session they have at the end of a few days acts to reinforce the pouting behavior and the whole annoying chain of events preceding it.

There is a behavioral "glue" that keeps chains together. Each response in a chain acts as a cue for the next one and alternatively as the reinforcer for the response just before it. Some chains are glued together better than others, based on their performance frequency and how long they have been in practice. Compulsive-behavior chains are glued together very well. For example, Figure 1-2 shows a house-cleaning compulsion:

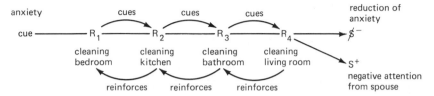

FIGURE 1-2

We are not talking about normal cleaning. Compulsive house cleaning can occur many times a day. In essence, finishing the bedroom is a cue for starting the kitchen. Kitchen cleaning literally reinforces cleaning the bedroom (which came before it) and also cues the next step, cleaning the bathroom. Cleaning the bathroom reinforces the behavior which precedes it, cleaning the kitchen, and also provides the cues for cleaning the living room. This process continues until the final reinforcers are reached, in this case, a reduction of anxiety—probably through exhaustion—and negative attention. Each response member of a chain has been bound to the ones around it through conditioning. As long as each response in a chain automatically cues the next one and is reinforced by the same response it cues, the chain will roll on to the end and be ready to start the next time the right stimulus cue is offered.

What we must remember about chains is that they are cyclical. They have a starting point, which we call the *initial cue*, and an ultimate end point, which is the final reinforcer in the chain. While there is always a final reinforcer in every chain, there are many more immediate reinforcers along the way. So people are not left without incentives along the road to the final consequence. Since it may take a while for the final reinforcer to be delivered, it is often difficult to discover what the final reinforcers are. However, with training and practice, the skill of identifying complex behavior chains comes more easily.

There is a major advantage in looking at problem behavior in patterns or chains. Behaviorists have discovered some interesting tendencies about them.

Rule 1. *The longer the behavior chain, the harder it is to extinguish.* Patterns of behavior that take a long time to be played out, or take much effort to perform, will be more difficult to get rid of. It also suggests that if you try to extinguish a long chain by removing the final reinforcer, it's going to take a long time for the procedure to decrease the chained behavior. In a long chain, such as the one in Figure 1-3, the removal of the final reinforcer would extinguish R_4, which would then work to extinguish R_3, and so on. If the identified problem behavior is at the

Cue———— R_1 ———— R_2 —/— R_3 —/— R_4 —/→ S^+

FIGURE 1-3

beginning of the chain, a simple extinction procedure would not be the primary treatment of choice. But it might be helpful along with some other procedures.

Rule 2. *The first members of a chain of behavior are the easiest to extinguish.* The first steps in a behavior pattern were probably the most recently added to a person's behavorial repertoire, and as such are not well established. Therefore, since they are the newest and the weakest response members, they will be more vulnerable to extinction than other behaviors in the chain. If we could extinguish the first members we could have a way to stop the chain from beginning in the first place.

Rule 3. *Once a chain starts, it will likely go to completion.* It is harder to stop a fistfight once it has started than to stop it when words begin to fly. For therapeutic purposes, it suggests that active intervention will be more effective towards the beginning of chains. It is harder for people to control themselves and be rational once they are caught up in the middle of their problematic behavior.

Rule 4. *The longer a chain, the weaker the disposition to start it.* Behavior patterns that take a lot of time or emotion will not be seen as frequently as shorter, less energetic ones. A knockdown, drag-out fight won't be as frequent as bickering.

Rule 5. *If a chain is extinguished or broken in its middle, the rest of the chain is left intact.* This chain phenomenon is one of the critical issues for behavior change. In fact, it goes a long way in explaining why some interventions work and others don't. It also gives an empirically demonstrable explanation of that Freudian nemesis, symptom substitution. If we consider that every pattern of behavior has a beginning cue, a number of identifiable steps with their own reinforcers, and then an end where the final reinforcer is delivered, then we see there are actually many places in a chain where an intervention can be aimed. If the intervention is aimed at breaking the chain in the beginning or middle, then that much of the chain up to that point of the break will be changed, assuming the intervention worked. But what of the rest of the chain after the break? It's left intact. The remainder of the chain, which includes that important final reinforcer, is left as part of the person's behavior but without a cue to get it started—almost as if half the highway to St. Louis from your own town disappeared. You have no apparent way of driving to St. Louis, but if you could figure out how to get your car to the intact part of the highway, it would be easy to get to the Mississippi River. Stimulus control techniques will help explicate this point further.

Stimulus control.   Interventions that deal with only the first part of behavior chains are powerful but also problematic. Behavior Therapy calls them *stimulus control* (S-control) techniques. Their value is that they are often immediately effective, especially since they deal with the weakest part of the chain, the first members. They are also relatively simple techniques which require little or no "in depth" psychotherapy. However, because they leave much of the chain intact, a number of problems can develop.

Let's take a simple example to explain the power and problems of S-control interventions.

1. Almost every Friday Bill and Sally come home after work between 5:00 and 6:00 P.M.

2. Within a few minutes they start bickering about bills, where or what to eat, and so on.

3. It usually escalates to a knockdown, drag-out fight, with yelling and screaming.

4. Bill usually walks out to get his own dinner, Sally slams the door and locks herself into the bedroom.

5. Later in the evening or the next morning they make mad, passionate love and feel rather sheepish about their fight.

Our assumption in this chain is that coming home after a hard week's work sets off the chain; and by definition what they are working for at the end of the chain is to spend time alone for a while, and then be more intimate. This is not so much an interpretation but a description of what happens. If we wished to interpret, although it is not necessary, we might say that they have not learned the skills to come home and request "alone time" before they make closer contact with each other. So they have developed a chain of behavior allowing them to be alone first. It may not be constructive for their marriage, but it is functional.

An S-control intervention would help Bill and Sally break their chain between steps 1 and 3. There are an infinite number of S-control possibilities, including: going out to dinner or drinks before going home; making a list of argumentative topics and refusing to discuss those; working on problem solving or fair fighting so the argumentative issues are dealt with more effectively; self-monitoring themselves so that any time they begin feeling irritation they deal with it by making requests, and/ or sharing their feelings. Any of these S-control techniques might indeed break the chain between 1 and 3. But steps 3, 4, and 5 are left intact. What this means realistically is they may not have dealt with their apparent need to be alone before making close contact with each other. S-control techniques finesse the issue by simply arranging that the chain won't start. If, by chance, through communication, problem solving, or by being in a happier atmosphere, Bill and Sally communicate their need to be alone, then the reinforcers at the end of the chain will be delivered anyway. This is called the *snowball* or *avalanche* effect. Often an S-control technique will dictate that the needs implied at the end of a chain are met without direct intervention. For instance, a child may be frustrating a teacher by running around the room for negative attention (a positive reinforcer). The teacher intervenes at the beginning of the chain to reinforce the child's in-seat behavior with a point system. The teacher is so pleased with the new behavior, he or she starts giving positive attention. Attention was what the child wanted in the first place. By arranging to stop the problem behavior at the start of the chain, and putting a more appropriate chain in its place, there was an avalanche effect and the child ended up getting the attention he or she needed.

This is a common phenomenon and explains why S-control techniques work without doing any further psychotherapy. But what happens if life doesn't naturally deliver what was needed at the end of a chain? The client is left with an important reinforcer that cannot be delivered because the original chain is broken. There is obviously a need or deprivation state this final reinforcer was fulfilling, and there is no longer a way to get it. One of two things will happen: the client will either revert back to the old behavior that got into the chain to get the final reinforcer (regression); or a client can be creative and find a new way to get to the reinforcer, that is, learn a new chain to attach to the remnant of the old one (symptom substitution).

Thus, after a successful S-control intervention, Bill and Sally, in a real state of deprivation for alone time on Fridays, might either revert back to the fighting (regression) or begin making excuses to come home late (symptom substitution).

In Behavior Therapy it is not only the power of the technique applied but also where in the chain it is applied that determines the maintenance of a newly learned behavior. Since all operant behavior is ultimately controlled by its consequences, it is necessary to attend to interventions at the end of chains for permanent behavior change. If an S-control intervention is all that is contemplated, the therapist should make sure the needs represented by the reinforcer at the end of the chain are taken care of. Otherwise, a consequence-control intervention should be implemented as well.

You might hear the comment that Behavior Therapy deals only with symptoms and not with underlying issues; or behaviorists deal with too specific behaviors and not with "personality characteristics." "Symptoms" and "specific behaviors" are part of longer complex chains of behavior that we call *underlying issues* and *personality characteristics*. If you can break a small chain by instituting appropriate S-control and consequence control techniques, it is often the case you will see an avalanche effect on much broader response classes of behaviors, such as underlying issues and personality traits.

Given the necessary reservations, S-control techniques alone can be very effective. For weight control, compulsive behavior, smoking, and drug problems there have been promising results. What is generally demonstrated is that a reasonably good percent of clients will respond to S-control interventions without further work. For instance, the behavioral diet, which teaches how to interrupt the beginnings of the eating chain, works well for many people. It demands that you continue to eat what you like to eat, but learn new habits of eating to control the cues that start eating chains. When the diet fails, it is probably because these S-control techniques do not directly deal with the final consequences of the eating chain. These consequences include, among *many* others, negative comments to oneself about being overweight and negative comments from other important people. If these kinds of reinforcing consequences are powerful, and not naturally replaced with positive attention to oneself and from others, the diet will likely fail in the long run, even if there has been an initial substantial weight loss. The same phenomenon can be seen with smoking behavior. What makes the control of smoking even more difficult is that not only are there the reinforcers for smoking, as in eating, but there is a chemically addictive reinforcer as well: nicotine. It is likely that when an addictive reinforcer is involved in a behavior problem, the normal behavioral procedures do not work as easily.

As we continue to explore other therapies, keep in mind the concept of the behavioral chain and the *chain rules*. We will find that the effect of techniques from other psychological theories can be better understood using the conceptualization of the behavior chain.

Modeling and behavioral rehearsal. People learn large chunks of behavior by watching others. They copy what they see and learn more quickly than if they had to be painstakingly taught, step-by-step, as in shaping. Think how hard it would be to teach a child how to swing a bat by shaping each step. Fortunately, just by demonstrating how the behavior is done, most children can copy it. In fact, many very critical behaviors are learned through the modeling process. Learning to walk and speak are two of the earliest.

When the modeling process breaks down, as it seems to with retarded and autistic children, behaviorists have begun to learn how to teach children to watch models and copy their behavior. It is a painstaking process, sometimes taking months and even years. But the effort is well worthwhile because without the ability to observe models and copy their behavior, speech is impossible, along with many other behaviors needed for self-sufficiency.

We don't completely understand how in the normal environment people become important models for children. It is obvious that parents are important. As we grow older the characteristics of a person that will make him or her a powerful model are complex. People who are associated with power, prestige, popularity, success, warmth, strength, or beauty could be models given the proper circumstances. The whole advertising industry is based on the idea that successful, popular, sexy, pretty, and handsome people can model buying products in a way that will induce us to copy their behavior. And often we do.

In therapy the modeling process is hopefully more significant than buying beer or cosmetics. Therapists need to be effective models for their clients' new behaviors. When clients need to learn skills that their therapists do not have, groups are particularly helpful because there are more potential models to watch. While there is not a thorough and comprehensive therapeutic technology utilizing the powerful modeling phenomenon for outpatient problems, it plays a role throughout the therapeutic process. In the future we will see more clear and systematic inclusion of modeling techniques in therapy.

Behavioral rehearsal is one of the techniques used in modeling. It is essentially a more systematic approach to what has been called *role playing*. A client is asked to practice or rehearse a newly learned behavior before trying it in the natural environment. The rehearsal will usually grow out of a suggestion by the therapist after a new behavior has been discussed as an alternative to present behavior, or after having watched a model. In either case it is important to make the rehearsal as near reality as possible so that generalization to the environment is enhanced. Groups are particularly good for this.

A rehearsal of a new behavior, or the approximation of one as in a shaping plan, will likely be more successful if the behavior is modeled first. The modeling and behavioral rehearsal situation should be made as close to specific real-life reinforcement and punishment contingencies as possible. The timing and quality of reinforcers coming to both the model and the client need to be realistic. If, for example, a client expects anger as a consequence for attempting a new assertive response at home, then regardless of whether that consequence will actually occur or not, the client should be prepared for it.

Behavior Therapy can certainly not lay claim to behavioral rehearsal. It is a pervasive part of almost all therapies. Yet, like many of the techniques discussed in the behavioral approach, it is by the careful behavioral specification of what makes the technique effective that therapists increase their power to help people.

Assertive training. There is much ado concerning assertive training, and with good reason. It is a relatively clear stepwise process for taking more control of one's life. Simply put, assertive behavior gets people what they need or acts to remove something they don't. All organisms, human or otherwise, wish to manipulate their environment to maximize survival, comfort, and satisfaction. These attempts at environmental manipulation are called *assertive behaviors*. When children are going through the "terrible twos" and continually saying no to parents, they are experimenting with manipulation. How parents develop reinforcement or punishment contingencies for these early manipulation attempts will greatly affect a child's ability to say no in later life.

While there are probably an infinite number of possible assertive behaviors, they usually fall into the following categories therapeutically:

1. the ability to say no (or yes)
2. the ability to make requests or demands
3. the ability to express negative or positive feelings
4. the ability to initiate, maintain, or terminate conversations
5. the ability for self-disclosure
6. the ability to perform under duress

Assume that all of the above six behaviors are on a continuum. Each of us can do some of them better than others depending on the circumstances. Regardless of one's early childhood conditioning, it is usually possible to teach people more effective assertive skills through assertive training.

The process of assertive training is relatively straightforward. It is helpful to identify with which assertive behaviors a person is most concerned. Then find a representative situation where the lack of an assertive response occurred. Next reenact the original scene, give feedback to the person, model another way to be a little more assertive, do a behavioral rehearsal, give feedback, and go through this cycle again.

What is tricky about the process is that you must be sensitive to two major issues: first, if you expect people to be very assertive when they have been relatively passive before, you will be setting them up for failure. Therapists need to use shaping and successive approximations so that each assertive attempt will be possible and successful. For example, helping a person merely acknowledge he or she feels angry could be a tremendous step to being able to look and sound angry. The second important issue concerns the kinds of contingencies that inhibit people from being assertive. Behavior therapists talk about how people are reinforced in their present environment for nonassertive behaviors, often on long intermittent schedules. There are very powerful contingencies that inhibit assertive behavior. Often they were learned during childhood; now they are maintained by people in the person's present life. For instance, the inability to make a demand on one's spouse could be negatively reinforced by the anger a person receives after making the demand, even if the demand is eventually met. Or the inability to self-disclose personal history could be conditioned by experiences of having had personal information used against you. It is important for the therapist to know what kind of contingencies are presently operating that make assertive behavior more difficult, so that these contingencies can be dealt with directly.

The assessment process, through the use of chain analysis, is extremely helpful in this regard. Remember, while stimulus control at the beginning of a chain can be powerful in helping a person change his or her behavior, it is the final consequence that ultimately controls that behavior. If people learn more assertive behaviors but do not act on those contingencies reinforcing nonassertive behavior, they could be in for big trouble. It may sound good to be able to say no. Can the the client live with the consequences? If the consequences seem insurmountable, then we need to teach clients not only to say no but also to effectively assert themselves towards those threatening aversive consequences.

An interesting example of asserting oneself against a potentially punishing consequence is a newly emerging behavioral technology called *covert* or *cognitive assertive training*. Covert behavior, you will recall, occurs partly in your head, such as thinking, imagining, and dreaming. There is every reason to believe the same laws that govern overt operant and respondent behavior also govern covert behavior. Thoughts, images, dreams, and concepts continue to occur because they are reinforced; those that are not remembered have been either extinguished or punished. If you can imagine the consequence of an assertive behavior, you may be able to decide how you will handle the situation.

For example, if after you say no you imagine you will feel guilty, you may wish to extinguish those covert behaviors that mean "guilt" to you. Guilt is made up of a combination of overt and covert behaviors. To be behaviorally specific, first you do something that is observed; then you tell yourself or hear someone tell you intermittently that you "should" be doing something else; finally you must agree with yourself or that person in order to feel guilty. You can choose to assert yourself to the person passing judgment by telling him or her you do not wish to hear his opinions of your behavior. That would be an example of an overt assertive behavior. You can also decide to refuse to agree with the judgments in your mind. Telling yourself that those judgments may be right for others but are wrong for you is an assertion against a message you give yourself, that is, the agreement to the "should." By practicing this covert assertion you can literally extinguish guilt.

Since there are so many "internal messages" we give ourselves, it is an exciting concept to realize that by behaviorally specifying what those covert messages are, we can deal with them in much the same way that we deal with overt behavior. Thus we have two powerful assertive options when we wish to manipulate our environment more effectively. We can overtly act to differentially extinguish and shape the behavior of those around us; and we can covertly assert ourselves directly on the messages that contribute cues and consequences to the control of our behavior. In Figure 1-4 we see an example of how both processes can work together.

The therapist's options for helping Jerry assert himself could start in either the covert or overt domain.

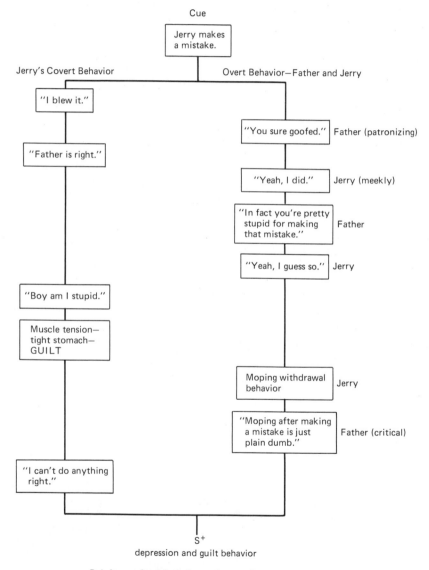

Cue

Jerry makes a mistake.

Jerry's Covert Behavior

Overt Behavior—Father and Jerry

"I blew it."

"You sure goofed." Father (patronizing)

"Father is right."

"Yeah, I did." Jerry (meekly)

"In fact you're pretty stupid for making that mistake." Father

"Yeah, I guess so." Jerry

"Boy am I stupid."

Muscle tension— tight stomach— GUILT

Moping withdrawal behavior Jerry

"Moping after making a mistake is just plain dumb." Father (critical)

"I can't do anything right."

S+
depression and guilt behavior

Reinforcers for this chain are the negative comments from Father and negative self-comments that occurred in the last steps. Both culminate in behaviors Jerry calls depression and guilt.

FIGURE 1-4.   Example of an overt-covert chain of behavior

Overt. Jerry never deserved to be told he is stupid. While he may wish to receive corrective feedback about his behavior, he does not need to hear personal attacks during that feedback. Thus, in order to feel better about his mistakes and use them as learning tools rather than negative psychological bludgeons, Dad's comments are going to have to be extinguished. In addition, by looking at this chain we notice that Dad's negative attention is likely an instrumental reinforcer not only for the guilt but for making mistakes as well. Jerry is probably cued to make mistakes when his father is around if he is in a state of deprivation for his father's attention, such as it is.

While Jerry would need to go through an assertive shaping process, his final approximation would likely look like this: "Dad, I don't want to be told I am stupid again. I am willing to listen to your opinion of my performance, but I will not tolerate personal attacks on me such as calling me stupid, dumb, or inept. If you cannot find another way to give me feedback then I don't want to hear it. Do you understand?" Jerry is essentially breaking this behavior pattern near the beginning of the chain before the negative statements start. While this may be the only intervention he needs to attend to, his assertion alludes to the important impact of the chain's consequence. Negative attention from Dad is likely a reinforcer for Jerry. His assertion is essentially demanding that Dad withdraw—extinguish—negative attention as a reinforcer and substitute something else. Since neither of them have much experience with "something else," their relationship will probably be uncomfortable until they develop a new chain ending with a more positive interaction.

Covert. We are dealing with the same issues here, but the therapeutic attack is different. Jerry says to himself that Dad is not correct and he is not stupid. He could also learn to relax after mistakes since it is very difficult to feel guilty and relax at the same time. The effect of his covert assertions would be seen in a change in his overt behavior. By asserting himself against his own negative thoughts Jerry will in essence be withdrawing an important reinforcer from the behavior chain. Not only will Jerry be extinguishing his tendency to make mistakes when his father is around but he will likely be withdrawing the overt reinforcers for Dad's negative comments as well.

An interesting by-product of the kinds of covert statements we make about ourselves is tied to the concepts of self-image or self-esteem. What people say to themselves about their behavior is the behavioral definition of these concepts. When Jerry was saying he was stupid he was making a judgment about his behavior, and more generally about his existence—a statement which could easily be construed as part of his self-image. Please note, however, that Jerry's covert comment about himself was part of a larger reinforcement contingency in a chain of behaviors that included reinforcers from his father. In fact, the negative statements about his performance are actually reinforcers in the chain originally conditioned based on Jerry's need for attention from his father. Jerry ended up giving himself the same kind of reinforcer he got from his father—negative statements—and thus participated in the intermittent reinforcement of his own behavior. In addition, these covert reinforcers became Jerry's opinion of himself—his self-image. Thus a person's self-image is partly developed by covert reinforcers conditioned in chains of interactional behaviors with others. People often do not see the connection between what they covertly say about themselves and the reinforcers for the very behaviors they consider problematic. However, through an assessment of behavior chains it becomes clearer how covert behavior interacts with overt interactions to condition our evaluation of ourselves.

Thus a comprehensive assertive training program can have many side benefits beyond the simple ability to develop specific assertive skills. It can have a major impact on not only how we successfully manipulate our environment but on how we feel about ourselves as well.

The relationship between operant and respondent behavior. Having discussed the theory and techniques of respondent and operant behavior it is time to demonstrate how they frequently interact with each other. While it is true that operant procedures don't work well on problems controlled by antecedent stimuli, and respondent procedures likewise will not be very effective on responses maintained by consequences, there is a connection between them. For example, recall how a dog phobia was conditioned. After a painful or frightening experience with a dog, an anxiety response is Classically Conditioned which is ultimately under the control of the antecedent stimulus, the sight of a dog. However, just after the anxiety response was respondently conditioned, an operant negative reinforcement contingency was tacked onto it. In this new contingency the anxiety acts as a cue for an escape or avoidance response so that the child can get away from the dog. This is a normal reaction to a fearful stimulus and thus naturally ties the respondent behavior to an operant contingency, shown in Figure 1-5.

The decrease in anxiety that results from escaping a fearful stimulus, or avoiding it in the first place, is a powerful negative reinforcer. Since this reinforcer comes at the end of a chain of events that started with the sight of the dog, it acts as a final reinforcer and ties the respondent into the operant chain.

The negatively reinforcing decrease in anxiety by itself would be enough to maintain an escape or avoidance response. But this chain of behavior that starts with a Classically Conditioned response and ends with an operant contingency can also be positively reinforced. First, positive attention is often given to people, especially children, when they have had a phobic reaction. While this sympathy or support is most often an appropriate consequence to a fearful experience, it can actually lead to reinforcing a phobic response if the child habitually has been in a state of attention deprivation.

Second, negative attention as a consequence for anxiety and avoidance behavior can be a potent reinforcer. It is very common for the victims of long-term debilitating fears to force many people around them to conform to their lifestyle. This is

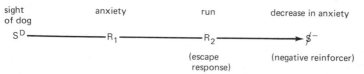

FIGURE 1-5

especially true in families. For instance, people with agoraphobia (the fear of going out) will be unable to leave their homes and members of their families will have to do all of the shopping and errands for them. While the family members may be generally supportive, it can get pretty frustrating over the years to have one's life continually centered around someone who apparently is not able to psychologically take care of him or herself. This frustration, when displayed on an intermittent schedule, becomes one positive reinforcer for agoraphobia.

Following our example of the dog phobia, children notice some interesting consequences to their fear reactions. If the fear does not eventually go away, as do most childhood fears, then the family may have to go out of their way for the child to avoid dogs; plans may consistently have to be changed and special requests made of friends and relatives to accommodate the child. Even though the fear and anxiety are real enough, the child is in a rather powerful position of being able to manipulate a number of people, and possibly frustrate some of them as well. Depending on how members of a family allow children to express anger and be involved in decision making will partly dictate whether this type of negative attention will reinforce a phobia chain. Figure 1-6 suggests the three ways a respondent dog phobia could be operantly reinforced.

Another area where the respondent and operant domains have become more integrated is in biofeedback. There are a number of responses that until recently have been thought to be only under respondent control. These include blood pressure, heart rate, and intestinal contractions. Incredibly, rats have been taught to control these responses by giving them operant negative reinforcement. Research with humans has been progressing as well with promising results. It may well be that if we can get feedback on internal body responses we will be able to control them operantly.

PRACTICE

The Role of the Therapist

Behavior Therapists are first and foremost teachers. They make the assumption they have learned a body of knowledge for problem solving that can be shared with others. Once clients have learned Behavioral Laws, techniques, and procedures, they can use these skills to help themselves and others modify behavior.

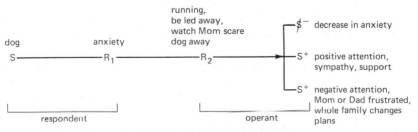

FIGURE 1-6   Respondent Behavior Operantly Reinforced

In this teaching role the therapist uses two basic strategies: an *instigation or direct approach* with clients; or a *mediator-indirect approach*. As instigators, behaviorists may try to directly reinforce clients for making changes to meet whatever behavioral goals have been set. In this context the client-therapist relationship can be very important. There are, after all, very few functional reinforcers that therapists can use other than those that come out of forming good relationships. Praise, negative feedback, or confrontation are usually more effective the better the relationship is. However, there are Behavior Therapists who do not emphasize the professional relationship. Instead they instigate behavior change in clients by using instructions and contracts that make use of reinforcers developed in the therapy session and the natural environment.

The second role for a Behavior Therapist is the mediator model of intervention. In this role therapists sometimes never have direct contact or even see the target clients. An example of this approach would be working with parents of a disturbed child when the child rarely if ever came in to see the therapist. There are a number of advantages in using the mediator model. All too frequently an identified client cannot or refuses to enter therapy. In these cases, others in this person's life can seek help anyway. Since in Behavior Therapy a problem is defined as undesirable behavior on the part of a target client *and* being inappropriately reinforced by relevant others, there is every reason to work with the people who mediate reinforcers. The mediator model is used extensively with teachers in schools, parents, and supervisors in the work setting.

THE BEHAVIOR THERAPY TREATMENT PROCESS

Behavior Therapy has a very explicit sequence of events that are to be followed by both researchers and therapists alike. They are shown in Figure 1-7. While the steps may be further delineated, these are sufficient for our purposes.

Problem specification. This is one of the most difficult steps. Clients need to be helped in translating their problems into concrete identifiable behaviors. It is specific behaviors that are extinguished and reinforced. Therefore, we must have them clearly specified. For example, feelings are important, but it is what people *do* when they are feeling that is amenable to modification.

Baseline. Clients are asked to literally count the number of times a problem occurs over some specific time, usually a week or more. This figure is used to monitor whether behavior is changing during therapy, and how much progress was achieved at termination.

Contracting and goal setting. Contracting first occurs during the initial stages of treatment, but it is also continues throughout as part of the therapy. The initial

FIGURE 1-7
The Behavior Therapy Treatment Process

contract is an agreement between the therapist and the client concerning what kinds of things will occur during therapy and what responsibilities both will have. Later in treatment, the contracts will concern specific treatment objectives and should always include: 1) what the client will do; 2) what the therapist will do; 3) the time limit of the contract; and optionally, 4) what will be the consequences for performance and nonperformance of required behaviors in the contract. Goal setting is the skill of helping clients identify what they wish to be doing as an alternative to their problems, as well as how much they wish to decrease the identified problem behavior. To help both the therapist and the client be more accountable, setting a goal always includes setting a date when it is believed the goal can be met, or at least evaluated.

Assessment. This is probably the most skillful step of the behavioral treatment process. It is the stage where Behavior Therapists are separated from those who are simply trying to modify behavior. Since most of the procedures in the behavioral approach are extremely specific, it is relatively easy to read a few books and start delivering artificial reinforcers or extinguishing behavior with very little training. There are many people who are doing just that—they are not really doing Behavior Therapy as it is meant to be done, but they may be successful in modifying behavior. To do good therapy, you must carefully assess the controlling conditions for the identified problem behavior. This means identifying the controlling antecedents and consequences of the specified behavior for the last five or ten times it occurred, and is called a *functional analysis*. Each incident can be broken into three segments: before, during, and after. For each segment the therapist asks about who was present, when it occurred, what happened, and where. The questioning continues until it seems that the incident is over. After doing this a number of times a pattern, or behavior chain, becomes apparent which is then amenable to the chain rules discussed previously. It is only by going through this type of assessment process that we can get a concrete sense of what type of intermittent reinforcers are maintaining the problem behavior chain. Good assessment helps the therapist find out what the client has been working so hard to achieve, what needs are ultimately being met, and who is delivering the reinforcers helping to maintain the pattern of problem behavior. In addition, people who could potentially become part of the intervention and possible reinforcers to use for new behavior patterns become clearer.

It is true people can learn how to manipulate and control others. Unfortunately, the simple modification of behavior without investigating controlling conditions of prior response patterns often leaves clients with unmet needs, and should be avoided. Behavior Therapy is meant to help people get their needs met, not to simply control behavior.

Intervention. All of the data is collected and a plan of intervention formulated, taking into consideration what is possible in the natural environment and what will most likely succeed. A good assessment should help dictate the best treatment plan. The intervention strategy is discussed with the client, modifications made as necessary, and instituted on a time-limited basis to see how it works.

Evaluation. After the treatment plan has been instituted, it is constantly under scrutiny by everyone involved. It is a rare plan that does not need changes as time goes on. Because every treatment plan includes monitoring along the same lines as was done during the Baseline step, it usually becomes apparent quickly whether the intervention is helping people change their behavior toward the established treatment goals as was desired.

Maintenance. Once treatment goals have been reached, the final challenge to the therapist and client is to work out a way that the newly learned response patterns won't be lost in the future. Behaviorists have two basic strategies to help people maintain behavior in the natural environment: schedules of reinforcement and self-control. In the first case, we know that unless newly established behavior is put on an intermittent schedule of reinforcement it will be more vulnerable to extinction. If artificial reinforcers have been used, natural ones need to be substituted. But no matter what reinforcers are currently being utilized, behavior must be on an intermittent schedule to be maintained. Usually this will occur naturally. Self-control, the second maintenance strategy, requires that the clients learn to reinforce themselves. If it turns out that people in a person's life support new behavior with very few reinforcers, then clients can develop the ability to support themselves as well.

Termination Criteria

Clients appropriately terminate in Behavior Therapy when their treatment goals are met. Goals may have to be upgraded or downgraded during therapy, but the basic criteria for termination remains the same. Therapy success or failure is essentially determined by what percentage of the goal was reached and how fast.

The Therapist's Response to Resistance

Conceptually, resistance is not usually mentioned in the behavioral approach. If clients are not doing what they initially set forth as their behavioral goals, it is because an appropriate reinforcer has not been found. Remember, motivation is defined by states of deprivation. A client who is not performing a desired behavior may not be in a great enough state of deprivation for available reinforcers. Therefore, if a client is resisting change, behaviorists either try to find a more potent reinforcer or help the client put him or herself into a greater state of deprivation for an existing one. If this is not possible then the client will either have to change goals or decide not to change, since no behavior will occur unless a viable reinforcer for it can be found.

The Therapist's Response to Transference and Countertransference

Again, the phenomena of transference and countertransference are not an integral part of Behavior Therapy. The client-therapist relationship is not used as a focal point in therapy. As previously mentioned, when the relationship is used it is basically as a context for the therapist to reinforce client behavior in the environment. There is no reason, however, that behaviorists could not utilize these phenoma when they are defined in behavioral terms. Later in the book I will discuss transference and countertransference in behavioral terms.

SUMMARY

Behavior Therapy is a highly structured attempt to scientifically approach human behavior. Beyond philosophical controversy, it has empirically demonstrated remarkable effectiveness in helping people change their behavior over a wide variety of presenting problems. Utilizing research with both animals and humans, behaviorists have established what they consider to be Laws of Behavior in both the respondent and operant domains. Behavior Therapy is considered by many professionals as one of the major foundations of psychotherapy in the twentieth century.

REFERENCES

AYLLON, T., and N. AZRIN, *The Token Economy*. New York: Appleton-Century-Crofts, 1968.

BANDURA, A. *Principles of Behavior Modification*. New York: Holt, Rinehart, and Winston, 1969.

FRANKEL, A. J. "Beyond the Simple Functional Analysis—The Chain: A Family Therapy Case Study." *Behavior Therapy*, 1975, 6, 254-260.

MAHONEY, M. J. *Cognition and Behavior Modification*. Cambridge, Mass.: Ballinger, 1974.

MILLENSON, J. R. *Principles of Behavioral Analysis*. New York: Macmillan, 1967.

SCHWARTZ, A., and I. GOLDIAMOND, *Social Casework—A Behavioral Approach*. New York: Columbia University Press, 1975.

SKINNER, B. F. *Beyond Freedom and Dignity*. New York: Knopf, 1971.

————. *Contingencies of Reinforcement*. New York: Appleton-Century-Crofts, 1969.

————. *Verbal Behavior*. New York: Appleton-Century-Crofts, 1957.

SUNDEL, M., and S. S. SUNDEL, *Behavior Modification in the Human Services*. New York: John Wiley, 1982.

THARP, R. G., and R. J. WETZEL, *Behavior Modification in the Natural Environment*. New York: Academic Press, 1969.

ULLMAN, L. P., and L. KRASNER, *A Psychological Approach to Abnormal Behavior*. Englewood Cliffs, N.J. Prentice-Hall, 1969.

WATSON, D. L., and R. G. THARP, *Self-Directed Behavior*. Monterey, Calif.: Brooks/Cole, 1972.

WENRICH, W. W., H. H. DAWLEY, and D. A. GENERAL, *Self-Directed Systematic Desensitization*. Kalamazoo, Mich.: Behavior delia, 1976.

WHALEY, D. O., and R. W. MALOTT, *Elementary Principles of Behavior*. New York: Appleton-Century-Crofts, 1971.

WOLPE, J. *The Practice of Behavior Therapy*. Elmsford, N.Y.: Pergamon Press, 1969.

REFERENCE JOURNALS

Behavior Therapy. Published by the Association of the Advancement of Behavior Therapy, New York. Vol. 1, #1: 1970.

Journal of Applied Behavior Analysis. Published by the Society for the Experimental Analysis of Behavior, Inc., University of Kansas, Lawrence, Kansas. Vol. 1, #1: 1968.

CHAPTER TWO
GESTALT THERAPY

BASIC PHILOSOPHY

Gestalt therapy came out of the psychoanalytic traditions. Fritz Perls, whose name is to Gestalt as B. F. Skinner's and Sigmund Freud's are to their respective approaches, was originally trained in the psychoanalytic atmosphere of Europe when Freud was still alive. For a number of reasons, some personal, Perls rebelled against Freudian theory and began to develop a psychology that was a dramatic departure from the norms of his day. Where Freud felt that aggression and sex were the basic motivational drives of human behavior, Perls hypothesized that eating and hunger were more important. He drew from a variety of other ideas as well to make what is now known as the first "humanistic" psychology. Such areas as existential philosophy, bioenergetics, and Eastern philosophy were integrated into Gestalt, a German word meaning "whole."

Perls refused to look at human psychology as necessarily dealing with pathology, where people were neurotic or psychotic and needed to be "cured." Rather, he viewed people as continually growing throughout their lives, each person uniquely struggling with different issues. Thus clients were not mentally ill, just stuck in their growth cycles. Instead of looking into what was sick, Perls chose to look at what was beautiful, creative, graceful, and fulfilling in life, and guided the goals of his therapy toward personal enrichment rather than cure.

Fritz and Laura Perls, who was also influential in developing Gestalt, attempted to integrate the body and the mind into a total psychological view. Humans are not just thinking beings. The total organism is involved in every thought and action. Feelings are not the same as thoughts; they involve the muscular structure before they get to a level of awareness. Thus, people cannot feel confused—confused is a thinking behavior. If you feel angry, you are experiencing a sensation of tension somewhere in your muscles, a characteristic tension unique to you, that eventually can reach a cognitive awareness of anger. Gestalt asks that we consider our whole organism as an integrated system, each part contributing to present awareness. In fact, when we are unsure of what we need, Gestalt suggests we utilize our whole body as a tool of discovery. One shouldn't be surprised to hear a Gestalt therapist saying there is wisdom in your fingers, feet, or stomach. When people are unaware of their anxiety, their bodies often respond with nervous behavior before they are cognitively aware of the feeling.

When people come into a Gestalt growth experience, an assumption is made that there are major unresolved issues in their lives. Whatever symptoms the person brings are symbols of these basic unresolved issues—they represent the tip of an existential iceberg. Existential philosophy, whose founder was Jean Paul Sartre, suggests we are essentially alone and constantly struggling to break out of this isolation. Life in a universal sense has no meaning. The only meaning life can have is what meaning we give it in our present moments. The way to resolve a client's initial presenting problems as well as the bigger, more existential ones, is through making better contact with people. Thus the goal of therapy is to help people make use of their existing personal and interpersonal resources to resolve specific problems and more central life issues as well.

Gestalt therapy has occasionally been associated with nonconformist lifestyles that are unconventional, to say the least. The therapy itself neither supports nor condemns nonconformity, but it does encourage people to experiment. Within reasonable boundaries, there is an emphasis on allowing people to attempt to fulfill their needs in diverse ways. Through experimentation with others it should become clearer whether behavior is truly congruent with getting important needs met. Gestalt generally believes that repressing needs and behavior keeps people from doing the kind of work that is so necessary for creative growth. The approach is very concerned with clients' knowing what they need and want from others and allowing themselves to get it.

The Gestalt Prayer summarizes the philosphy of the approach:

THE GESTALT PRAYER

I do my thing, and you do your thing.
I am not in this world to live up to your expectations
And you are not in this world to live up to mine.
You are you, and I am I,
And if by chance, we find each other, it's beautiful.
If not, it can't be helped.

THEORY

The "here and now."   Because we live only in the present, all of the learning that is possible exists in the now. During a therapy session, any problem clients have is somehow being acted out in relationships with the therapist and whoever else may be there. It is up to the therapist to help clients acknowledge how they are acting out their concerns with those present. The process isn't always obvious; in fact it is often obscure. But if we assume that all problems ultimately stem from a person's inability to make contact with others, then there is always a vehicle available in the here and now for bringing any issue into the present.

The emphasis on the here and now is almost synonymous with Gestalt. Both the past and the future are important, but they can infringe on the present, impeding the ability to get needs met. The past, or history, is considered wisdom which people draw upon when necessary, but the ability to choose to be in the present or with the past is important. An emphasis on history can keep people from being aware of the richness and creative potential of the moment.

It is at the present moment when all of the therapeutic work occurs in Gestalt. There are no antecedents or consequences—only the moment. If we are able to take care of ourselves in each of our here and nows, then the future will take care of itself. Thus, anxiety or fear about a possible future event is nothing more than a screen for discovering what we need now. All feelings are signals of present unfulfilled needs. There is no feeling that cannot be taken care of in your present moment. The Gestalt approach teaches us how to do this.

Unfinished business.   Unfinished business represents an unmet need from the past. Many things people start, both tasks and feelings, are not allowed to be finished for one reason or another. When an important need is not met over a long period of time, it gets stuck as energy within people's bodies. If they are not able to get this need met, the energy will either develop into a physical symptom or be channeled into misdirected anger or anxiety. For example, anger is a natural reaction to being hurt, either physically or emotionally. Children who are not allowed to be angry carry this unfinished experience into adulthood, acting it out in diverse ways. People who habitually refuse to say no may end up feeling chronically anxious when faced with a deluge of incompatible requests. In both cases, as children these adults were not allowed to do what was natural in taking care of themselves: to become angry and say no. Any time a natural expression of feeling is repressed, it creates unfinished business with those who demand compliance.

This is not to say, however, that people should allow all expressions of feeling regardless of the outcome. Life is full of unfinished business, much of which will never get dealt with. In fact, Gestalt therapists believe that it is the tension between past unfinished business and present experience that is the wellspring of creativity. And almost by definition, those people with whom we are the closest are the ones with whom we have the most unfinished business. However, there are times when issues from the past fairly beg to be finished in order for us to effectively go on with our lives. In these cases we cannot ignore the signals, which include serious relationship problems, psychosomatic symptoms, and debilitating anxiety.

When working on unfinished business, the most important question to ask is not *why* we get stuck but *how* we get stuck; *how* we keep ourselves from getting what we need. The "whys" are certainly interesting and usually include parent-child dynamics. But insight in Gestalt therapy is worthless unless along with it people identify what specific behavior they are performing in the here and now that is keeping them from getting their needs met. Regardless of whether clients get insight or not, they can see what they are presently doing to resist contact with others and change that behavior to get their needs met.

Organismic self-regulation.   The concept of organismic self-regulation is central in the theory and practice of Gestalt therapy. Clients will constantly be told to "trust the process—trust *their* process." People are born with an innate ability to get their needs met. The organism knows what it needs and learns quickly how to effectively communicate to get those needs met. Through growing up in families and society, children learn to inhibit their natural tendencies to take care of the organism as nature meant. Part of this process is of course necessary for the survival of civilization; but often this learning goes far beyond what is helpful. For example, little boys and girls cry whenever they are sad or hurt. As they grow up some of them learn to drastically inhibit the crying response because of family or cultural norms. Unfortunately, our bodies, or organisms, cannot inhibit some natural tendencies as well as we might like. Therefore, if crying is characteristically repressed in situations where our organisms are demanding that response, unfinished business will develop. Gestalt theory says that our organisms are built to take care of themselves if we will only allow them to. Essentially, the entire therapeutic model is based on helping people learn to trust that their organisms will take care of them—unlearning all the ways we have been taught to keep ourselves from naturally getting our needs met.

Personal responsibility.   It is not uncommon to hear Gestalt therapists say that people do not have the power to emotionally hurt others. Instead, we are responsible for our own feelings. We *choose* to feel hurt. This concept of personal responsibility for our feelings and behavior is one of the hardest to understand and accept for those still uninitiated into the Gestalt fold. Most people generally take responsibility for their behavior but just don't put it so literally. If you reject me and I feel hurt, you are not responsible for my pain. The facts are: you performed a behavior and I ended up feeling hurt. This is quite a different view from my saying, "You hurt me." In the first case I have the chance to look at how I am reacting and can choose to react differently regardless of what you do; in the second case I am blaming and giving you the responsibility for how I feel.

Not being responsible for others' feelings does not give people license to go around doing whatever they want, regardless of the outcome. I will do whatever is necessary to protect myself if I am consistently around someone with whom I feel hurt. If a client ends up feeling pain based on my behavior, I may not be the cause, but that does not mean I don't care. I do very much. But by not taking responsibility I am giving the client the gift of permission to take responsibility for his or her own life, and feel the power of that experience.

The Awareness Cycle

The structure for the Gestalt therapeutic process is called the Gestalt Awareness Cycle (*see* Figure 2-1). It can also be called the Experience Cycle. Both problem solving and personal growth start with the *awareness* of a need. Since there are so many stimuli to be aware of, Gestalt suggests that our perceptions will be guided by our present needs. Once a need is acknowledged, we *mobilize* our energy trying to meet the need. We literally begin mobilizing physical energy to either talk or move. Assuming that we are able to mobilize ourselves, the next step is the *action* necessary for getting the need met. The action will be verbal and/or physical. An appropriate action will put us into *contact* with the person or thing best able to meet our need; and finally assuming the need has been effectively met by our actions, we will *withdraw* from the experience and start the cycle over again. An example of this is eating. We become aware of hunger in ourselves; we mobilize our energy to move, the energy is used to walk to the icebox; we make contact with the food by eating it; and then once we are finished we withdraw from food until the next time we are hungry.

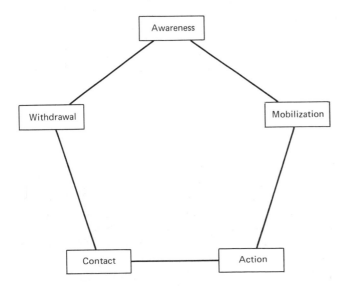

FIGURE 2-1   Gestalt Awareness Cycle

A person who is effectively going through the Awareness Cycle looks graceful, purposeful, assertive, at ease. One who is stuck with unfinished business will exhibit symptomatic resistances, most of which are easily observable. The cycle may be conceived as occurring during a moment, or for a lifetime. Each time we breathe in and out we are completing one small cycle. To be able to show how much we care for someone might take a lifetime.

The Awareness Cycle is so central to the theory and practice of Gestalt that it is well worthwhile to analyze each step further. In addition, we shall see it is the resistances at one or more of the steps of the cycle that are the focus of therapy.

Awareness.   The way we know what we want or need is through an awareness of ourselves, other people, and the environment. Awareness occurs only through the use of the five senses: seeing, touching, hearing, tasting, and smelling. With these senses we perceive the world and interpret our surroundings. The more ability we have to use these five senses, the more we will be able to know what we want and how to get it.

Nature provides little children with a wonderful curiosity to explore and test each of their senses. As they get older, they literally lose the ability to experience some of them. This comes about by a process of learning in our families and our culture. For instance, children use their noses freely, often reporting reactions to others. If someone smells bad, they feel free to mention it. This behavior is usually not well tolerated in many homes. Many children are taught to suppress their comments when people don't smell good. Eventually, over the years, some will literally lose the ability to notice and discriminate subtle body odors. Frankly, the loss of the ability to smell body orders is probably not significant. But the *process* that inhibits the smelling experience also inhibits much more essential senses that can seriously keep people from getting their needs met. For instance, children have a natural frustration response, especially when they don't get what they want. In some families this behavior is not acceptable. As the years go by these children learn that if they show anger they are punished, beginning an important piece of unfinished business: the inability to naturally complete the anger process. Many people who have grown up with this kind of learning actually do not consciously know when they are angry. They have been systematically conditioned to ignore those cues that mean anger. It is a fairly safe assumption that since anger is such a universal phenomenon, both in the human and animal world, it must be a natural way of reporting to yourself and others that something is seriously wrong and needs attention. In order for the process to work, one must be able to be aware of those muscular and glandular body cues that mean anger and then be able to communicate them effectively. People who have lost this ability will probably not be able to act on a situation that is hurting them. This, then, is a prime example of how we lose an important awareness through early childhood learning, one which is often necessary in getting our adult needs met. I might add that many people know when they are angry but were not allowed to naturally communicate their feelings in their families. Although the natural instinct was conscious, the energy it generated for action was misdirected. This type of behavior will be scrutinized later.

Mobilization.   While this step of the Awareness Cycle may in fact occur in a split second on the way to action, it can also be protracted. Think of how much time some people procrastinate before actually starting a task. Many students typically put off papers and serious studying until the last minute. In these cases it takes quite a while after the awareness that there is a job to be done to mobilize the energy to start it.

Action.   While the number of behaviors leading to contact are too numerous to describe, those that seem to be goal directed and purposeful are easily observed. In this stage of the Awareness Cycle we are concerned with performing only those behaviors that will most effectively make contact with the people or things helpful in getting our needs met.

Contact.   Contact is an approach to anyone or anything. It includes seeing, hearing, tasting, touching, and smelling. If you are aware that someone is in a room, you are in minimal contact with them, although they might not be in contact with you. In order for contact to be reciprocally maintained with a person or thing, there must be a sense of movement. For instance, remember when you were first dating? Sitting in a movie, hands touched, as if by chance, and hearts pounded. Neither of you dared to move as you held hands for the first time. After a few minutes, your hands started feeling clammy and eventually you probably lost the sense of where your hand stopped and your date's hand started—a sort of numbness set in. This is a good example of how there must be movement for contact to be experienced and maintained. You can do the same experiment with eye contact as well. Staring intently into someone's eyes becomes pretty old unless eyes move back and forth.

Psychologically, emotional contact is similar to physical contact, because you make contact through the use of your five senses. There is a line where your contact stops and another person's starts. This sometimes imaginary point is called a *contact boundary*, and is an important part of Gestalt psychology. When two people approach each other, there is an unstated line over which neither will encroach— a territorial imperative, if you will. Each relationship defines this boundary line for a wide variety of situations. In a more abstract sense, boundaries are also formed between two people by what they will tolerate in each other's behavior, what behavior they like and don't like in each other, and by what actions they will take to acknowledge and accentuate the differences between them. When two people do not acknowledge the obvious differences between them, or try to maximize their similarities, they are in a state of *confluence*, very much like what happens when you hold hands for too long. Keeping good psychological contact means helping people to be comfortable with their differences, knowing what they want to tolerate from each other, and allowing them to more freely express their likes and dislikes. This is analogous to the movement necessary for keeping good physical contact.

What is important about making contact is that you choose how much contact you want. The question of choice is central in Gestalt. There is no rule stating that high contact is better than low contact. Sometimes we need to withdraw into ourselves, while at other times we need the intensity that high contact brings. The ebb and flow of contact in relationships is as important to honor and respect as the ebb and flow of the tides. It is a natural and renewing phenomenon.

However, assuming a person wants higher contact, there are a number of guidelines that Gestalt suggests for making higher contact with yourself and others. In order to make high contact with someone else, you have to first be able to make higher contact with yourself. Physical support is the first way to get in better touch with oneself by centering your body in a sitting or standing position. Generally this means sitting or standing straight. Gestalt therapists believe that people have a hard time supporting themselves emotionally unless they are supporting themselves physically as well. In addition to physical support, the ability to breathe abdominally is also helpful. Those of you who have played a wind instrument, had singing lessons, or taken yoga know how to do this. The rest of us need to learn the skill of breathing with the stomach instead of with the chest. Done slowly, it is an excellent technique for relaxing at will, thus allowing oneself to settle down and find out what internal cues need to be attended to. Staying in the here and now also helps make higher contact with the self. Any joy, problem, or concern is always occurring in the present, so that consciously attending to present stimuli acts as a support. And finally, slowing down, both verbally and physically, is usually very helpful in giving self-support. It is very hard to know what is happening if you feel yourself "whooshing," or moving too fast. You could make a case for saying that all of these self-supporting techniques act to help a person slow down body processes.

Once a person has enough contact with the self to know what he or she wants, it is easier to make higher contact with another person. Gestalt also has some suggestions to enhance the possibilities for higher contact with others. Use "I" messages. Instead of saying "It seems hot," you will make higher contact if you say, "I feel hot," taking responsibility for your own experience. "It" takes the responsibility from you. Making statements instead of asking questions will also act to increase contact. Instead of saying, "How are you feeling?" try saying, "I want to know how you are feeling." This is quite different from saying, "How do you feel?"—not necessarily better, just more contactful since it is clearly acknowledging your need to know.

It is more contactful to speak concisely. Usually very few words can effectively convey an idea, a feeling, or a request. The general rule of thumb in Gestalt is that the more words a person uses, the lower the contact. There are some people who suffer from a chronic condition of diarrhea of the mouth. These people usually have a great deal of trouble making contact with others. Most of us tend to use too many words when we are upset and thus decrease our contact with the very people from whom we are needing something. Along with the concise use of words, the ability to make use of similes and metaphors will heighten contact. Your behavior reminds me of a giraffe; when you laugh like that I feel like a feather in the air; you vacillate like a yo-yo. These kinds of images enrich communication and heighten contact. Great speakers are able to touch people from a distance partly because of the wealth of similes and metaphors in their speeches.

There are a number of other behaviors that tend to increase contact: physical touching (the quality of the touch is important!) sharing feelings, wants, fantasies; using people's names; speaking directly to a person; making statements of recognition and, of course, staying in the here and now.

While these are general guidelines for heightening contact with yourself and others, the best way to know how to get better contact is to ask for feedback and to experiment. What is high contact for one might be anathema to another.

Withdrawal. This last step in the Awareness Cycle, while not as dramatic as Action or Contact, is just as essential for effective need fulfillment. Withdrawal is what it implies. After any contactful experience there needs to be time-out to let the learning of that experience be integrated into the organism's wisdom. If this time is not taken there is a good chance that learning will be lost in the rush to the next contact. Withdrawal can occur as the physical removal from people or a place, sleep, or a refusal to communicate with others. If people do not acknowledge the need to occasionally withdraw from each other as part of the ebb and flow of intimate relationships, they will find that distance occurs naturally anyway. Organisms need to integrate highly contactful experiences. Unfortunately, some of the ways withdrawal comes about in relationships are not as nourishing as others because of how it is instigated. People can separate from each other in anger as well as in love.

Motivation. Clearly it is the Awareness Cycle that defines motivation in Gestalt therapy. Once an organism becomes aware of a need, which always involves physical sensations, it is driven to get this need met. What the Awareness Cycle delineates are the steps people go through in this motivational process.

Fritz Perls suggested early in the development of Gestalt theory that there are basic drives at the root of motivation, much as seen in Freudian theory. However, he seriously departed from the traditional view of the libido and aggression as the central unconscious drives. Rather, Perls looked at hunger, the need to eat, as the most basic drive. He considered aggressive drives as well, but in relation to hunger, the development of the teeth, and chewing in particular. Hunger is, after all, one of the first needs a baby must struggle to meet after it is born. As we shall see, the hunger drive fits very well as a symbol for explaining how people learn to both physically survive and psychologically make contact with others. For instance, one of the important breakthroughs clients can make is to begin feeling the natural sense of disgust that comes when doing something unhealthy for one's organism. This disgust reaction, so important to change and growth, can be ultimately traced back to the eating response, which is of course driven by hunger.

Resistances to Change

At the core of how Gestalt therapy works are the resistances. Gestalt is unique in the way it uses this concept both theoretically and in practice. *Resistance* is ultimately defined as saying no to someone or something. In the therapy setting, resistance is associated with saying no to perceived therapist requests, particularly. Thus, resistance is defined as part of relationships and the process of making contact in the Awareness Cycle.

Another of the unique ways resistance is described in Gestalt is in its availability for observation. While many thought and physiological reactions may accompany resistance, Gestalt therapists believe that there is always a visible or verbal component. It is never necessary to interpret that a client is resisting; it always involves motor behavior and thus can be seen. In general, interpretation of any kind is anathema to Gestalt, as it imposes therapists' projections on clients' experiences. But nowhere is interpretation more unacceptable than when working with client resistances. In fact, since every problem is finally defined as a contact issue, we do not even talk about resistances to working on problems, we talk about resistances to contact which always involve observable or verbal behavior.

Resistances are organized in Gestalt by how we stop ourselves from getting our needs met. The five stages in the Awareness Cycle are all potential points where people have learned to keep themselves stuck with unfinished business. There are characteristic resistance behaviors associated with each step, which allow therapists to identify whether a client is stuck at awareness, mobilization, action, contact, or withdrawal (*see* Figure 2-2). Remember, the question to ask is not *why* but *how* people keep themselves from problem solving and getting their needs met. The resistance behaviors are these "hows."

Resistance to awareness. People resist awareness by feeling numb, refusing to use their five senses to feel internal sensations. These behaviors offer cues to therapists that there are resistances to awareness; in fact, these behaviors *are* the resistances. When people are refusing to feel, they will respond to "What are you feeling?" with "I don't know" or "Nothing." They are literally not aware of the sensations in their bodies. One important giveaway is when you see energy in their muscles—movement or tension—or can hear a strain in their voices, while at the same time they are saying that they have no feelings. It is a good Gestalt rule of thumb to assume that one is always feeling something. It is impossible to have no body sensations, unless you are dead.

Another type of numb behavior is more difficult to assess: a person looks relaxed and comfortable in a problem situation that would bother most people. He or she may not literally be seeing or hearing here-and-now stimuli.

There is nothing wrong with keeping one's head while all around people are losing theirs. However, an unhappy situation may persist if you are not able to make the kind of contact with them that will further a problem-solving process. It is rather common for people who have good skills in resisting awareness to characteristically

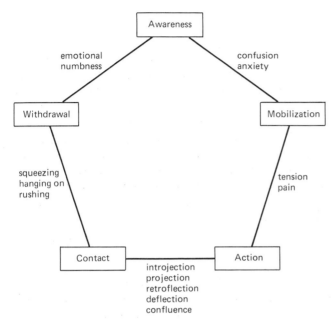

FIGURE 2-2 Gestalt Resistances

respond to anger, hurt, or fear with apparent relaxation instead of allowing their internal feeling cues to guide them into higher contact. These people are likely not completely relaxed. It takes energy to look and sound at ease when one's organism is not. Somewhere in the body there will be energy in the form of tension, pain, or glandular activity, such as sweating. In these cases it is up to the therapist to be aware of how behavior is incongruent with the present situation and share that possibility with the client. Therapists do this in two ways: first, they ask clients to report what they see and hear in the present situation. Differential perceptions are then highlighted. Second, clients are asked to carefully check in with their bodies, assessing any body sensations. If they become aware of incongruent here-and-now perceptions, or new body sensations, there is a good chance they are using resistances to awareness to keep themselves stuck. If, however, clients do not discover anything new, Gestalt therapists will not push their interpretations. Instead, they will continue to help clients find out how they are resisting solving problems and making contact. Gestalt spends a lot of time teaching people to be more aware of their bodies and environment. There are many awareness exercises geared to help people expand their sense organs, not only to know better what they are feeling but also to be able to enrich their enjoyment of life.

Thus there are two major classes of resistance behaviors to awareness: the first can be observed when the verbal behavior concerning feelings is not congruent with the motor behavior; the second can be inferred and checked out when a person apparently acts incongruently with environmental stimuli.

Resistance to mobilization.   The resistance to mobilizing one's energy is either confusion or anxiety, both of which are observable. People may be aware of their feelings but don't know what to do. Suggestions just add to the confusion. It is generally easy to know when people are confused just by listening to them; there are overt cues as well. Rapid nondirected movements of arms, hands, legs, or parts of the face are confusion cues. Anxiety is observed in nervous habits, sweating, shaky voices, rapid movement, and tense muscles. Most of the time clients will also verify their anxiety experience with therapists.

There is yet another set of cues that can aid the therapist in identifying resistance at the mobilization stage. How people sit, or support themselves, has a direct bearing on how well they know what they want and how to get it, as you will recall from our discussion on contact. There is a remarkable difference in the feelings related to posture. People stuck at the mobilization stage will likely sit or stand in a slouched position or put strain on their bodies by the way they position themselves.

Clients who become aware of what behavior they are engaging in to resist mobilizing their energy can choose to do something different. Anxiety is, after all, basically muscle tension. The same muscles we use to move ourselves around we also use to make ourselves anxious. By learning to relax those muscles, for instance, the blocked energy will be freed. Not only will it become clearer what we need to do but there will now be the energy to do it!

Resistance to action.   Now, assuming clients have some idea of what they are feeling, what they want, and are mobilizing to take some action, there may be resistance to taking the action itself. Long-term undirected energy, such as confusion and anxiety, often leads to physical tension and pain if it goes on long enough. Many people experience headaches, migraines, body aches, or other psychosomatic complaints at this point of the Awareness Cycle.

Actions that make close contact are inherently risky, especially when people are covering new ground. Unfortunately, or fortunately, depending upon one's perspective in life, any action leading to contact with another person is inherently unpredictable. The outcome will vary from acceptance to rejection. Thus, contact has risk involved with it. Risks seem much greater when people are feeling vulnerable—or perhaps people are more vulnerable when the risks are greater. In any case, actions that result in high contact are often difficult and tension or pain can be a way to resist them. It is interesting to note that tension and pain can literally keep a person immobilized—in a state of inaction.

Resistance to contact.   The resistances to contact in the Awareness Cycle are the most well known and the most complex. There are five basic resistances that occur here, and we will discuss each of them. Remember, there is nothing inherently wrong with being resistant to contact, unlike other therapies where to be resistant is undesirable. On the contrary, in Gestalt it often becomes necessary to help people become more resistant. Resistances to contact can be very healthy—depending on whether you are choosing to be resistant or whether the resistance represents an inability to get what you want.

1. *Introjection.* Introjection is the process by which we let things and ideas into our organisms. At its most primitive level, it is the eating process; but it is also the way we learn and accept values, attitudes, and morality. These are called *introjects*.

The world starts introjecting when we are born. Our first instinctual response, after breathing, is to suck for milk. In order to survive we have to trust that whatever is put into our mouths is good and healthy. A significant event occurs with the advent of teeth. When babies get teeth, they can prevent food from going in. Children can begin to make significant discriminations about what goes into the mouth with a set of teeth to not only chew food but also to bite whoever tries to force in unwanted food (*see* Figure 2-3). Perls called this phenomenon *dental aggression*.

It is a fascinating experiment to watch an adult eat. Some take small bites, some large; some chew slowly, some gobble; some spit out inedible bits of food, some swallow whole. This eating process, since it is so basic and conditioned at such an early age, can be perceived as analogous to how a person takes in values, attitudes, and critical feedback. Children learn all kinds of rules concerning how to live in our families and culture. Rules such as "Don't put your finger in a light socket," and, "Look before you cross the street," are functional. Some of the interpersonal rules we learned turned out to be functional as well. But some of them didn't. Such rules as, "Don't show your anger," "Don't cry," "Don't trust members of the opposite sex," or, "Don't be vulnerable," may have been functional in surviving a family system, but they and many like them may not be helpful in living a fulfilling life as an adult. Furthermore, we learned how to swallow rules, values, and attitudes, just as we learned how to take in food. Some of us swallowed whole the introjects we were taught; others took them in very slowly (possibly irritating our parents all the while!); yet others learned to be very suspicious and reject them outright. These introjection processes were vital to learning how to be in our families. But as adults they also may be nonfunctional. Thus, there are two introjection issues in Gestalt: the introjects themselves and the process of introjection.

Just as in eating food, if people take in values or rules that are not good for their organisms, they end up with a stomachache. The organism wants to get rid of this undigestible tidbit, so the natural process is to throw it up. People usually learn to inhibit the natural vomiting response, so the food, or introject, goes through the

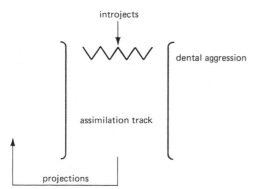

FIGURE 2-3
Introjection-Projection Process

assimilation track, some of it getting absorbed and perhaps making for more problems, with the rest being expelled. With eating we can learn to change the introjection process physically and use dental aggression to keep unwanted food out. We can also learn to spit food out if it doesn't taste good, take smaller bites, and generally be more discriminating about what goes into our bodies. Similarly, with values, rules, and feedback we can look at how we accept them and learn new ways to take them in so that we only "eat" what is good for us.

To better understand introjective resistances, let's look at some examples. There are people who are very sensitive to negative feedback. When they receive it, they do not symbolically exercise dental aggression by saying, "I don't like the way you are putting me down and I won't tolerate it"; or, "I want to hear how you feel and what you don't like about me but I can't handle it today"; or, "If you want to tell me what you don't like about me, tell me what I am doing that you don't like instead of putting me down." If sensitive people don't protect themselves from abuse, then they symbolically "eat" the feedback and get a stomachache, or worse. At the other extremes are the people who continually practice dental aggression. They won't listen to anything. What they are missing is the necessary feedback that helps to start and maintain intimate relationships. Symbolically, they are starving and literally need to open up.

It is important to learn a balance between these two extremes. People need to be able to psychologically clench their teeth at times. Indeed, when people get mad they instinctively clench their jaws. Showing teeth when angry is common across the animal kingdom and symbolizes the need to protect oneself when threatened. Conversely, it is often good to open up to listen to things you don't particularly want to hear because there may be some important learning in the feedback. But even then, we need the self-assurance that we don't have to accept all of what we hear.

In addition to learning new styles of introjection, getting rid of dysfunctional introjects is an important process in making higher contact. Therapists usually have a sense when clients are dealing with a dysfunctional introject. It will cause a continual upset about the same situation. The introject may even make a person physically ill. It is not uncommon for people who are dealing with dysfunctional introjects to feel nauseous. In fact, before an introject is finally expelled from their organism, they will need to get in touch with the natural sense of disgust that is part of eating unacceptable things. You might notice that a real sense of disgust is very similar to nausea.

A case example will help to show how the whole process works. As a child Bill learned from his parents that "you should not hurt people." This is the introject. Another lesson that Bill learned very early was that he had better do as he was told or life would be very unpleasant for him. So he basically followed his parents' wishes. Thus, among the many lessons of childhood, Bill learned the introject or rule, "Don't hurt others," and learned a process of introjection, "Accept rules without much question." When Bill as a young adult left his family, he began to experience some difficulty in relationships with women. He formed relationships well enough, but a pattern was emerging where he usually ended up being dropped by girl friends. He didn't understand since he was always so nice and he tried especially hard not to hurt them.

There is nothing inherently wrong with the introject, "You shouldn't hurt people." In fact, it's a pretty functional rule for surviving in most cultures. However, as with most introjects, it does not leave any room for exceptions, or at least, important qualifications. If a person believes it is wrong to hurt people, it will be difficult to give negative feedback, since there is always a risk that people will feel hurt. It is fairly common in relationships that people do things to hurt each other. A person who is being hurt has a limited number of choices to take care of him or herself in these situations: 1) tell the other person what it is you don't like and request that he or she stop doing it—this option risks that the other person will also feel hurt; 2) say nothing and continue being stepped on; 3) leave the relationship.

One of the reasons that Bill couldn't keep close relationships was a function of the introject that he had swallowed as a child. When a person will not set boundaries concerning what he will and won't tolerate in a relationship, it sets up a situation where there is little contact around some very important issues. Bill's introject acted as a resistance to contact by not allowing him to tell girl friends how he felt about their behavior toward him. By allowing himself to give negative feedback, he would have established better contact boundaries, and made more intimate contact by breaking the confluence of his relationships.

In order for Bill to increase his contact with friends, he will need to consider the value of his "don't hurt" introject and how he wants to qualify it. In addition, it would be helpful for him to look at how he accepts rules and feedback—his introjection process. With or without therapeutic guidance, Bill should consider making new rules that are more functional in his present life. This process, which is called *destructuring* an old introject and *restructuring* a new, more functional one, usually involves a degree of emotional pain. The pain is analogous to what happens whenever something is destroyed, and then has to be rebuilt. There is an element of saying good-bye to old habits and to the people who taught them to us. But it is the destructuring process itself that is intrinsically painful and necessitates a high input of energy to complete.

The therapist guides this process of destructuring an introjection resistance by helping the client develop the natural sense of disgust that comes when anything undigestible enters the body. As we will discuss further in the "Practice" section of this chapter, it is by heightening client dissatisfaction with the present state of affairs that will eventually get him or her disgusted enough to spit out the introject and replace it with a more functional one.

2. *Projection.* In its purest state, the projection resistance is not unlike its cousin in Freudian Theory. People put what they are feeling or experiencing onto someone else. When it is done by choice we call it empathy; when it is done as a resistance more traditional therapists may see it as a problem. Gestalt, on the other hand, accepts the use of projection as another way to resist or increase contact. It is neither good nor bad.

In addition to the more traditional view of projections, Gestalt adds another dimension; projections include how we expect people or things to act in the future. A person who expects that close friends usually end up leaving, brings an important dynamic to new relationships. Other projections could include: "Members of the opposite sex end up hurting me"; "Nobody can help me when I'm feeling down"; "People aren't going to like me on first encounters"; "I don't come off well in intelligent conversation." What is so interesting about projections is how we selectively use our perceptions to make sure that the expectation will come true, even when there is very little cooperation from others. For example, consider this projection: "When I am in a group people will put me down." In any group of ten people there are going to be those who are willing to fulfill this prophecy with very little encouragement, or will naturally be turned off by your behavior. However, there will also be people who like you and give positive comments. When people are into a projection, they are especially sensitive to those behaviors that will fulfill it. When those behaviors occur, they can say, "Aha, I told you it was true." Some people will often have no memory of positive events—just the negative ones. It is as if their ability to see and hear reality were limited by their selective perceptions. At those times when people are into a projection and no one is conveniently fulfilling it, they have another option: they can act in such a way as to make sure that someone will meet their expectations. In the previous example, if the group were a particularly positive one, one could always get negative comments by being obnoxious. Then, of course, he or she could say, "I told you this would happen. It always does."

Projections keep people from making contact by not allowing them to see present stimuli and what is available to them in their here and now. The classic example of this is when two people are trying to problem solve and one says to the other, "You're angry with me." The other says, "No I'm not." "Yes you are." And so on. If the second person is not angry and cannot convince the first that he or she is not, he will become frustrated, thus fulfilling the prophecy. It is very difficult to make contact with someone who is not perceiving the same basic here-and-now reality that you are. Being in a projection means there will be very little contact, since people are literally perceiving different stimuli in the same situation with an inability to find some common ground.

In order to get rid of a projection and improve contact between people, a number of steps need to be taken. First, you have to accept the possibility that when you are feeling threatened or vulnerable you may go into a projection. There will be interferences with your ability to perceive here-and-now stimuli as awareness functioning is selectively inhibited. People truly believe what they are seeing and hearing is all that is there. And what makes life even more confusing is that at times they may be right. Thus, a person with an ongoing projection initially needs help from others to verify perceptions.

For example, if a client is sure that others are angry and can be convinced that he is wrong through corrective feedback, then he can try "owning" the projection. Owning a projection means that you take the feeling or expectation in the projection and apply it to yourself. Thus, the client who was projecting anger might own his projection by asking, "Am I angry and don't realize it?" Remember, if people try owning their projections, and it still doesn't fit with their present experience, they can always continue operating with their original perceptions, even if they are making poor contact. Sometimes people just don't make good contact with each other, and as it says in the Gestalt Prayer, "It can't be helped."

After you have become aware of a projection, the next step is to systematically check it out. This is not as easy as it may sound. Obviously individuals are not completely honest with themselves or with others. So the process of checking out realities is fraught with pitfalls. There needs to be a reference person or group you can trust.

There are a number of good cues that help signal the onset of a projection. Overreactions and underreactions are usually signs. Another cue concerns how people give up projections. For instance, I suggest you look depressed. You say you are not depressed. At this point, the question is whether I can give up the projection or insist on my original perception that you are depressed. If what I was trying to communicate was the projection, "When I look like you I feel depressed," then I am open for corrective feedback. But if I continue on with that perception in the light of your denial, I am telling you, in effect, that I know you better than you know yourself. This is obviously not true. At that point there is the possibility that I am depressed and am refusing to own the feeling myself. But even if I am not feeling depressed myself, if I continue with this perception of you I will be using my projection to resist contact. It doesn't matter whether I am right or wrong, or whether I am really feeling depressed. If we are not generally responding to the same here-and-now stimuli in a situation, then our contact is very likely to be poor. Hanging onto a projection in the face of corrective feedback always tends to decrease contact. Of course, as I have said before, there is nothing wrong with using projections for lower contact; but it should be a question of choice, not habit.

In order to completely get rid of a projection resistance it is necessary to go back to the original introject that spawned it. Look at Figure 2-3. Notice again how the process of an introject works. Unless it is initially spit out, the introject enters the organism and remains undigestible. Eventually it comes out as a projection on the world. There is no predicting exactly what kind of projection will come from a single introject. For instance, the introject, "You should not trust members of the opposite sex," could come out as, "I expect to be hurt in close relationships, "I expect men/women to put me down," or, "I'm not able to enjoy sex." Since life presents different kinds of experiences to us all, there will be a wide variety of possible projections that could be derived from any introject. However, once the projection has been indentified and labeled, a natural regressive process occurs back to the origins of the projection, the introject. Similar to dealing with any introject, a natural disgust reaction will have to be invoked to get rid of the introject, and thus the projection stemming from it.

The whole therapeutic process, then, is to first identify projection behaviors, when clients perform them, and begin accepting feedback about others' perceptions of present realities. As this process is going on, clients will probably begin to get in touch with the introject behind the projection, and can then deal with it. It is of course possible to work on a projection without going back to the original introject. People can gain good control of their projections by becoming aware of them and consistently checking them out with others. They may decide not to confront their origins. After all, life is full of things on which to work, and all work does not have to be finished. In Gestalt, clients work only until they feel finished, at whatever point that may be. If therapists don't like it, that's their problem—clients are the best judges of what is good for them. Trust the organism.

3. *Retroflection.* Retroflection resistances are performed in two interesting ways: 1) doing to yourself what you would rather do to others; 2) doing for yourself what you would rather have others do for you. In addition, a positive retroflection is one where you work to support yourself; a negative retroflection is when you work to hurt yourself.

Any behavior you do to yourself that doesn't feel good is a negative retroflection. These behaviors include putting yourself down, depression, self-depreciation, and guilt. All of these self-abusing behaviors are retroflections, or doing to yourself what you would rather do to others.

Consider the feeling of guilt with its accompanying behaviors (as we did in the behavioral chapter): 1) you do or say something; 2) you hear a message that you should have done it differently; 3) you agree with the message; 4) you put yourself down with an internal statement such as, "What a dummy I am," or, "I am a terrible person," with attending physiological reactions. The fourth step is the retroflection which not only doesn't feel good but also doesn't motivate a change in behavior. If it did, then you wouldn't feel guilty again. Never feeling guilty is of course absurd, since it is a normal human experience. But it does no good to feel guilty about the same things again and again if the situation is not resolved. Therefore, once again we must ask what is the function of kicking oneself. The Gestalt answer is that a retroflection is a way of resisting contact. If contact were made it would likely be to the person who is "laying on the guilt" or more specifically, the person who is telling you what you should or shouldn't have done. The retroflection is coming from a part of you that symbolically represents whoever originally gave you the message, and represents some unfinished business with him or her.

If negative retroflections become a characteristic way of treating oneself, they are being used to continually resist contact with those with whom we have unfinished business. It is far safer for us to punish ourselves than to make riskier, higher contact by confronting the people who are critical of our behavior. These retroflections represent the unfinished business that always persists when we do not stop people from consistently judging our lives.

The way to get rid of a negative retroflection is to "undo it" by literally turning self-depreciating statements from "I" messages to "you" messages. Thus, "I am a terrible person," is turned around to, "You are a terrible person." Of course, in undoing the retroflection one must find the appropriate person to whom to direct it. What makes this process very difficult is the real risk involved. The people with whom you are close are not likely to be pleased with your questioning their values and rules, much less deciding to change them in yourself. However, the choice is whether to dysfunctionally continue kicking yourself, or to let that energy flow to the person who is helping to make your life difficult.

Depression is another common retroflection. In traditional forms of Freudian psychology, depression is generally thought of as anger turned inward. Gestalt psychology looks at depression similarly, but with the added dimension of its basic function being a retroflective resistance to contact. Depression is a very natural human experience, if not a pleasant one. It appears to be nature's way of expressing loss. Allowed to follow its natural course, depression can be viewed as healing, a way for an organism to turn inward, break contact with the world, and assess how to deal with a new set of circumstances. When depression becomes a characteristic way of behaving, it becomes dysfunctional.

The Gestalt interpretation that depression is a retroflection, something you do to yourself which you would rather do to others, is again based on the idea that it is not natural to hurt yourself; but it is less risky than making contact with someone with whom you are angry. Whenever we experience a serious loss, or repeatedly feel helpless to change intolerable situations, depression is a possible organismic response. For instance, depression resulting from a death will usually cause a person to turn inward. The grief process can also include anger relating to the unfairness of the death, or directed at someone who is considered responsible. Making contact for support is also an eventual part of the natural depression cycle which finishes with acceptance of the new reality.

But there are many people who chronically react to life with depression, not just as part of the normal ebb and flow of contact. In these situations the depression becomes a means for avoiding the risk of letting people know how they feel and making demands on them. This retroflective habit and the feeling of helplessness can be so ingrained that any alternative suggestions fall on deaf ears. The risk is projected to be too great, even when reality suggests that it is not. Frankly, though, part of the perceived risk is often quite real. For example, take the stereotypic situation of a depressed housewife. She may be aware that what she needs is to have a career, but is fighting a husband who wants her to stay home to cook, clean, and take care of the children. She has likely learned from parents that her role is to stay at home and be a "good wife," and parts of society reflect these values. In order to get out of the house, she will have to confront all three of these factors. Each of them represents a very real risk. Her husband could divorce her; her parents could withdraw their support; her circle of "friends" could judge her harshly and she could lose their support as well. Is it any wonder that so many housewives who want careers choose depression instead? It can take skill, training, and, yes, courage to undo this retroflection and put the anger where it belongs—on the people who are demanding that she remain in a role that no longer meets her needs. The basic question we must ask ourselves when we are depressed, or into any negative retroflection, is whether we wish to continue to hurt ourselves, or undo the retroflection and take risks. The choice is often difficult, but it is ours.

The most severe form of depression is of course suicide, and in Gestalt this is retroflective murder. It is the result of a severe retroflection resistance to contact over a long period of time.

The positive retroflection is certainly not as unpleasant as the negative, but it can be a lonely experience performed in the extreme. Basically, a positive retroflection includes supporting yourself. Just as in every resistance we have discussed so far, it has its good points. If you are in a situation where no one will praise you, it is helpful if you can effectively praise yourself. If there isn't anyone who will make your breakfast, it's good to have the ability to feed yourself. However, taken to the extreme, the ability to support oneself can make people so independent that they feel they don't need people. Remember the definition: a positive retroflection is doing for yourself what you would rather get from others. If you've done a good job, it feels good to get praise. Giving the praise to yourself is fine; but if you feel no one else will like your work, or that their opinions would weigh too heavily on you, then you are using a positive retroflection to keep from making contact. There is always a risk in asking others for their opinions. It makes you vulnerable to them; they may not want or be able to give support; they may give you the opposite of what you wanted. Most people need a balance between their ability to support themselves and their ability to ask for support from others.

People who are viewed as extremely independent often feel they can't depend on others to take care of them. This represents unfinished business in important past and present relationships. As long as they don't have to depend on anyone to get their needs met, they will not be vulnerable. Being vulnerable is risky. It's easier for positive retroflectors to support themselves and avoid contact.

It is often hard to determine when a positive retroflection is being used to inhibit contact and when it is helpful. The best rule of thumb is to look at how people characteristically behave when they feel threatened or scared. If people seem to need support and characteristically refuse it, it is possible they are using a positive retroflection resistance to contact. Also, if you hear a statement to the effect that "you have to depend on yourself because you can't depend on others," that is a good cue, too.

4. *Deflection.* The deflection resistance to contact can be one of the simplest to spot, and at the same time can be extremely subtle. It is a hit-and-miss proposition with your environment. While it appears a person is putting enough energy into a relationship to make good contact, in reality the energy is being misdirected and missing its mark.

The simplest kind of deflection is when people change the subject. If you want to talk about your feelings and suddenly find yourself talking about someone else's problems, you have let yourself be deflected. Or if a friend starts talking about your old girl or boyfriend, making you uncomfortable, you may try to change the subject to one that is less annoying. Changing the subject is the most basic form of deflection.

Deflections occur at emotional as well as content levels, and this is where they are hard to recognize. For example, if clients are hurt and instead show anger, they are deflecting one feeling for the other. There is nothing inherently wrong with this process unless people have no choice in the matter. We are frequently not aware that a strong feeling is really a deflection from another more vulnerable one which would be too risky to share. There are many times that showing hurt takes more risk than anger. If people are not getting what they need from a relationship, it might behoove them to consider if they deflect vulnerable feelings, such as fear and hurt.

Couples who are intimate often use deflections when they have disagreements. For example:

ANN: When you put me down at parties it hurts me, I get angry, and I want you to stop it.

BOB: Well, you do it to me. (deflection 1)

ANN: I do it to you because you do it to me first. (deflection 2)

BOB: You've been putting me down ever since we first got married. (deflection 3)

ANN: God, you're being just like your father, a real bastard. (deflection 4)

This fight could go on for a long time, escalate further into a full-blown war, and still the issue of Bob's hurting Ann at parties would not be addressed. How did this happen? In deflection 1 Bob immediately deflected from Ann's topic by bringing up one of his own. Perhaps Bob has been harboring some resentment (unfinished business) that Ann has been putting him down at parties, or just doesn't want to deal with this confrontation. Regardless of the reasons, he has deflected the discussion to his agenda. There is a standard rule of thumb in Gestalt that only one person's agenda can be dealt with at a time. In this case, Ann and Bob have not decided who will have the floor first, and as a result Ann is almost assured that her request for a change in Bob's behavior will be lost. Her choice here is to take up the offered deflection, joining in a collusion to deflect from her wants, or to ignore the deflection and demand that he listen to her first. As you can see, Ann picks up the deflection with a vengeance and starts defending herself. Bob then continues deflecting by going into history and getting out of the here and now, which is one of the standard ways of deflecting from contact and escalating an argument from a relatively small issue into a big one. Ann then offers another deflection by bringing Dad into the picture. Since there is always lots of unfinished business with our parents, it is a pretty safe bet that bringing them into arguments will be deflective.

When a deflection is offered you don't have to take it. If you do, then you are also responsible for using this resistance to keep from making contact. There is a tendency to blame the other person for deflecting, and forget that we actively participated.

There are other subtle ways to deflect from contact that are certainly not as dramatic as what happens in a fight, but may accomplish the same end. When a person in a group says, "I'll take feedback from anyone"; "What I want to say . . .";

or, "Let's discuss that," they are offering little deflections from making contact more directly. In and of themselves, these small verbal deflections are not significant. But when a pattern of them emerges, it is at least reasonable to consider that a person uses deflections as one of his or her basic resistances to contact.

The clues therapists use to detect deflective resistances are generally observable. The person receiving deflections often reports feeling confused, not quite knowing what happened. The deflector most often feels misunderstood. If you characteristically feel that people just don't understand the way you feel, it would be worthwhile to consider whether you are a sender of deflections into the world.

Therapists do very well at the art of deflecting. We are unwitting experts at it. For instance, a client gets angry with me. Instead of facing how I feel when someone who is depending on me gets angry, I might say, "Let's talk about your anger." That comment is a deflection from my feelings, which could be verbalized as, "I feel uncomfortable when you are angry with me." Another example: Client, "I don't think you are helping me so I'm going to terminate." Therapist: "It sounds as it you are angry with me." This is a deflection from a common feeling among therapists of either fear or irritation with clients who want to leave before we therapists think they should. It is much riskier for therapists to admit that they can be vulnerable and hurt by clients.

To stop using deflective resistances to contact, we must first know how and when we are using them. Then we need to know what we are deflecting from. This may not be a simple process since there is usually a lot of unfinished business related to emotional deflections. Along the road to making higher contact, clients can experiment with refusing to perform the deflection behaviors and substituting alternatives. In Gestalt it is not important *why* people are deflecting, but *how* they are doing it. Once their deflective behaviors are clarified, they have the power to choose to perform differently to make higher contact.

As with all of the resistances we have discussed, deflections can be as helpful as they can be harmful. When contact is too much for you, a well-chosen deflection can be a godsend. Humor is a good example of how a deflection can lessen contact on one hand, and leave you open for contact on the other. If you think about the kinds of things we laugh at, you will notice that they are often not funny. We laugh when comedians make fun of themselves and others. We laugh at people's foolishness and ridiculous stereotypes. These are not inherently funny, but by laughing and not taking serious things seriously, we leave ourselves open for further contact and feel better. In fact, a deflection can be done contactfully if it is done through negotiation. When two people jointly decide to deflect, it is called a *contactful deflective activity*, an agreement to jointly deflect.

There is so much one could be working on in life that we would go crazy if we spent all of our time trying to "grow" and problem solve. Thus, it is important to choose what issues will be faced and what unresolved issues will be deflected, or as we say in Gestalt, "bracketed." When an issue is bracketed, it is left to be resolved later. For two people to survive and enjoy a relationship, it is essential that there be agreement that some personal and interpersonal issues be bracketed. Otherwise, there will be very little time to rest and enjoy.

5. *Confluence.* Whenever two people do not recognize the boundaries between them, they symbolically mesh into each other. Their lives will be comfortable, not exciting; they will be in agreement about almost everything; they will be bored. Even when the agreement between two people is not stated, there can be a collusion about how the relationship will be conducted. For instance, in the well-known Gestalt "top dog-underdog" relationship that many people feel is part of their married lives, there is often an unsaid rule demanding one of the partners be considered the top dog and the other the underdog. Furthermore, the rules go on to demand that these roles not be seriously challenged and that they be basically accepted. If people are happy in their assigned roles, who is to say that their relationship should be modified. But it is often the case that one partner is not happy, and yet will not risk a challenge to the confluent system. It is more important to keep things "cool" than to risk breaking the confluence. In this way confluence keeps people from making contact. You frequently hear couples using the royal "we" when they are discussing their relationships instead of discriminating between what each of them thinks separately. There is an emphasis on how the two people are alike and how they agree rather than an acknowledgement of their differences—indeed, an appreciation of their differences. In order to break confluent systems, people have to recognize and accentuate the differences between them. Setting contact boundaries is painful because people who habitually use confluence are usually afraid that differences will put distance between them.

Good and healthy dynamics are a part of this resistance, too. It would be a nightmare to come home every night to see your furniture rearranged. You like to know that some things won't change, that there will be continuity to count on. But if there is too much security, you will probably get bored. Two people can get so enmeshed that they can no longer see each other or themselves. Like all the resistances, there needs to be a balance between confluence and boundaries; but most important, people need to be aware of whether they are resisting contact by habit or by choice.

Resistance to withdrawal. The basic resistances to withdrawing are rushing and hanging on or squeezing. Rushing is moving so fast that there is no time to integrate an experience. It is a physical as well as mental phenomenon. A person can be seen moving quickly, jerkily. Speech will usually also be rapid. In therapy the client will finish up one important piece of work and want to move on to another. Rushing thoughts are common.

Hanging or squeezing an experience occurs when people are afraid to let go, for whatever reason. A person will be reluctant to leave, will maintain eye contact, and continue trying to communicate.

Withdrawal as a resistance to contact works in a variety of ways. After sharing high contact, if people rush from that experience to the next, they will inevitably be attempting to make contact with others who recognize their own present needs for withdrawal. This attempt will tend to discount what contact did occur. Conversely, refusing to leave a highly contactful experience can be thoroughly exhausting, not only diluting what contact was there but also making further contact very difficult. In addition, nothing can be more irritating than one person trying to hang on while another recognizes the need for withdrawal. The functional outcome of all of these withdrawal resistances to contact is to put psychological if not physical distance between people.

Working out of rushing and hanging on requires clients to know, as usual, how they do it. The ability to either slow down or let go is one that can be learned and practiced, regardless of one's history. The organism needs time to withdraw from contact, but not so much time that life can't go on. There is no formula for how much withdrawal is best in a given experience. But once people learn to trust their organisms they'll know how long to let an experience nurture them and when to say good-bye.

Polarities.   Beyond the resistances in the Awareness Cycle, Gestalt integrates two other important concepts into clients' work: *polarities* and *dreams*. Gestalt work on polarities looks at opposites: good-bad, soft-hard, strong-weak, powerful-vulnerable. While the humanist movement has generally supported the contention that humans are basically loving and nonjudgmental, Gestalt suggests that this view deletes a significant part of human experience. If we try to ignore the negative parts of ourselves we are working with less than what we are—complex, sometimes gentle, sometimes brutal creatures with tremendous potential to lovingly create and horrendously destroy.

Working with polarities brings out the positive and negative parts of our existence. The negative parts are in what is called *the shadow side*. Discovering the attitudes, values, and behaviors in our shadow side can tell what our developmental tasks are and what we need to do to live a more fulfilled life. The shadow side is considered to contain the disowned parts of ourselves we do not wish to acknowledge.

There are many stereotypic examples of polarities. Men tend to try to keep their femininity in their shadow sides, including all those attitudes, values, and behaviors with which femininity are associated. They generally try not to show their emotions, dress too extravagantly, or be too gentle, especially in public. Unfortunately, some supposedly feminine characteristics are also human characteristics. In that sense, the energy men use to keep their femininity in the shadow makes them less able to be natural and interferes with getting needs met. Another example is the powerful-vulnerable polarity. Many people feel that it is better to be strong than vulnerable. Again, it is natural to be vulnerable at times. If we permit ourselves that experience, some very exciting things can occur, including real intimacy. Often people feel that if they experiment with a disowned part of themselves, it will take over. Be vulnerable for a minute and you'll fall apart; men, be gentle and you'll become homosexual; women, be assertive and you'll become aggressive and castrating.

The goal of polarity work is to clearly separate and heighten polarities so that they can be understood, experienced, and integrated. It is possible to be and feel both powerful and vulnerable at the same time. It is possible to be simultaneously gentle and strong. Once a polarity is separated, acknowledged, and owned, there exists the possibility to integrate the attitudes and behaviors the opposite poles represent. This is not to say that people have to accept everything they find in their shadow sides. There are many things in there we do not choose to accept as part of our behavior. However, by acknowledging their existence, we can better control them. For example, the urge to kill ourselves or others is in the shadow side (I hope). Owning the feeling does not mean we have to act it out. But acknowledging it exists can be an important message that something is very wrong and needs immediate attention. You can choose to ignore it, listen to it, integrate part or all of it. In this case, refusing to own such a hostile feeling keeps us from getting important needs met, at best. At worst, disowning the urge to kill can allow sinister forces to be unwittingly exposed or even explode without apparent control. Working on polarities is an exercise in accepting what it means to be human.

Dreams. Dreams fulfill a number of needs representing important present concerns. They are existential messages to the self, telling us what are the major issues in our lives. In an incredibly creative way they show where we are stuck in our growth and what is lacking in our ability to cope; they call attention to unmet needs and states of deprivation. Everything is in a dream: the existential struggles, the missing parts of our personalities, our fully integrated parts, and the disowned unintegrated parts of our polarities. Since dreams are uniquely created from our own experience, they must then represent projections of ourselves—it is the only material with which we have to work. No matter who or what we dream about, we are using these people, things, and places as symbolic projections of ourselves. We are creatively putting them into our dreams to play out some dynamic in us.

Dreams that are happy are more easily owned and remembered. We can accept the message about ourselves, acknowledging its reality. However, if the dream is unpleasant, indeed, even nightmarish, it usually represents those parts and feelings that we do not wish to accept or acknowledge. People who do not remember their dreams are likely at a point in their lives where they are afraid to confront some present relationships and their existential state of being. Continual nightmares are more persistent reminders of the same dynamic.

Gestalt therapy uses a fascinating and unique method for therapeutic dreamwork. It is a process of owning the symbolic projections in a dream and acting them out until the meaning of the dream becomes clear. Dreamwork can be an exciting and profoundly moving experience for clients if therapists remain facilitators and keep interpretations to themselves. Only dreamers know the true meaning of their dreams.

When a dream becomes foreground in therapy, Gestalt therapists will listen to as much of it as can be remembered. It is not necessary to have a complete story—a dream fragment will do. The symbols and people associated with the most emotional and physical energy in the dream are clearly described. Then the client is asked to speak for each identified part, pretending to actually be that part. For example, if I had dreamed about a storm, I would begin "I am the wind . . ." and describe my role in the dream. By going through all of the identified symbolic projections in this way, the meaning of the dream can become clear.

Another interesting method for working through a dream involves using a group. Each important part of the dream is assigned to a group member and the client literally arranges the people for a dream reenactment. The dreamer walks through the experience again, interacting with the group members who are acting out the dream projections. This *dreamwork as theater* technique is obviously more dynamic than asking the client to personally speak for all the parts and can also clarify the meaning of a dream.

No description of Gestalt dreamwork would be complete without a case example. Sarah reported to her group that she had been having an uncomfortable recurring dream for the last year. She was a middle-aged divorcée, a schoolteacher, and lived alone. She dreamed she was running down an endless railroad track balancing on one rail or the other, but not on the ties. Every quarter mile or so she would pass a small station, but would never stop, only hurry on. These stations were for the most part empty; she wasn't too sure what was in them. The track was running through farmland and forest, but she never saw any people. As she continued along the track, she became tired and went slower and slower until the dream ended.

When Sarah "Gestalted" the dream she became the rail, the ties, and stations. "I am the metal rail of the railroad track. I am shiny and cold. I feel you, Sarah, running along top of me, but you don't seem to be too well balanced. I really don't mind your feet on me. In fact, it's sort of as if you are scratching me and feels good at times. When you slow down your feet don't scratch so well, but I really don't mind." Next the ties: "I am the ties. I am very aware of you rushing by. You seem to be very careful not to step on me, which is surprising, because you don't look very comfortable up there trying to keep your balance all the time while you get more and more tired. If you walked on me you wouldn't have to balance yourself. I think it's pretty stupid for you to keep walking on the rails." Then the stations: "I am the stations. I wish you would stop and rest in me. I don't seem to have much furniture to rest on, but I do look over some pretty countryside. You look pretty tired, especially after a while. I don't understand why you don't stop."

After Sarah finished her discourse, the therapist asked her if she had become aware of anything now that she was finished. Sarah reflected for a minute and then replied that the dream seemed to be related to some recent thoughts about entering middle age after so many years of struggling to arrive at a place where she could be comfortable. At this point she couldn't be more specific.

It was not necessary to do anything more with her present insight since she had had very little time to withdraw from her dreamwork experience and see more fully what it meant. However, her therapist asked if she would be interested in finishing the dream now. If Sarah's organism was ready to finish up the work this dream represented, she could take the opportunity now. She chose to do so. Sarah returned to her dream, but this time she was writing a new script, so to speak. Instead of continuing on walking down the rail, she decided to stop in one of the waiting stations and processed her experience with the group: "I am tired so I will stop in this next station. It is rather barren, but there do seem to be a few pieces of old antiques in the corners. And the view is very pleasant. I can see where I have come from and feel a little sad that I did not stop to look at the views from the other waiting stations." The therapist said, "Look around the waiting room carefully. Do you see any more furniture? Are there any people there with you?" Sarah: "No, there is no one here with me. I am aware that I feel more relaxed and comfortable. I am really enjoying looking at the view. The trees and farms are very pleasant."

When Sarah was finished, the therapist again asked if she had become aware of anything during her work. She replied that she was surprised how nice stopping at the waiting station had been. "I have been hurrying so hard to get somewhere and getting nowhere. When I stopped it was nice. Maybe that's all there is. It's not such a bad place to be."

Sarah's dream apparently represented her ongoing struggle to find the existential meaning for this period of her life. You will notice that the therapist's role was to set the structure of her work, not to offer interpretations of what the dream symbols meant or to guide her experience to some specific predetermined end. It was Sarah's dream; it was her work; and any meaning she found in her dream was what she interpreted for herself.

PRACTICE

The Role of the Therapist

The therapist is the most experienced client in the room. While this role is congruent with Gestalt theory, it is a profoundly difficult one to follow. First, since many clients expect therapists to take care of them, or at least to tell them what to do, it is easy to be lulled into parental-type roles. Furthermore, there are a good number of therapists who enjoy being appreciated as charismatic leaders and don't want to be considered as experienced clients. Be that as it may, Gestalt is at its best when Gestalt therapists demonstrate to their clients that in the room are two adults who are working for better contact with each other. Therapists need to be themselves with all of the strengths, weaknesses, creativity, and insecurities that come along with being human.

This is not to say Gestalt therapists don't work hard. Indeed they do. The major difference between the therapist and client role is that therapists must be keenly aware of everything that is going on while clients are learning these skills. It takes tremendous concentration and energy to maintain this level of awareness for long periods. Therapists learn how to use their awareness functions as efficiently as possible by going through their own personal-growth experiences as part of Gestalt training. As they gain experience in facing their own resistances to making contact, very often as clients in professional growth groups, they are then able to better help clients face the same issues.

It is the relationship between the therapist and client in the here and now that is the basis for personal growth. No matter what problems clients may bring into a session, the issue always ultimately boils down to how clients resist contact in the here and now with whomever is present. Honest and open therapist behavior is crucial to developing a helpful relationship. Professionals who practice Gestalt find that while they let themselves be natural, they are often taking some real personal risks. It takes skill and self-assurance to allow yourself to be vulnerable, afraid, or hurt with a client and still maintain a sense of your own power. If therapists are able to respond with honest feeling reactions while maintaining control of themselves and a sense of their personal power, they are providing a wonderful model for clients. Since Gestalt strongly supports the concept of organismic self-regulation, therapists are supposed to be for the most part nondirective. People are their own best therapists.

The Gestalt Treatment Process

There is a relatively systematic therapeutic process that gives both therapists and clients guidelines concerning what behavior is expected of them. It may seem strange that Gestalt should have any kind of definable process at all. After all, Gestalt is sometimes purported to be the creative, no-holds-barred, do-your-own-thing therapy. Indeed, some apparently curious therapeutic techniques can be seen in Gestalt experiments. What kind of systematic process could possibly be associated with hugging trees, smelling oranges, or "touchie-feelie" exercises?

In fact, it is by the very nature of Gestalt therapy that there has developed a structure for personal growth. Gestalt is concerned with the integration of polarities in the human condition. Having either a fixed or a freewheeling therapeutic process would represent the very principles that Gestalt is trying to avoid. What does seem to reflect the reality of life is the ongoing struggle between the imposition of a learning structure and the freedom for real creativity. Somewhere between these two seemingly incompatible polarities lies the best learning model for each of us. Gestalt tries to uniquely find that balance.

The Awareness Cycle provides the basic framework for each session, with therapists using their awarenesses to suggest possible resistances, depending on what stage of the cycle the client is stuck. There are six steps in the Gestalt therapeutic process (See Figure 2-4). The umbrella that covers them all is the knowledge that no matter what kind of problem a client is dealing with, it is somehow occurring in the here and now.

Awareness. Therapists begin each session by asking clients what they want to do. If they cannot respond clearly to that question, it becomes the initial focus of therapy. For adults not to know what they want to do implies that they are stuck in the Awareness Cycle; they are using their inability to answer the question to resist contact. Assuming that the client knows what he or she wants to do, the next question the therapist may ask is, "What do you want from me?" Again we have a situation where two adults should be able to state what they want to do in their

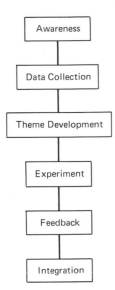

FIGURE 2-4
Gestalt Therapeutic Process

time together and what they want from each other. Beginning therapy like this immediately lets people know that they are responsible for guiding their own growth. Clients frequently expect that the therapist will tell them what to do, and may even verbalize that assumption. There is nothing inherently wrong with giving opinions often. Rather, it is better to support people to be responsible for developing their own best learning experience.

It is not uncommon for there to be power struggles in the initial stages of treatment as clients demand to be taken care of and therapists continue to insist that everyone will be responsible for his or her own behavior. It is essential that clients learn to identify their feelings—they are the guide to knowing what you want. Learning this skill is necessary for problem solving with anyone. If you don't know what you want, there is an excellent chance you won't get it.

At the awareness step of the therapeutic process, therapists would likely probe for feelings, ask you to support yourself and breathe, and ask what you were aware of in the here and now. There would be sufficient time during this process for you to become more aware of your organism. Often, just by guiding clients into supporting themselves better and slowing down, they become aware of their feelings and what they want.

Data collection—Assessment. At this step therapists use their own awareness functions to collect information about what the client is doing. There are certain areas that are likely to be more productive for awareness than others. Energy dynamics are important. How much energy is the therapist investing in the interaction and how much is the client? Is there an imbalance? What is most obvious about a client? Personal characteristics, how a person looks, mannerisms, or abnormal behaviors are examples. You don't have to always mention the obvious, but is extremely important to be aware of it. Often, it is only the therapist who has the courage to mention an obvious characteristic when no one else will.

Body behavior is a rich source for the therapist awareness. Since our bodies express what we are feeling regardless of what we say, it behooves the therapist to attend to where there is muscular energy. This includes positions, movements, and expressions. The tone of voice is of course also worth some attention, especially if it seems incongruent with overt behavior. When watching overt and verbal behavior it is important to be dumb, not to interpret. The simple reporting of what is seen or heard is sufficient.

At the same time therapists observe a client, they must be very aware of their own reactions as well. If you were a Gestalt therapist I would ask you to consider: What are you feeling? Where is your muscle tension? What is your overt behavior saying? How are you looking and is it congruent with what you feel? What do you want from your client and are you getting it?

Knowing where you stand in response to a client's behavior is very important for a number of reasons. First, it is highly likely that no matter what your reactions are they are similar to how others behave when confronted with your client's resistances to contact. Thus, being able to assess your feelings when interacting with a client can let you work with here-and-now dynamics similar to what happens in the natural environment. Second, unless you are continually aware of your own organism, there is a good chance you will unwittingly become part of the support system for the client's resistances to contact. Almost by definition, clients will be subtly asking you to help them resist. By keeping a sense of yourself, you can more effectively deny that request. Third, self-awareness is essential for self-support. In order to be open for contact with clients, we must stay grounded. Therapists must contend with their own resistances to contact, too. It is helpful to be able to choose whether you wish to use them or not. And fourth, therapists have expectations of clients. When clients don't meet these expectations we often overreact. This is called a *counter-transference* and will be further discussed later in the chapter. Suffice it to say for now that sharp self-awareness can make countertransference an effective therapeutic tool unique to Gestalt therapy.

When enough data has been collected so that you can see a pattern, it is then fed back to the client for perusal. Based on reactions to the feedback, a theme begins developing that will act as the umbrella for therapeutic work.

Theme development.   A theme is a fundamental concept in Gestalt. It is the emergence of something clear which can be labeled. The labeling of what you are needing to work on is important. In fact, the process of watching themes emerge, synthesizing and identifying them, is a significant part of a client's learning process. There are so many issues on which a person can work that it becomes a necessity to find a common umbrella for them—a condensation all of the concerns have in common. A theme will emerge given the time and freedom for clients to experiment.

Themes can develop around any group of issues. They start emerging immediately; at least one is picked for each session. As therapy continues, it becomes clear which of many themes is becoming most important and seems to be more at the root of the client's concerns. The resistances in the Awareness Cycle, especially the resistances to contact, are common themes. But there are no rules concerning what labels to use. Metaphors make excellent labels for themes, such as a little boy in the candy store for someone who tries to do too much and ends up sick and exhausted; or a shy elephant theme for a powerful looking person who is afraid to be assertive. It is important that the therapist not direct the theme; rather allow the client to follow one theme, and then another, until a form of synthesizing occurs that is unique to the client's experience.

The experiment—The therapist response to resistance.   Once a theme has been established for a session it is time to design an experiment. The basic parameters of the experiment should emerge from the work on theme development. It is the opportunity for clients to heighten their resistances at an impasse, or to try something new after a breakthrough. The most active movement clients make is in the designing of and participation in here-and-now opportunities to confront their problems. An ancient Chinese proverb states: "I hear—I forget; I see—I remember; I do—I understand." This is the basic premise behind the experiment. Talk, insight, and modeling can only go so far; it is the act of taking risks and attempting to make contact where real learning occurs.

As you will recall, resistance in Gestalt is ultimately the act of saying no to contact. Since the therapist is the only person present in one-on-one therapy, that is where the resistance is directed. A large percentage of what therapists do in the experiment is to help clients heighten their resistances to contact. For example, if a client is not able to respond to the question, "What do you want to do?" she is telling her therapist she won't answer the question. After some probing a theme might develop describing her inability to know what she is feeling, or an expectation that she be told what to do. Once a theme is established, an experiment can be designed to help her take responsibility for her behavior by heightening this resistance. There are an infinite number of ways to do this. She could announce that she refuses to tell the therapist what she wants no matter what. In fact, the declaration could be greatly exaggerated.

This strategy does two important things: first, it lets clients experiment with taking responsibility for their behavior. The client in the example is trying on for size how it feels to adopt the experience as her own rather than its being imposed on her by others. It gives clients new perspectives when they own their power to say no instead of feeling helpless and confused. Second, heightening resistance in this way allows the therapist to utilize the energy stuck in the body to heighten a sense of disgust. There is nothing more difficult than trying to confront clients' resistance head-on. It often just makes them more resistant. And for good reason. Remember, we develop resistances to protect ourselves, and people who confront us will likely face a stone wall unless we feel safe. By heightening the resistance, exaggerating it, and making clearer the function it is playing, the client may still decide the situation is not safe enough or that she likes the status quo. But if the resistance is truly nonfunctional in the person's here-and-now existence, her organism may respond with profound disgust, beginning the process of spitting out the introjects and projections that have kept her from making contact.

Gestalt therapists do not fight resistance. The old adage you can lead a horse to water but you can't make it drink is true. You can support clients in clarifying their position and then lead them to the impasse by heightening the resistances that characteristically keep them from getting their needs met. But you cannot lead them through the impasse. The only way people will move beyond their resistances to make better contact is if they get so disgusted with their position it makes them sick—sometimes literally—or if they make their environment safer for themselves. Gestalt offers real relief for therapists in this approach to resistance. By helping clients use its energy, it takes the therapist out of the fray, so to speak, and allows people to experiment more freely for themselves.

An example of how a therapist can support a client in dealing with resistance is often seen in the first stages of therapy. For instance, after going through an experiment where a resistance to knowing what she wanted was heightened, it became clear that the client was refusing to make better contact for fear of being too exposed by the "powerful" therapist. The therapist helped her set contact boundaries stating what topics she wished to discuss and those she didn't; how much probing she wished to tolerate; and how she could withdraw with the therapist's support if she felt too vulnerable. This process allowed the client to begin feeling a sense of her own power to design an experience supportive of her organism, and allowed the therapist to convey respect for the client's resistance.

Another technique used in Gestalt to heighten resistance is the well-known "double chair." While a resistance is saying no to contact, it is also saying no to an internal impulse to break through the resistance. Thus it is possible to polarize these unintegrated parts by literally putting each on one of two chairs or pillows. The client then carries on a dialogue, changing chairs as the conversation continues. Clients literally move from chair to chair as they change roles. For example:

CHAIR 1:   I'm not going to let you know what you want or what you are feeling.

CHAIR 2:   Why not?

CHAIR 1:   I don't know.

CHAIR 2:   Is there any way I can get you to tell me?

CHAIR 1:   I don't know.

THERAPIST: Try answering, "No matter what you do I won't let you know what you are feeling," and see what happens. (therapist is trying to help client heighten the resistance even more)

CHAIR 1:   No matter what you do I won't tell you what you want to do in therapy or what you are feeling.

CHAIR 2:   (to therapist) I don't know what to say. I guess I'm finished.

THERAPIST: What is the part of you in that chair feeling?

CHAIR 2:   A little frustrated. Helpless.

THERAPIST: What did you learn from this experiment? What did you become aware of?

CLIENT: That one part of me seemed awfully stubborn.

THERAPIST: I became aware that the part of you in Chair 1 did not seem helpless at all. It seemed very powerful and stubborn to me. Where would you like to go from here?

CLIENT: I don't know.

THERAPIST: Ah, I'm talking to the part of you in Chair 2. What shall we call that part?

CLIENT: Umm, how about the wishy-washy part.

THERAPIST: Okay, how about Chair 1?

CLIENT: A mule.

THERAPIST: I'm going to ask my question again, and this time I would like to hear from the mule. Where would you like to go from here?

CLIENT: I'm not going to let you know what I want no matter what you do.

THERAPIST: I believe you. I am very aware of how powerful you look to me now. Your voice is strong and you are sitting up straight.

CLIENT: Yeah.

This example is typical of how the double chair works in heightening resistance and separating polarities, and how carefully and slowly we need to work with people. Dramatic breakthroughs, when and if they come, are the culmination of many small experiments over time, building to a climax. It is a real skill to help clients structure experiments that are not too easy or too hard, that take advantage of and enhance their creative potential, heighten a resistance, and allow people to face their here-and-now struggles to make contact.

The techniques in dreamwork, speaking for the parts of the dream, and dreamwork as theater, are also in the purview of the experiment. There is no end to the creative expression possible once a theme has been labeled. Experiments can utilize a client's ability to sing, draw, write, play an instrument, or dance. Every expression of the human spirit can be integrated into the experiment. It partly depends upon what talents therapists and clients bring into the therapy setting, but it also depends on how willing each can allow their own creative energies to flow together.

Feedback. After the experiment is finished, a common therapist response is, "What did you learn from your experience?" or "What did you become aware of?" It never fails to amaze me that clients often have perceptions from their experiments that are quite different from those watching. Sometimes they perceive more or less than observers think they "should," but therapists need to support any self-awareness, regardless of its apparent importance to others. We can't very well ask people to trust their organisms and then refute what their organisms are telling them.

Although it is standard to ask clients what they learned out of their work, one should not be surprised if they report they learned very little. This happens in the best of therapy situations. However, if it is a common occurrence, therapists need to examine what is happening, and not happening, between the two of them. There are many things a therapist can do to better support the growth process, such as confronting a transference and countertransference or breaking a confluence. But one thing therapists do not need to do is feel responsible for their clients' failures to learn from their experimentation. Rather, I would wonder with my clients how they are consistently allowing themselves to design and participate in experiments that are apparently not supportive to their growth. People are responsible for their failures as well as their successes.

After the client has had a chance to reflect on his or her experiment, therapists share their personal reactions as well as awareness of overt and verbal behavior. Since there is so much to be aware of in an experiment, therapists need to be selective, using the same principles we have already discussed in the awareness step of the treatment process.

Integration. It is incumbent on therapists to make sure that clients withdraw so that what was learned can be integrated into the wisdom of their organisms. If clients do it for themselves, therapists need do nothing but remain silent. Otherwise, it may be necessary to suggest that the work end; ask for silence; or remind the clients to be sensitive to when their organisms have had enough. And of course if the resistance under scrutiny is rushing or hanging on, then it can become the theme, and experiments can be structured to ultimately support the withdrawal process. The general rule of thumb is the greater the energy that went into the experiment the more withdrawal will be needed before going on.

There are no rules concerning how many times you should go through this treatment process in a single session. It depends on the people involved, whether it is an individual or group therapy, and how much time there is. I have seen the whole process completed in fifteen minutes, including theme development and a meaningful experiment. I have also seen it take the traditional fifty-minute hour and much longer. Again, a lot depends upon how much energy goes into each of the steps in the treatment process as to how many times one would go through it in a single session.

Termination Criteria

Clients terminate when therapy is no longer necessary or healthy for their organisms. In the same way we know when any situation is finished, our organisms tell us it is time to withdraw from the therapy experience. In some cases a specific goal might have been reached. But it is also just as likely that a more nonspecific existential growth issue is clearer now and the client is ready to withdraw to ponder the experience.

There is also the possibility that for some reason or other therapy is just not working out for the client. In this case, the organism will also know that something is wrong in the same way we display symptomatic behavior when the Awareness Cycle is not running smoothly. It is of course the client's as well as the therapist's responsibility to suggest that a clinical relationship is not satisfactory. That communication leaves open the possibility for modification to the client's advantage.

But when any situation persists, including therapy, where people are not getting their needs met, they can attempt to make better contact in the hope for change. Failing that, for whatever reason, their only other choice is to continue suffering or to leave. It makes no sense to blame either party for the failure of a relationship. If, after a reasonable attempt to make things better, a relationship still does not meet the needs of *both* the therapist and client, one or the other should terminate. The key phrase is "a reasonable attempt," and that can only be defined by one or both of the people directly involved.

It is very difficult to discuss a "premature" therapy termination in Gestalt. That term is usually used by therapists who feel that their clients "should" have stayed longer. If, however, we really believe in organismic self-regulation, then clients must know better than anyone when they are ready to leave. This is not to say they cannot be confronted with their decision. Indeed they can. In any relationship, when one person decides to leave without the other's agreement, there will be feelings that need to be shared. If, after these discussions, the client still wishes to terminate, the therapist can hopefully support the decision of another adult to get his or her needs met elsewhere, even if it means terminating the relationship. Of course, this is sometimes difficult for therapists to do since they, like the rest of the world, are human. Therapists who generally feel that they know what clients need better than the clients themselves, will be more prone to "premature" terminations.

The Therapist's Response
to Transference and Countertransference

Gestalt uses both transference and countertransference in a unique way. Transference is when clients project expectations onto their therapists as well as behavioral characteristics and feelings that are not entirely real to the here-and-now relationship. It is a normal experience and many of us do it, especially with authority figures. In the structured intensity of a therapeutic relationship it can occur all the more easily. Whenever we assume that someone is supposed to take care of us and we give him or her the power to do so, there is an excellent possibility that a transference will occur. You don't have to have years of clinical education to understand why this happens. When we put ourselves into situations where people have more power than we do, either perceived or real, it sets up a scene from our earliest learning experience: the family. This is where we first faced being in situations where people had more power than we did; where we frequently felt helpless and often were. When this kind of stimulus presents itself, there is a reasonably good chance that what will re-emerge is the unfinished business of parent-child relationships.

In Gestalt, we assume that clients come in with expectations and projections based on unfinished business. But we also assume that no matter how buried in the past these transference issues may be, they *always* have some basic connection to the here and now. Since in a one-on-one session the therapist and client are the only show in town, there must be some stimulus the therapist presents to support the transference. Therapeutic relationships, then, become a rich source for delving into what unfinished business is represented by the transference and determining what the therapist is actually doing to support it in the here and now. By the very nature of Gestalt, therapists must be available to explore here-and-now dynamics with clients and not assume that everything that a client expects and projects is based on the past. This is one more reason that Gestalt therapists need to have good self-support so that they are not threatened (unduly!) by this dynamic experience.

Countertransference is the opposite of transference. While a client comes in with expectations and projections, so does the therapist. There is sometimes an assumption that therapists are giving, altruistic creatures whose only goal is to serve their clients. We therapists should not try to fool ourselves into believing that we expect nothing from people who are apparently depending on us. People do psychotherapy as a profession for a variety of reasons, the most important of which is *not* an altruistic desire to save the world. While world and people saving may possibly be a pleasant by-product of our work someday, we do it because it meets very important personal needs. In Gestalt, we assume that therapists' basic goals are to take care of themselves and in that process the client will hopefully be taken care of, too. People who do not provide sufficient support for themselves cannot adequately support others. Therefore, as always, therapists need to exercise good self-awareness to make sure their needs are being met, as well as their clients' needs.

The countertransference comes into play when therapists are not fully aware of what they are expecting clients to do for them. It is unnatural to expect that people can participate in a therapy session and leave all of their unfinished business at home. There are a number of common basic needs that psychotherapists expect clients to meet. The countertransference is established when clients do not cooperate and resist meeting these needs. They include: 1) the need to be responsible; 2) the need to be loved; 3) the need to make contact; 4) the need to be in control; and 5) the need to be respected. Depending on a therapist's history of unfinished business, one of these might be more an issue than another. And each client offers therapists the possibility of a unique countertransference dynamic.

1.   *The need to be responsible*: This is probably the most common issue for beginning therapists. We expect clients to "get better" or be successful so that we can feel good about our practice. If they don't, we somehow feel responsible. The sympton of this countertransference is usually guilt.

2.   *The need to be loved*: Many therapists like to be caring, supportive, and empathetic. In return, they expect to be appreciated. Unfortunately there are clients who not only will resist being taken care of but they have the audacity to be thoroughly unappreciative of all that caring, too. Therapists who tend to this countertransference might try to maintain a top dog-underdog relationship with their clients, with you-know-who trying to stay on top.

3.   *The need to make contact*: Some therapists use the psychotherapy setting to make closer contact with people, often better than they experience in their nonprofessional lives. When clients resist, therapists get hurt and angry. These feelings are usually intellectualized, however, and come out as statements directed at the client, such as "I do understand that you are angry with me. Tell me more about that," or, "So you want to terminate suddenly today after coming to see me for six months. Why don't we discuss it further." The intellectualization is a resistance to making contact about feeling reactions to client behavior.

4. *The need to be in control*: Many clients want their therapists to be on top, which meets the needs perfectly of those therapists who like being in control. All of us want some control of our relationships; however, it's a question of degrees. Therapists who encounter clients who also have a great need to be in control will find themselves in constant power struggles.

5. *The need to be respected*: Some people in the profession, even those of us who write books about psychotherapy, expect people to admire and respect us for our prowess. Unfortunately, all too many clients do not cooperate with this expectation. When this happens, therapists involved with this countertransference selectively give more attention to those who show respect than to those who do not.

In general, therapists will know when they are into a countertransference with a client when they consistently experience over or underreactions of feelings. If a pattern of guilt, hurt, anger, sadness, fear, or depression emerges in the therapist over time; if there seem to be too many power struggles; or if the therapist is acting defensively, it is worth considering whether there is a countertransference going on.

What makes the Gestalt approach to countertransference unique is its allowing the dynamic to become an open part of the here-and-now clinical process. First, since Gestalt believes that it is in the relationship between client and therapist that growth occurs, anything that seriously inhibits contact should be dealt with. And nothing inhibits contact like a good transference or countertransference. Second, since the therapist is only the more experienced client in the room, and human to boot, it is absurd to think that he or she will be able to keep all of his unfinished business out of therapy. Since it is there, why not share with a client how the therapist also resists making contact. Third, just as therapists support transferences to some extent, so do clients support countertransferences. In fact, it is highly likely that the irrational feelings being evoked in the therapist are also evoked by the client in other important relationships. Therefore, it is important for therapists to share how their clients are not meeting their expectations, even though they shouldn't be expected to. Very often, clients will experience a déjàvu feeling and learn how they have supported these unhelpful projections in others.

For example, assume you have a need to be responsible with clients. One of them whom you have been seeing for quite a while is going nowhere, stuck. In fact, recent sessions have been rather boring and you've left feeling frustrated. You find yourself feeling more and more guilty, and wondering what you've done wrong. It is very possible a countertransference is occurring, since you are not responsible for how your client performs. Being concerned is different from taking responsibility and feeling guilty. If, and this is a big "if," you are at the place in your personal growth that you have integrated the abilities to be vulnerable and share your weaknesses, while at the same time keeping a sense of your own ground and self-support, then you have a real opportunity to help your client. It could go something like this:

THERAPIST: I have been aware that there has not been much energy between us for a while and I haven't felt too good about it. I wonder how you've felt.

CLIENT: Yeah, I feel like I haven't been getting anywhere. I've been wondering if I should continue therapy. Maybe no one can help me.

THERAPIST: I don't believe that but I do understand how believing you are getting nowhere can be discouraging. Do you find yourself in many situations where nothing seems to be happening and you feel like giving up?

CLIENT: Yeah.

THERAPIST: I believe it. I've been thinking a lot about our sessions and have become aware of a couple of things I want to share with you. First I became aware of being bored in our sessions. By "bored" I mean there is very little energy between us. I've walked out of our last few sessions feeling frustrated. I found myself wondering what's going wrong, how I might have failed you.

CLIENT: You haven't done anything wrong.

THERAPIST: I know. I want you to listen to how I felt, and how I feel now. When I was with you I began feeling worried, sad, and guilty that I had failed you. Then I realized that it was you who was failing me.

CLIENT: Me? How?

THERAPIST: I expected you to get better so that I could feel successful. I am irritated with you because you haven't been doing better. (pause) I want to know how you feel about that.

CLIENT: I understand.

THERAPIST: That's what you think. What do you feel?

CLIENT: I don't know. I didn't think I was supposed to get better so you could feel good. I thought I was supposed to get better for me.

THERAPIST: You sound angry to me. Are you?

CLIENT: Maybe a little.

THERAPIST: I'm glad you have some awareness of what you are feeling. You are quite correct. I have no right to expect you to perform so I can feel good. But let me tell you what that has done to me. First, I did not let myself feel how bored I was with our sessions because if I did I would have had to admit to myself that I was not being successful. Then when I became aware of it a few weeks ago I did a real trip on myself. Instead of letting you know how I felt about being bored, I retroflected my feeling into guilt. I clearly have a problem, but I plan on doing something about it with you now.

CLIENT: What?

THERAPIST: I am going to do the same thing I have told you to do with a negative retroflection: turn it around and direct it to the person with whom you need to make more contact to solve the problem. (pause) I am unhappy that you do not bring more energy into our therapy sessions. I want you to take more initiative; I want to hear more about what you are feeling; and I want to hear about what you are feeling about me, particularly the negative feelings. And I want you to know that from now on, I will work not to let myself feel guilty; instead I will tell you how I feel about your behavior and what I want from you when I feel bored or when there is too little energy between us. Now, how do you feel about all that?

CLIENT: A little overwhelmed. (pause) I wonder, does this have anything to do with why I don't seem to be getting anywhere?

THERAPIST: To the extent that there are others like me who don't give you feedback about how they feel, it does. I know that this is not the only place in life you have felt stuck. It's very possible that you support people in giving you as little feedback as possible.

CLIENT: How do I do that?

THERAPIST: Let's look first at how you do it with me, how you have accepted the lack of energy between us. For instance, would you be willing to tell me now as an experiment three things you don't like about my work with you?

To reiterate, when therapists use a countertransference as a therapeutic tool, they must remember to be sure of their ground and self-support, make clear that it is their projection and not end up making it the client's problem, and let the client know how they will be working to make better contact in the future.

It is my experience that the work connected with the transference and counter-tranference in Gestalt therapy can be a high point for both the client and therapist, often leading to the most exciting growth in the therapy experience.

SUMMARY

Gestalt therapy offers a comprehensive theory and practice methodology attempting to integrate creativity, philosophy, and a personal-growth model into the problem-solving process. There are many unique features in the practice of Gestalt, including its insistence on dealing with the here and now; dreamwork; polarities; and the dynamic use of transference and countertransference. Gestalt's philosophical influence has surely been felt in what is now called the *humanistic therapies*. Its technology of treatment, too, has been widely utilized. As we shall see in the next chapter, Transactional Analysis has incorporated many Gestalt techniques into its treatment methodology. Clearly, the genius of Fritz Perls laid important foundations for significant contributions to the field of psychotherapy.

REFERENCES

FAGAN, J., and I. L. SHEPHERD (eds.). *Gestalt Theory Now*. New York: Harper & Row, Pub. 1970.

HATCHER, C., and P. HIMELSTEIN (eds.). *The Handbook of Gestalt Theory*. New York: Jason Aronson, 1976.

KEMPLER, W. *Principles of Gestalt Family Theory*. Salt Lake City: Desert Press, 1974.

PERLS, F. S. *Ego Hunger and Aggression*. New York: Vintage Books, 1969.

———. *Gestalt Therapy Verbatim*. New York: Bantam, 1969.

POLSTER, E., and P. POLSTER. *Gestalt Therapy Integrated*. New York: Brunner/Mazel, 1973.

SHEPARD, M. *Fritz*. Sagaponack, N.Y.: Second Chance Press, 1980.
SIMKIN, J. S. *Gestalt Theory Mini-Lectures*. Millbrae, Calif.: Celestial Arts Publish-
    ing Co., 1976.
SMITH, E. W. L. (ed.). *The Growing Edge of Gestalt Therapy*. New York: Brunner/
    Mazel, 1976.
ZINKER, J. *Creative Process in Gestalt Therapy*. New York: Brunner/Mazel, 1977.

REFERENCE JOURNALS

American Journal of Orthopsychiatry. Published by the American Orthopsy-
chiatric Association, New York. Vol. 1, #1: 1930.
Voices. Published by the American Academy of Psychotherapists, New York.
Vol. 1, #1: 1964.

CHAPTER THREE
TRANSACTIONAL
ANALYSIS

BASIC PHILOSOPHY

Transactional Analysis, colloquially known as TA, was founded by Eric Berne. He integrated some basic psychological concepts into an interactional psychology that included ideas compatible with Gestalt and Behavior Therapy. As it evolved, TA took on what might be called a "people's" language, using terminology common in playgrounds, the theatre, and supermarkets. Its apparent simplicity and the charismatic talent of early TA practitioners allowed it to catch on in some places as almost a folk psychotherapy.

TA is unique in its approach and application. The basic theory is compelling in its simplicity and logic. Of all the psychotherapies it is the easiest to understand. Because of the necessity to work with interactional behavior, TA is mostly practiced in groups. Since the terms used are unique, there is a socialization period where clients learn how to label what they do. In fact, it is not uncommon for there to be introductory sessions that are conducted much like regular classes.

Almost all intensive TA training is done privately outside of university settings, by TA therapist trainers, who become TA trainers by teaching other people to be TA trainers, ad infinitum. This type of training model has had important implications for TA. First, it has made training more accessible to people without the traditional professional degrees usually associated with psychotherapy. And since TA has its own internal accreditation standards, it has lent some validity and quality control to the practice of therapists who have completed the TA training programs. However, because there has not been a general inclusion of intensive TA training into university graduate schools, its acceptance among academicians and some professionals has not kept pace with its apparent acceptance with the lay public who utilize TA therapy.

In contemporary practice, TA is rarely done without combining it with some Gestalt. All of the Gestalt techniques are applied to fit into the TA framework, and an observer would not be able to see easily how Gestalt theory is part of the therapy. Transactional Analysis basically views people as part of relationships, with their behavior a function of past interactional learning experience and present dynamics. Problems are defined not only as particular situations but also as the behavior patterns that lead up to and continue on after a problem situation has occurred. TA also makes heavy use of the concept of personal responsibility, a la Gestalt, which suggests that people are ultimately responsible for what they do.

THEORY

Ego States—Parent, Adult, and Child

While one might look at the Freudian superego, ego, and Id as analogous to the Parent, Adult, and Child ego states developed by Eric Berne, the comparisons are only superficial. The TA ego states are directly operational in therapy and are immediately descriptive of specific behaviors, whereas the superego, ego, and Id are theoretical constructs. Essentially, the Parent, Adult, and Child are three mutually exclusive categories that together account for all covert and observable human behavior.

Parent behavior includes moral indignation, statements that suggest rules to live by, and nurturing behaviors. Adult behavior includes factual statements and reports of a person's perceptions and feelings. Child behavior includes all of our feelings, natural curiosity, and is the wellspring of our needs. The Parent acts as the part that both nurtures and governs; the Child tells us what we are feeling and wanting; and the Adult reports what is happening with the Parent and Child as well as what the environment is like. Our Parent is similar to our real parents or whoever raised us; our Child is us as a child. You can tell a lot about a person's parenting history from watching him or her now; likewise, you can see what a person was like as a child by seeing his child behavior in the present. These TA ego states are more than terms to a therapist. Every overt and covert action clients perform represents being in the Parent, Adult, or Child. An ego state can be identified by what people say, how they respond, and how they look. Even a person's posture has characteristics of each of the ego states.

Parent. When you were growing up, it was important to learn survival rules to live by. Your parents modeled and stated rules and how they should be followed. In TA these rules are called *parental injunctions*. You watched carefully what your parents did, how they acted, and what rules were necessary to comfortably survive life in the family. These behaviors were internalized as you grew up. We are not only talking about obvious rules such as, "Don't cross the street against a red light," but also about injunctions concerning how to relate to others and how to handle and express feelings. Any statement that includes the words *must, ought to, have to,* or *should* are parental injunctions. Examples of parental injunctions include: you *should* never show weakness; people *ought to* vote; I *must* always be on time; you *have to* finish everything on your plate. These rules, and all the others like them, are learned either by directly relating to parents or authority figures, or by watching what they do, perhaps in lieu of what they say. For instance, parents might tell children that they should not hit other people. But if the parents hit their children or each other, their children might obviously learn a different rule. Similarly, if parents try to teach children that they should express their feelings, all well and good. But if at the same time Mom and Dad emotionally hurt each other in ways that frighten their children, the rule learned might be, "You shouldn't show your feelings." One of the challenges in TA therapy is to help people understand that the most important injunctions they live by were formed in their early years. People frequently assume that the rules of which they have some awareness were developed contemporarily. TA suggests that unless there has been a conscious redecision process, the basic rules by which we live were learned from our parents or parent surrogates in the primary family.

Parent behavior is divided into two major categories: the *Critical Parent* and the *Nurturing Parent*. The Critical Parent is just what its name suggests—it judges behavior. This has positive and negative aspects to it. On the plus side, it is surely helpful to be able to judge what is good or bad, and to be able to constructively evaluate work and performance. On the negative side, unsolicited criticism, especially when it is a pattern of interaction, makes for very unpleasant relationships. There is a real difference between saying, "You *should* have done better," as if God were speaking on high, and saying, "I would have liked for you to have done better." As we shall see, these two statements are coming from two different ego states—the first from the Critical Parent and the second from the Adult. Seemingly small semantic differences loom large in TA practice.

Not only did we learn how to be critical from our parents but how to nurture as well. In order to have grown to adulthood with any sanity at all our parents had to teach and model nurturing. The most obvious way the Nurturing Parent in us was learned was by the direct caring we received from parental figures as children. All of those behaviors that act to take care of and emotionally support people are in the domain of the Nurturing Parent. These include empathy, praise, understanding, and the kinds of caring and protective physical contact that parents give to children. When there is a nice balance in the Parent, a person can be constructively critical and utilize nurturing skills as part of intimate relationships. Imbalances emphasizing either side of the Parent can make for trouble.

Adult. The adult is essentially a feed-in feed-out computer. It is the part of us that uses the five senses to perceive what is reality. Without a well-functioning adult, people lose contact with the world. This computer function works well on its own unless it gets contaminated (*see* Figure 3-1). It can get contaminated by the Parent

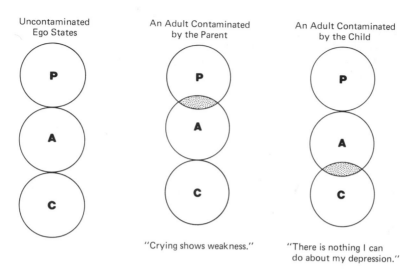

Uncontaminated Ego States

An Adult Contaminated by the Parent

An Adult Contaminated by the Child

"Crying shows weakness."

"There is nothing I can do about my depression."

FIGURE 3-1 Examples of Uncontaminated and Contaminated Ego States

and/or Child, which skews perceptions. An Adult contaminated by a Parent, for instance, could report the apparent fact that it is a weakness to cry. This injunction is, of course, not a fact, but if the Adult reports it as one the Adult is contaminated by the Parent. An uncontaminated Adult would report that you have a personal rule that inhibits crying. Your Adult would acknowledge this injunction is obviously not a universal rule since there are strong people who cry. Therefore it is a rule that only applies to you—you feel weak when you cry.

An Adult contaminated by the Child would also report reality in skewed ways. For instance, chronic depression involves a Child-contaminated Adult. The Child overwhelms the Adult, who reports there is nothing that can be done to make a situation better. Since this is rarely the case, the perceptive functions of the Adult have been contaminated by the Child. A functioning Adult would report that the Child is sad or angry and would not preclude support that would be of aid in problem solving.

Child. There are a number of parts to the Child ego state. One is called the *Free Child*, the natural expression of feelings, curiosity, playfulness, and wonderment. People in touch with their Free Child are able to play and experience life as they once did when very young. There is an *Adaptive Child* state that tries very hard to please, especially other parent or authority figures. The *Parental Child* works to be what he or she perceives to be correct grown-up behavior. Sometimes people have never had a real childhood because parents demanded that they act like "proper" adults. And of course there are situations where children were forced by circumstances to grow up fast. The "Little Professor" looks like the smart little boy or girl who is above childlike games and attitudes. He'd rather be cerebral. Then, of course, there is the acting-out *Brat* or *Naughty Child* who is out of control and hell on wheels.

The kind of child we were in our youth defines the child in our Child ego state. However, since no one was only one kind of kid, the Child ego state has many facets. But it is common for there to be a predominant behavior pattern that labels the Child into one of the above categories. It is the Free Child in all of us that TA tries to unlock. That ability to feel free, spontaneous, creative, full of fun and laughter, is cherished and nurtured as part of the therapeutic process. But along with the fostering of the Free Child, the rest of the Child is not ignored. Remember, when we feel mad, sad, glad, hurt, or scared—five basic feelings in TA—it is the Child in us experiencing these feelings just as we did when we were little. No matter what part of the Child is speaking, it must not be ignored even if it is Naughty, Adaptive, or Parental. It must be listened to and taken care of.

Strokes and Transactions—Motivation

The basic foundation of TA theory is the stroke. There are two kinds of strokes—positive and negative—and one or the other is necessary for survival. This is meant literally. Without strokes babies will die and adults can become seriously disturbed. Strokes include any kind of physical contact, talking, or eye contact, and since they are so necessary to life, people in a state of stroke deprivation will be highly motivated to work for them.

It is much more pleasurable to receive positive strokes, colloquially known as "warm fuzzies." They feel good. However, if positive strokes are not forthcoming, negative strokes will do to satisfy the deprivation state. Negative strokes, also known as "cold pricklies," are not pleasurable. Often they hurt, such as criticism, or even cause pain, such as with hitting and spanking. Yet, since children must have strokes to live, they will work hard to get whatever kind is available in a family. It should not be surprising, then, that some children go to any lengths to get whatever strokes they can, no matter what the price. In a family where "warm fuzzies" are scarce, children may have to be very naughty to get any strokes at all. As we shall see when we discuss games, people develop a wide range of behavior patterns to get positive and negative strokes which sometimes look incredible to the uninitiated observer. After all, why would anyone "work" to be spanked? To get stroked is TA's answer.

Adults also need strokes to live, but unlike little children, their physical survival is usually not at risk. The basic TA premise that behavior is motivated by a need for strokes still stands, however. By the time we are adults we have learned many strategies for getting strokes, based on learning from parental models and childhood experiences.

The *transaction* is the means by which we get strokes from other people. It is a verbal and/or nonverbal interaction which exchanges strokes. Transactions are determined by whether the strokes being exchanged are complementary or crossed. Diagrams such as the ones shown here are used to analyze the type of transaction and the games being played. It is from the analysis of these dynamics that Transactional Analysis gets its name. Figure 3-2 is an example of a complementary or "straight" transaction. A wife says from the critical part of her Parent ego state: "You should have done the dishes tonight. It was stupid of you to forget." The hus-

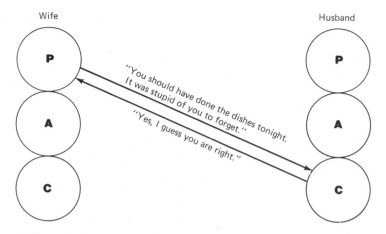

FIGURE 3-2 Parent-Child Complementary Transaction

band responds from his Child ego state: "Yes, I guess you are right." Another example, Figure 3-3: Fred says from his Adult: "I'm cold"; Sally replies from her Adult, too: "I'm hot." One more example, Figure 3-4: One member of a couple from the Child: "Let's go to bed and fool around"; the other replies from the Child: "Hot dog!" A complementary transaction occurs when the ego state being addressed by one person responds back. In the first example, the Parent of the wife was addressing the husband's Child. The Child responded and thus we have a complementary transaction.

However, when the ego state addressed does not respond in kind, then the transaction is crossed. Unless a crossed transaction becomes complementary rather quickly, communication will break down. For example, if a father addresses his son with a Critical Parent statement, Figure 3-5: "You are not taking good care of your-

FIGURE 3-3 An Adult-Adult Complementary Transaction

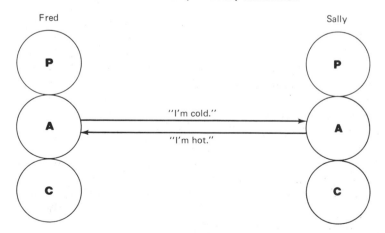

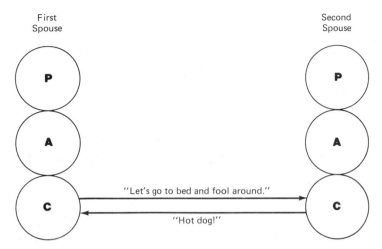

FIGURE 3-4 A Child-Child Complementary Transaction

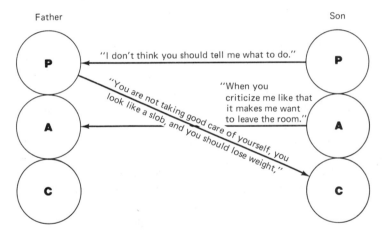

FIGURE 3-5 A Crossed Transaction

self, you look like a slob, and you should lose weight," he is likely requesting a Child response, such as a whiny, "Leave me alone," or a sheepish, "Yeah, I guess I need to take a bath for a change." However, if what Father gets back is an Adult or Parent reply, then the transaction will be crossed. As you can see, the Adult response, "When you criticize me like that it makes me want to leave the room," or the Parent response, "I don't think you should tell me what to do," will successfully cross the transaction. The son's reply has in effect told the father that he will not respond from his Child. If this transaction remains crossed, their exchange of strokes will cease. It is possible, however, that they may wish to continue stroking each other. In that case, one or both of them will have to take the responsibility to make the transaction complementary.

Time Structuring

There are six ways to spend time: withdrawal, rituals, activities, pastimes, games, and intimacy. In each of these ways of structuring time, strokes are exchanged in differing levels of intensity. In fact, they are usually discussed in the rank order of their opportunity for stroking and the amount of risk involved.

1. *Withdrawal.* A person may be physically present with others but is psychologically somewhere else. Daydreaming would be one example of withdrawal.

2. *Rituals.* These are simple, patterned communications used to exchange strokes, but on a very low level. Examples are: "Hello, how are you?"; "I'm fine"; or, "Nice weather we're having, isn't it"; "Oh, yes, but I've heard it might rain." Every culture has its simple communication rituals. They are important for making initial recognition of another's presence. There are, of course, much more complex rituals such as marriage ceremonies, bar mitzvahs, and funerals. These traditions are the cement of society. They provide for very low stroking, but are also comfortably predictable, and in their more stylized forms are often important societal rites of passage.

3. *Activities.* This means of exchanging strokes is what its names implies. Football, going to movies, playing games, and shopping could be included. More involved activities are work, child rearing, and any activity that seems to be goal oriented.

4. *Pastimes.* Pastiming usually involves conversations about simple topics to pass the time with others. While the exchange of strokes is not very intense, talking about baseball, work, school, sewing, or hometowns can be very pleasurable. People who have trouble pastiming often find it difficult to make friends because so much interaction is structured at this level.

5. *Games.* Games are a series of patterned behaviors that two people engage in as a way of exchanging higher intensity strokes and proving something about themselves. Unfortunately you usually end up feeling unhappy and lonely after the game playing is done. Since we need stronger stroking at times, games make a poor substitute for real intimacy, but often are the only way people have learned to get intense strokes. We will spend a section discussing games since they are such an important part of TA theory and practice.

6. *Intimacy.* This is the most meaningful and difficult form of structuring time. In order to reach intimacy there must be game-free, complementary transactions. Not only is it hard to give up the games people play but one must also face the much higher risks that are part of facing another person without the security of knowing what will happen.

Too much of an emphasis on any one of these ways of structuring time is not advisable. Rather, it is the ability to flow in and out of each with a sense of choice that makes for optimal stroking as you go through life.

Life Positions

What is at the foundation of how we feel about ourselves and are out to prove with game playing is the life position. It is basically a Child position and is learned, some TA theorists believe, before the age of five. There are four positions you can take and only one of them is considered healthy.

1. *I'm O.K.-You're O.K.* This is the healthy position. You believe that you are a good, caring person; you like yourself; you are responsible for your own behavior. Other people are also responsible for their behavior and are able to take care of themselves if they so choose. This is a game-free position.

2. *I'm O.K.-You're not O.K.* A distrustful Child occupies this position. In its worst form a person is paranoid. While you believe that you are O.K., the rest of the world cannot really be trusted to come through for you. People are not responsible for their behavior; they can't take care of themselves very well, much less take care of you.

3. *I'm not O.K.-You're O.K.* This is the position of a Child who is generally depressed. While everyone around you seems to be doing pretty well, you are just not able to cope. You don't like yourself very much and find it hard to take compliments—you may even feel you don't deserve positive strokes. As long as those in the environment take reasonably good care of people in this position, they will survive, but perhaps without much happiness. But if this support system falls apart for some reason, the person in the I'm not O.K.-You're O.K. position is in trouble.

4. *I'm not O.K.-You're not O.K.* A most depressing position—literally. Not only can't a person take care of him or herself but he can't count on anyone else to take care of him either. The Child is helpless and hopeless, a potentially suicidal position.

One of the major premises of the TA approach is that no matter with what "not O.K." position we may come out of childhood, we can decide to change it to an "I'm O.K.-You're O.K." position. There are no exceptions to this premise and it is an important statement of permission to change and grow.

Games and Rackets. A game is a series of moves, starting with a setup and ending with a payoff. Translated from the TA language, a game is a sequential pattern of behaviors, starting with an antecedent and ending with a consequence that are common to each particular game. It can take just a few minutes, or it can go on for days or longer before the final payoff is delivered. The games people play have ulterior motives along with the strokes that are exchanged. People are out to prove something about themselves and the person who is playing with them. While there may be an infinite number of things people can be out to prove with their payoffs, it is finally their life position that determines what kind of payoff they will be working for. Games, then, provide a means to exchange strokes for immediate stroking needs; they reaffirm one's basic life position through the payoff.

Each game has similar components: a setup, a number of moves, and the pay-off. It takes at least two to play; everyone participating is responsible for his part and gets something out of it. One of the more popular games is called *If It Weren't for You*. This game is particularly popular in marriages and other close relationships. It can look as if one spouse has a problem while the other wears the cloak of angels. The setup usually starts with some simple disagreement. As the moves escalate, one of the player ends up feeling guilty or depressed while the other feels that if it weren't for his or her partner everything would be fine. For example:

PLAYER 1:   I would like the invite the Smiths over for dinner next week.
PLAYER 2:   Honey, you know that I'm not comfortable around Mr. Smith.
PLAYER 1:   No wonder. You were so obnoxious to him that it's impossible for him to be nice to you.
PLAYER 2:   Well, he wasn't very nice to me either.
PLAYER 1:   How can we have any friends unless you are nicer to people. I have lost more friends because of the way you act around people.
PLAYER 2:   I know, I know.

The final payoff for Player 1 is the feeling that he or she can blame someone else for his inability to make and keep friends. Player 2, on the other hand, can feel persecuted, misunderstood, guilty, or depressed. Ultimately the payoff proved Player 1 was O.K., and Player 2 was not O.K.

Kick Me is one of the most common games. Almost everyone plays once in a while, some people more than others. Kick Me players set up situations in which they will predictably be given negative strokes. For example, if a person knows that by not taking out the garbage he or she will be yelled at, and he continues not to take out the garbage, he is setting himself up to receive negative strokes and be fig-uratively kicked. It doesn't feel good, but it beats getting nothing at all. Not only that but it proves again that he is basically not O.K., or possibly that he is O.K. and is being persecuted by not O.K. types.

Games work out very well in tandem. For instance, a Kick Me player works very well with an If It Weren't for You player; *Now I've Got You, You Son of a Bitch,* lovingly known as NIGYYSOB, works like a hand in glove with Kick Me. The Kick Me player is looking for negative strokes. The NIGYYSOB players are looking for a legitimate reason to get angry. They have been accumulating anger but don't have the permission to ventilate it. The NIGYYSOB game provides the opportunity. Here is one example of how it could go.

PLAYER 1:   I'd like you to help me to keep from overeating. Every time I take a helping, I'd like you to take away half of it.
PLAYER 2:   Okay.
             (some days later at a meal)
PLAYER 1:   I'm going to take some cake.
PLAYER 2:   Okay, I'll take half of it.
PLAYER 1:   Look, I've been doing real well. I want to have all of this.

PLAYER 2: But you said for me to take half of your food.
PLAYER 1: I know, but this once can't I please have the whole thing?
PLAYER 2: Well, okay, just this once.
           (later that night)
PLAYER 1: You broke your promise to me and let me have too much food. You should have known that I would try to weasel out of the contract. You obviously are not able to help me because you are so inadequate. You let yourself be pushed around too easily.
PLAYER 2: I'm sorry.

The good NIGYYSOB player sets up his or her partner is such a way that there is an excellent chance a promise or contract will not be performed as specified. Then he can prove that his partner is not O.K., and ventilate anger at the same time. Player 2, on the other hand, knows at some level that the contract agreed upon will be very difficult to carry out. So it gives him or her a perfect opportunity to fail and get kicked in the process.

Another common game is called *Uproar*. This one explodes, if you will, when there is a chance for a couple to have some intimacy, particularly sex. The game starts just when it is clear that sex is in the offing. The couple will end up in a fight instead of in a bed. The immediate payoff is to keep from getting close. Children (and others) love to play the *Let's Get You and Him to Fight* game. By just a few comments children can take the heat off themselves and get Mommy and Daddy fighting. One payoff is obviously to get anger directed to other sources and prove they're O.K. Another of the frequent games that is played in therapy is the *Yes-But* game. Yes-But players get people to give them suggestions but rarely take any of them. The payoff is to prove that nothing can really be done to help and that people can't be counted on anyway.

We could spend the rest of this book describing the many games that are part of Transactional Analysis. They range from relatively harmless to violent and life-threatening games. But whatever their intent, how hard people play them, and how dangerous they are, the names of these games are taken from common language and are descriptive in their own right. You can almost know what the games are like by reading their labels: *Blemish; Psychiatry; Cops and Robbers; Ain't It Awful; See What You Made Me Do; Schlemiel; Now He Tells Me; Wooden Leg.*

The point in all games, besides the strokes that are exchanged, is to prove basic life positions. People who participate are getting the intrinsic strokes and payoffs that game playing provides, no matter how much they may protest their roles. Acknowledging one's part in a game is an important part of TA therapy. It is this recognition that allows you to begin taking responsibility for your own behavior.

One of the cues that there is a game going on between two people is when there are recurring patterns of guilt, anger, depression, or fear. These feelings are real when they are experienced, but if they repeatedly occur it is likely they are a "racket" and part of a game plan. When clients continue to participate in transactions where these characteristic feelings keep cropping up, it is called a *racket*.

These feelings reside in the Child and are based on old messages and injunctions. By allowing ourselves to experience them again and again we are able to save them, as it were, for a later payoff. TA has a rather colloquial way of describing this phenomenon. We collect brown stamps of bad feelings until we fill our trading stamp book. Then we cash them in. Letting many little frustrations build up into a big blowup is a good example of stamp collecting. Similarly, a lot of fears and anxieties can be collected and turned in later for an anxiety attack. A number of seemingly insignificant irritations can be turned in for a severe depression. The feelings involved in rackets are really not the only ones we are experiencing. They are being used to repeatedly prove something and cover more vulnerable risky feelings in the Child.

One of the TA's many anomalies is the Karpman Triangle (Karpman, 1968). There are three basic roles you can have when participating in a game: rescuer, victim, or persecutor. No matter with which role you start, a switch in roles will always occur. Persecutors and rescuers often end up as victims. Victims frequently end up taking care of their former rescuers and sometimes persecuting them. For example, a husband who has spent years putting down his wife (persecutor) becomes crushed (victim) when she finally decides to leave him. Or a conscientious therapist who goes far beyond the call of duty taking care of clients (rescuer) ends up divorced, alone, and unhappy (victim) because his or her family was so neglected. If clients can identify their roles in the Karpman Triangle, they will have an effective tool for predicting the "switch" and finding the stoppers for the games that keep them in this endless role reversal.

The identification of games with their inherent payoffs is central to TA therapy. However, it is not simply an academic analysis. Any time you put a number of people in a room where one of the goals is personal problem solving, there will be ample opportunity for them to play games. This "in vivo" game playing gives TA therapists the material they need to help people understand experientially how they get themselves into trouble. Then they will be able to find game-free alternatives to getting strokes and achieving intimacy with straight transactions.

Scripts

The script is the final central concept in the Transactional Analysis of a client's behavior. It is the synthesis of many different messages from our parents dictating the more global issues concerning how we are to live our lives. Script messages range from the more dangerous, "Don't be (don't exist)," or, "You will be a failure," to more hopeful messages such as, "You will triumph regardless," and, "You will be happy." Ultimately scripts are categorized in two ways: winning or losing scripts. Having a winning script means you will be generally happy and successful in your relationships. People with losing scripts are frequently anxious, depressed, and experience chronic relationship problems.

These basic decisions about how people are to live their lives were made as children based on early messages from parents. These messages came from both the

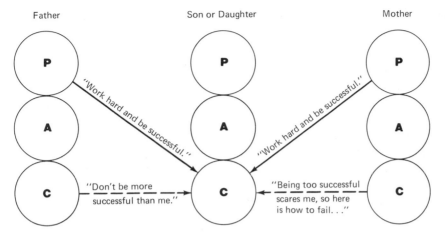

Father   Son or Daughter   Mother

"Work hard and be successful."

"Work hard and be successful."

"Don't be more successful than me."

"Being too successful scares me, so here is how to fail. . ."

FIGURE 3-6 Overt and Ulterior Script Messages

Parent and Child ego states of our parents and were often contradictory. For example, in Figure 3-6 you can see that the spoken Parent script messages are clear from both Mother and Father: "Work hard and be successful." But the more subtle and probably more powerful script messages are also coming from the Child of both Mother and Father. These are never spoken aloud; they are modeled by the games parents play in which children watch and participate. The father's Child message, "Don't be more successful than me," and the mother's Child message, "Being too successful scares me, so here is how to fail . . ." could very well turn out to be the foundation for a primary script message of, "I will never be successful in life," and lead to a losing script.

As part of TA therapy, it is incumbent on clients to look at these early-life decisions and decide whether they wish to change them as adults. It is always possible to make new decisions based on our present realities and develop a winning script. Making these decisions and actually putting them into practice is the culmination of much difficult therapeutic effort over weeks, months, and sometimes years.

The Cure

After traveling through the Parent, Adult, and Child, strokes, transactions, life positions, games and rackets, it is possible to end up with a winning script. This end point is generally called the *cure*. It certainly seems to be a misnomer, since TA definitely does not subscribe to the medical or disease model of psychology. The cure symbolizes becoming game free, being more flexible in one's time structuring, and generally developing a winning script. The behavior changes occurring in clients in TA therapy are wrought from a combination of factors starting with ego states and ending up in substituting intimacy for playing games. As we shall see in the discussion of TA's practice, there are a number of techniques that TA therapists use to bring about the cure.

Theoretically there are two major ways that people stop playing games: they come up with "stoppers" to the game, or they refuse the payoff. Consider an example: Bill frequently plays Kick Me with his parents, wife, and members of his TA group. While each incident is different, there is a common theme:

1. Bill agrees to do something even though he knows he has a history of forgetting.
2. He forgets to fulfill his commitment.
3. While people may be initially understanding of his problem and even try to help him remember, they eventually get angry.
4. Bill receives these negative strokes and agrees how irresponsible he was.
5. Bill says he is very sorry and promises to try to do better the next time. He feels guilty.

The journey Bill must take to the cure begins with his recognition of when he is behaving in his Parent, Adult, and Child ego states. The therapist will help him be more in touch with what his Child is feeling, the difference between his Critical and Nurturing Parent, and strengthening his ability to speak from the Adult. Through this process Bill will come to see that his Kick Me game is an archaic pattern of behavior first learned as a child. Bill also realizes that the major way he received strokes from his father was through this game. His mother supported the game, although indirectly, by complaining to his father that he was being too harsh on Billy, but furtively explaining to Bill that his father really couldn't help it and had to be accepted as he was. Since Bill needed strokes from his father, he learned that the best way to get them was to make mistakes and be irresponsible. True, the strokes he got were rarely pleasant, but they were better than no strokes at all. Thus, in his present adult life he is continuing to seek strokes in an old, familiar way. In fact, it should not surprise him that he looks for people who tend to be critical since they give the kind of strokes he can most easily accept.

Bill's present reenactments of Kick Me are being played out not only with others but are also part of the internal Parent-Adult-Child (P-A-C) dynamics. His Critical Parent is a copy of his dad, and the Child in him is acting exactly as he did many years ago. His own ego states make up the important dynamics of the game without any other people present, as a way of stroking himself, so to speak. We learn to stroke ourselves in the same way we were stroked as children.

Bill's decision to give up Kick Me will not come easily. He will probably be motivated to seek an alternative because of current pressing problems in his relationships. But that will not make the pain of change any less. Consider what Bill will be giving up and risking by refusing to play Kick Me. First, it is a known entity. Getting strokes this way may not make him happy but at least he is receiving them. Being left in a vacuum of no strokes at all is very anxiety producing. To some extent, there may be a deficit of strokes during the transition from gaming to intimacy. Second, Bill is concerned that he will lose the people with whom he has played Kick Me, including his father. Again, it is entirely possible that those people who were part of Bill's past stroking patterns may not wish to give up playing games themselves.

Behaviorally, Bill can find stoppers for Kick Me by only taking on commitments he knows he will fulfill. He needs to listen to his Child and take on fewer responsibilities that don't appeal to him. At the same time, he will need to practice refusing the critical statement and guilt payoffs. On one hand he can let people know he isn't perfect and reserves the right to make mistakes; he will accept how others feel about his behavior but will not tolerate personal attacks. On the other hand he will activate his own Nurturing Parent to support his guilty Child and help the Child get angry instead of feeling guilty. Another way of doing this is by refusing to say he is sorry and instead owning that he didn't want to perform in the first place. He might consider that he was using the game to express anger, too. In TA, love is truly never having to say you're sorry—TA therapists mean this quite literally.

The implications of this treatment strategy are important both to Bill's present and past relationships. Since Bill and his father have spent a long time playing games, it will be just as difficult for Dad to change as it will be for Bill. Parents have a vested interest in the games you play and your resulting script. The way parents play games with children and exchange strokes is one basic way they stay in contact. If you stop the game playing there will be a void in the relationship. Initially no one will know how to exchange strokes without playing the games of yesteryear. In addition parents will likely be uncomfortable with the decisions you are currently making since some of them go against their own parental injunctions and scripts. Their vested interest in maintaining the status quo may be violated by your new decisions. What can result from this situation is a period of strained relationships. After some initial strain, new stroking patterns often emerge and the parent-child relationship is maintained and strengthened, based on even more straight and intimate transactions. Thus, the risk for Bill in giving up games is clear. There will be a reorganizing in his pattern of relationships. People may be upset when he demands straight transactions and refuses to play games. They could be disappointed and scared with his new life decisions that go against their own parental injunctions; they may be threatened that they will lose his stroking, too. The process is not altogether bleak and painful, however. If parents or partners are willing to support changes; if there is enough motivation to keep relationships alive, as there often is, then Bill's new behavior will be a stimulus for them as well and will likely result in more intimate relationships.

Becoming game free, which has also been called becoming script free, rescripting, or developing a winning script, is of course not all that happens during therapy. Concurrent with the development of game-free behavior is the redecision process, which occurs first with decisions not to play specific games. The most important redecision is the one that changes the script message. By reliving the early childhood scenes where our script messages were first learned, it is possible to confront them and for the Child to decide not to perform for the archaic Parent anymore. In the example in Figure 3-6, this would take the form of the Child saying, "I have been living like a failure for you and I'm not going to do it from this moment on. I'm going to be a winner." The process of making these major redecisions can be quite dramatic and moving and is often the high point of therapy.

PRACTICE

The Role of the Therapist

By virtue of the demands of the theory, TA therapists must be versatile in their role. Part of the time they are in a teacher-student relationship with clients, especially since the concept of P-A-C and transactions have to be learned early in the therapeutic experience. But as therapy progresses, TA therapists generally get more nondirective. There are "four Ps" that are supposed to guide therapists in their relationships with clients: Protection, Permission, Potency, and Power.

1. *Protection.* Therapists must be able to utilize their Nurturing Parent to support and protect a client's vulnerable Child. In addition, they should protect that Child from physical and undue verbal abuse to the extent that it is possible, especially in the group therapy setting.

2. *Permission.* Therapists should develop an atmosphere where clients have the permission to take the risks necessary for change. There need to be messages that support honest communication and confrontation in the group and the freedom to act out one's Child in nonviolent ways.

3. *Potency.* Good therapists have the ability to reach people, get through to them, when others may not be able to. An example is the scene where someone is talking about killing him or herself, scaring the hell out of everyone present. The therapist must demonstrate the potency to transact directly to the person's very Hurt and Angry Child and not be frightened by the threat.

4. *Power.* Ultimately, therapists must be in reasonable control of what happens in the therapy sessions and cannot allow themselves to be manipulated into positions that are not therapeutic for their clients. Assertive skills, the ability to express negative and positive feelings and to make demands and requests, are very important. Real power comes from the ability to behave game free by choice, and to the extent that therapists have that skill, they will be powerful.

Of the many gifts TA has brought to our understanding of human behavior, I believe one of them has been to conceptualize how therapists who have their own personal problems can still help clients. To say that therapists are human begs the issue. The reality is that therapists have the same kinds of problems in their lives that many of their clients have. There is a myth among the populace, probably spread by therapists, that people who have been trained in psychotherapy have "got it all together." The myth gets perpetuated by the dynamics of therapy, where vulnerable clients want someone to take care of them and to give advice and guidance.

It is indeed fortunate that we can expect and receive help from people even though they cannot always help themselves. The old adage, "Physician, heal thyself," is of limited value in psychotherapy. Within the wide range of what is considered normal behavior there is so much variance that if we expected a perfectly game-free therapist to help us, we would go without help because they don't exist.

How, then, can therapists really help if they have problems similar to their clients? TA teaches that the differences between the Nurturing Parent and the Hurt Child are two distinctive behavioral classes. A person can effectively nurture someone else even if he or she cannot do it for himself. But even more germane is the kind of parental injunctions and life scripts a professional brings to the therapeutic experience. There are many injunctions that tell people they should take care of others and sacrifice themselves. There are parental injunctions that tell us we are able to see others' problems clearly but not our own. People can be conditioned to have a very problematic personal life and a very successful professional life, depending on their life scripts, the kinds of games they play, how hard they play them, and the types of parental injunctions that control their behavior.

Certainly, those therapists who "have their heads together" will be more effective with a wider variety of people than those who don't. But frankly, beyond the obvious extreme of serious emotional problems, I have a very difficult time deciding just who has it all together and by how much. I have seen too much of the private lives of perfectly normal people. I know many therapists who are quite effective and have very problematic personal lives. TA does gives some insight into how this could be possible.

The TA Treatment Process

There is a general sequence of events that takes place in TA therapy. While it is not as clearly mapped out as in Behavior Therapy or even Gestalt, it can be gleaned from reading the TA literature and participation in the training and therapy. So much of what is done is not sequential; rather it occurs throughout the treatment process. However, it is possible to put some of the major treatment events in stepwise order, realizing the actual therapeutic techniques that make TA work occur in each phase (see Figure 3-7). After describing the general sequence, we will discuss how TA therapists use a number of interesting techniques to put the theory into practice.

Socialization into TA theory. Many clients do not enter into the therapy knowing how to label their ego states, look at transactions, or identify games. In addition, the idea of working for strokes and receiving payoffs may be foreign and needs to be clarified. Some of this learning surely occurs through participation and observation. But it is a necessary step before any real work can be accomplished. The therapist's role here is to both be a teacher and facilitate others in the group to share what they have learned. Some TA therapists conduct pretherapy classes or workshops to teach the basic terms and concepts.

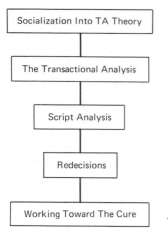

FIGURE 3-7
The TA Treatment Process

The Transactional Analysis—Assessment.   As clients become more comfortable in their groups—most TA is done in groups—they begin having more opportunities to observe and participate. They should have many chances to diagram transactions while becoming more familiar with experiencing their own ego states and games. By this stage the therapists' task is much more complex. They begin attending to body and verbal behaviors which are important cues in identifying ego states. The nuances of behavior associated with each ego state, facial expression, posture, and tone of voice, become clearer for each client under the therapist's guidance. It is also with the therapist's help that each client begins labeling personal games and payoffs. While there are some attempts to find stoppers and alternatives to game playing at this point, it will be some time before the client is able to become game free.

Script analysis.   As part of the natural process of analyzing games with their attending payoffs, it begins becoming clearer what one's script messages are and how they were learned. Another way therapists help clients assess their scripts is by looking at how they are presently leading their lives and helping to recreate some of the early childhood scenes where decisions were made about scripts.

Redecisions.   Actually, the process of making new decisions has been occurring in small ways throughout the process up to this point. Every time clients decide to begin looking for alternatives to games and refusing payoffs, they are on the road to the big redecision to drop their archaic script. There will come a time when clients decide to become winners and start being much more successful in practicing game free behavior. Until the Child makes a decision to give up the old script with its associated script messages, the occurrence of game-free behavior will be uneven. This declaration to become game free can be seen in the reenactment of early-childhood scenes, but it is also inferred by a person's present behavior. You are either game free in important present transactions or you are not. If not, there is still a part of your Child that has not been sufficiently taken care of.

Working toward the cure. This step is not so much part of a sequence but is integrated throughout the other four steps in the treatment process. Typically, there are a number of techniques that TA therapists use, some unique to TA, some borrowed from Gestalt. These include: contracting, the "hot seat," homework assignments, attending to body behavior, the double chair, the use of present transactions for practicing new behaviors, and the modification of semantics—the way people use language.

Of course every therapy group is conducted differently, but for the purpose of instruction let us assume that the following represents a typical TA group. The group starts out with everyone reporting how they did the previous week in general, and particularly their success on their homework assignments. Then they make a contract for what they want to accomplish during the group session. Since weekly groups usually run from one to three hours, it is not always possible for everyone to have a chance to work; therefore the group contract has to be one that can be fulfilled regardless of whether the client ends up on the hot seat. In-group contacts could include the wish to work in group that day, staying more in one's Adult during group interactions, practicing a Nurturing Parent role instead of a Critical Parent, or refusing to accept negative strokes if any are offered. After everyone has had a chance to report and make a contract, the therapist asks who wants to work. Essentially, the client who volunteers to work will be on what is called the *hot seat.* This term is also used in Gestalt and is called the hot seat because the person working is the center of attention and more available for confrontation and positive and negative feedback. It is a way of focusing attention on one person in a group setting but allowing for group interaction around that person. Whatever concern the client comes up with will usually involve some game occurring in the group. By assessing body language and transactions, the therapist can make judgments about what games the person is playing and what possible avenues are open for further work. It is not uncommon for TA therapists to use the double-chair technique borrowed from Gestalt. However, it can take on new dimensions in the hands of the TA therapist. For instance, once the client's ego state in a game has been determined, the double chair can be structured with one ego state in one chair and a second ego state in another chair. The complexities of this strategy should not be minimized. Remember, the Parent in us is ours, to be sure, but also represents the combinations of Parents from mother and father; similarly, the Child is with us now, but also is us as a child. Therefore, the parameters of the double chair can be structured for a present dialogue between a person's Critical Parent and his or her Hurt or Angry Child, or it could be put into the past where the Parent and Child in the double chair is a reenactment of early family scenes. In actuality, regardless of how this type of double chair is done, a dialogue between two ego states is both a representation of a client's present internal dialogue and a recreation of early childhood transactions.

As a case example, I shall present a double chair that starts with a Critical Parent–Hurt Child internal dialogue. It develops into a reenactment of an early childhood scene which is then replayed in a new way, and integrated back into the contemporary Parent-Child dialogue. While it is possible that this whole process could occur in one hot seat, it would more likely be synthesized over a number of sessions.

Therapist:	I am aware that you seem to be playing Kick Me with Jim and taking negative strokes today, Mary.
Mary:	Well, Jim is right. I am making a fool of myself when I approach men in singles bars. I get hurt when I ask a guy to dance and he refuses me. But what's really stupid is that I keep doing it and I keep getting rejected. I *know* I'm not going to get a nice guy and I always end up with a real louse. Then I feel even more shitty about myself and get more depressed. But a month or two later I'm back trying to pick up guys again. It's been this way for years. I just can't seem to find a man who I can have a good relationship with.
Therapist:	Why don't you put the part of you that calls you dumb on one chair, your Critical Parent, and the part of you that agrees on the other chair, your Child. Start the dialogue with your Critical Parent calling you dumb.
Mary as Critical Parent:	Boy are you dumb, kid. You should know better than to keep getting yourself into messy situations with men.
Mary as Child:	I know, I know. I just don't know what to do about it. I get lonely.
Therapist:	Little Mary, how old are you now?
Child:	About six.
Therapist:	And what are you feeling now?
Child:	Like I want to cry.
Therapist:	Why don't you?
Child:	Why should I? It won't do any good.
Therapist:	Mary, I would like you to stand up now and be in your Adult for a moment. Look at the people in these two chairs and tell me what you see.
Mary in her Adult:	I see a sad little six-year-old and a big person looking at her with disdain.
Therapist:	Do these people remind you of anybody?
Mary:	(with tears welling up in her eyes) Yes, it's my mother and me!
Therapist:	Then let's continue the double chair with you as a six-year-old talking to your mother.
Little Mary:	(with tears) Mommy, why are you looking at me that way?
Mary as Mother:	First of all, stop crying. I won't even talk with you until you stop sniveling. (pause) That's better. If you're going

to make it in this world you're going to have to be strong. Now tell me what's wrong.

Little Mary: I don't have any friends. I'm lonely.

Mary as Mother: It's just as well, Mary. You just can't trust people to take care of you. It's better if you learn to play by yourself. Now go play.

After further discussion Mary understands that the messages or parental injunctions she got from her mother included, "You have to be strong," "Don't cry," and, "You can't trust people." In the context of Mother's relationship with Mary's father, this was further translated into, "You can't trust men." The kinds of games through which she and her mother had exchanged strokes revolved in part around these issues. In Mary's adulthood, she continued trying to get negative strokes using the same games. There are many more dialogues that bore fruit for Mary, including a Child-Child dialogue with her mother, some talks with her father, and discussions with siblings. Eventually, one of the double chairs would bring us back to where we started, but now with redecisions and new demands on her Parent.

Mary: Mom, I hate the way you ignore my pain, and I won't take it anymore. I don't want to hear that I can't cry. I want to cry. I want you to take care of me and comfort me and make me feel better. If you won't I will find someone who will.

Mary as Mother: Who will you find?

Mary: I have my own Nurturing Parent now, because I've grown up. If you won't give me what I want I'll tell her to find me someone who will take care of me the way I've always wanted. I will nurture myself when I'm sad, even if there is no one else around.

Mary as Mother: That's what I've been trying to tell you for years. You have to be able to take care of yourself.

Mary: Only part of what you taught me was right. Other people *can* take care of me, too, and I will let them!

Mary is strengthening her Nurturing Parent so she can take care of her Child in ways she was never taken care of in childhood. She will be beginning a lifetime internal dialogue where she is constantly listening for the cues of what she feels and needs. Like any responsible Nurturing Parent, she will do what is possible to get her needs met, while supporting the process for accepting what cannot be accomplished.

Mary's new decision will also help her in seeking better relationships with men, although I do not wish to imply that her work is completed. She may need to find out much more about some of the subtleties of her script. But since she does not need to play her old games for negative strokes, her demanding positive strokes from herself and others will increase the probabilities of her forming good intimate relationships with men and women.

Another important technique used by TA therapists is the contract. There is always a contract for change that occurs at the beginning of treatment. This is more than just a statement of the desire to feel better. It includes agreements for therapy attendance, fees, and a commitment to work and interact in the therapy process. As time goes on, the contracts become much more specific and always relate to behavioral performance. For instance, a decision to stop playing a game will be followed by commitments about how this decision will be carried out, with whom, and when. A decision to be more in one's Free Child, or to stay in the Adult during arguments, would then include contracts specifying how, when, and where this new behavior would occur.

It is common for therapists to ask for week-to-week contracts concerning how clients want to continue therapeutic work in their natural environments. Some group therapists even encourage members to help one another outside the group to support their change efforts. There is usually an expectation that clients will report each week on how they did with their contracts. Just this weekly report can generate good therapeutic work. Success will give people the opportunity to receive warm fuzzies and experience how well they accept them; the ability to accept failure and still be in an I'm O.K.–You're O.K. position instead of figuratively beating oneself with a stick can also be dealt with if the contract is not completed.

One of the more interesting techniques in TA is its emphasis on how language controls our perceptions and behavior. For example, a client who says, "I'll try to be more in my Adult this week," will be asked to substitute the word *will* for *try*. In TA *try* is known as a "fail word." When you use *try* in a sentence, you are leaving open the option for failure. In the above example, the client is implying at the start that he or she would perform the best he could but might not be able to do it. Rather, saying, "I will be more in my Adult" suggests a commitment but does not imply perfection. Making a commitment does not mean people will not make mistakes, but by not leaving themselves an option for failure before they even begin, it likely increases the probability contracts will be fulfilled.

Critical Parent injunction words also get attention from TA therapists. If a client says, "I have to leave now," he will be asked to substitute *want* for *have to*. *Want* can also be used instead of *should, must,* or *need.* Instead of saying, "I need you," it is "straighter" to own that you do not need people like air and water. Rather, you "want" them, but could live without them if necessary. "You should clean your room," translates into, "I want you to clean your room." "I can't do it," is changed to, "I won't do it." Changing these words is an exercise in taking responsibility for your behavior.

Termination Criteria

As we have previously discussed, clients are finished with their work when they have reached a game-free point, also known as the *cure*. It is not possible to designate precisely when this happens and is based on a period of performance in the therapy sessions and reports on changes in environmental behavior and relationships. Termination decisions are of course basically in the hands of clients, but also involve feedback from therapists and other group members. It is not uncommon for people to go through upheavals in important relationships when they initiate game-free behavior and give up their losing script. Therapy will usually continue as a support until the dust settles, so to speak, and stable relationships are established. In addition to the ability to form and maintain intimate game-free transactions, the cure involves the ability to be in the Free Child mode—being spontaneous and having fun in life. Thus working on being more creative and enjoying life is part of what makes for a successful termination. Clients who leave TA therapy should be in the I'm O.K.—You're O.K. position and be able to flexibly structure their time as circumstances and their needs dictate.

The Therapist's Response to Resistance

Resistance in TA generally centers around "don't change" messages. The messages are behaviorally manifested when clients have great difficulty in finding alternatives to playing games and continue to work for payoffs that fulfill their losing script. Resistance may be directed toward the therapist, but it is embedded in the client's script and part of his or her general transactional patterns. What therapists face, then, is a Parent message saying the client can't change, and a Child in agreement. Therapists must try to strengthen the Adult, which is likely contaminated, and support the Child's confrontation with the Parent. The dynamics of change are completely analogous to what happens to children when they are confronted with the loss of their parents. They are scared, anxious, sad, and often desperately trying to hang onto something that is known and predictable. It is understandable that the Child in us tries to resist change unless our Parent offers the nurturing necessary to support us in insecure situations.

TA therapists generally approach resistance as a natural part of what happens when the Child is confronted with the need to change. It is dealt with as part of the ongoing treatment process and ends up developing a Nurturing Parent in the client who can support the Child when it gets scared or hurt, so that change is possible when necessary.

The Therapist's Response to Transference and Countertransference

The transference and countertransference fall perfectly into a Transactional Analysis. The transference can be seen as a Helpless Child ego state, having demands and expectations of therapists who are in a Parent position. Conversely, the countertransference is diagramed as a Parent having expectations of a Child.

Since there are times when therapists naturally take on a Parent role with clients, it is easy to see how this would set up the potential for clients to project their ·own Parents onto the therapist. They will of course try to play games in the process. Clients can become very frustrated as they struggle to find ways to get strokes from therapists who won't engage in game playing. This can also be a difficult time for therapists, since they are often being "baited" to join in the client's game. Children get depressed or very angry when they don't get the kind of strokes and payoffs they are used to.

The countertransference is set up when therapists start playing games with clients. Therapists need to have their Adult and Nurturing Parent in every therapy session. If they get stuck in an archaic Child ego state and lose a sense of themselves, there will be no winners. Therefore, it is important that TA therapists become game free and work from an I'm O.K.–You're O.K. position. Of course, this is an impossible ideal, but it is to be aspired to. The more self-awareness therapists have, the more able they will be to analyze transactions and what role they play in them. Therapists can stop playing games just like clients. This Transactional Analysis can become part of an open therapeutic process where clients see how therapists extract themselves from games by refusing to play and offer alternative stroking patterns leading to intimacy.

One of the more interesting aspects to how TA handles this particular Parent-Child dynamic is called *reparenting*. It is not a widely used treatment strategy because of the incredible investment therapists must make. Essentially, therapists become surrogate parents, allowing clients to return to their Child ego states for longer periods than is possible in short weekly therapy sessions. It is not uncommon for clients to live with the therapists for a time. You can imagine how this strategy goes far beyond the call of duty for the vast majority of therapists. And the possibilities for transference and countertransference are multiplied exponentially since the therapeutic relationship is so intense.

SUMMARY

After all is said and done, TA offers a unique view of the psychology of human behavior. Even with its distinct "unpsychological" terminology, it does seem to offer a theory and practice that is relatively easy to relate to. By tying the dynamics of what controls behavior to recognizable phenomena, it has attempted to take the complexity and mystery out of psychotherapy. To this end we can only applaud the attempt, no matter what its success.

REFERENCES

BARNES, G. (ed.). *TA After Berne: Teachings of Three TA Schools.* New York: Harper's College Press, 1977.

BERNE, E. *Games People Play.* New York: Random House, 1964.

——. *Transactional Analysis in Psychotherapy.* New York: Grove Press, 1961.

BROWN, M. and S. WOOLAMS. *TA: The Total Handbook of Transactional Analysis.* Englewood Cliffs, N.J.: Prentice-Hall, 1979.

GOULDING, R.L., and M.M. GOULDING. *Power Is in the Patient*. San Francisco: TA Press, 1979.

HARRIS, T.A. *I'm OK – You're OK*. New York: Harper & Row, 1969.

JAMES, M. and D. JONGEWARD. *Born to Win*. Reading, Mass.: Addison-Wesley, 1971.

KARPMAN, S.B. "Fairy Tales and Script Drama Analysis." *Transactional Analysis Bulletin*, April 1968, VII, 26, 39-43.

SCHIFF, J.I., and B. DAY. *All My Children*. New York: Jove Publications, 1977.

STEERE, D.A. *Bodily Expressions in Psychotherapy*. New York: Brunner/Mazel, 1983.

STEINER, C. *Scripts People Live: TA of Life Scripts*. New York: Grove Press, 1974.

REFERENCE JOURNALS

Transactional Analysis Journal. Published by the International Transactional Analysis Association, San Francisco. Vol. 1, No. 1: 1962.

CHAPTER FOUR
EGO PSYCHOLOGY

BASIC PHILOSOPHY

There are volumes written about the Freudian approach to psychotherapy. Unquestionably, Sigmund Freud was a genius. His was the first comprehensive theory of human behavior, and its impact is still widely felt not only in the psychology of human behavior but in literature, justice, politics, and government as well. Whether or not you like psychoanalytic theory, or its more recent offshoot, Ego Psychology, you cannot ignore it. Except for behaviorism, most psychologies developed since Freud have either been a reaction to Freudian theory or tangential attempts to augment it. Furthermore, even after all the years since Freudian theory was established in the 1920s, it is still the only comprehensive psychological theory used in psychotherapy that incorporates personality development into its scope and integrates diagnostic systems as well.

There are some important differences between the Psychoanalytic Theory (abbreviated PAT from this point on) of Freud and more recent Ego Psychology. PAT is concerned with human instinct and the nature of the Id, whereas Ego Psychology deals more with the relationship of personality to reality. Ego Psychology is concerned with the functions of the ego, the central mechanism that regulates the necessary compromises we make between the Id and the superego as we interact with the environment. In terms of therapy, psychoanalysts would tend to make more use of dreams, the entry into the unconscious. Their method would also include using free association and be generally historical in nature. While Ego Psychology therapists might touch on some of these techniques, they would tend to spend much more time on the functions of the ego, and the individual's ability to cope with the present environment. Thus, while basic Freudian theory underlies both approaches, there is quite a bit of difference in their practice and treatment goals.

The basic philosophy that guides the use of Freudian theory does not paint an altogether pleasant picture of the human race. People are driven by sexual and aggressive urges, and for survival must curb the expression of these drives. There is a constant struggle between the need to behaviorally express these sexual and aggressive impulses and the oppressive forces of society and civilization demanding their repression. This view of humans has not always found willing ears over the years among the many competing theories of psychotherapy. In fact, the controversies concerning the validity of Freudian theory have, at times, reached almost ridiculous proportions.

However, regardless of one's ultimate acceptance of Freudian theory, I believe it is incumbent on both the professionals and consumers of psychotherapy to have a basic understanding of it. Using both an historical and contemporary perspective, the concepts are too important and pervasive to be ignored in any comprehensive psychotherapeutic education, be it personal or professional.

THEORY

The Ego, Id, and Superego—Motivation

Ego Psychology starts with the familiar ego, superego, and Id. They are theoretical constructs, imaginary models of how our personality is made up. The ego represents all that we are aware of and our sense of ourselves. It is, for all practical purposes, what is conceived of as our personality and perception of reality. The personality is developed through the interrelationship of our early-childhood experiences and the primitive drives in the Id. It is the ego that acts as the executor of the conflicts and struggles going on between the sexual and aggressive urges in the Id, the values and moral attitudes of the superego, and the demands of reality.

We are born with the *Id*. It is a genetically determined drive left over from a more primitive time when survival of the human species was dependent on aggressiveness and, of course, the ability to propagate. Some of these instinctual urges are still necessary for survival, but with the coming of a higher civilization and the need to organize societies, the instincts in the Id needed to be controlled if people were going to live together cooperatively. For instance, in early times, those people who were the most aggressive could better compete for limited food supplies; similarly, those groups who most prolifically propagated themselves insured they would survive over those who did not. However, society began establishing rules against physical violence and indiscriminate sexual promiscuity. While these civilized norms were certainly more rational for helping people live together, they went directly against the irrational aggressive and sexual or libidinal drives of the Id.

All motivation for human behavior comes from the energy of the Id's instinctual drives. While this drive can be redirected, and is not always obvious as a motivator of behavior, it can always be interpreted as the driving force behind any behavior pattern. Another way this is expressed is what is known as the *pleasure principle*. Since the Id is so primitive, its needs seek immediate gratification without regard to consequences. In addition, attributes and values get associated with Id impulses, such as status, success, or wealth. The ultimate motivation for these behaviors can be viewed through the Id and the pleasure principle.

The *superego* is what acts as a censor of the irrational Id impulses. The superego develops through the process of modeling and identification with parent figures. Acceptable behavior in one's family and society; concepts of right and wrong; sexual identity and associated behavioral traits are all a part of the superego's function. Essentially, the superego is the internalization of a value system derived from many sources and experiences. As we shall see, its successful development in the early years of childhood is critical. Without an effectively functioning superego to censor Id impulses, antisocial behavior and conflict with society can result in later years.

It is the role of the *ego* that is most crucial and central in dealing with internal and external conflicts. The ego is able to perceive reality and begin problem solving. As the ego gathers up its resources to deal with a conflict, the need to block certain Id impulses becomes less and less. The ego separates present reality from past history, allowing for more accurate assessment of environmental demands. This, in turn, allows problems to be confronted, using data from the present, which of course increases the likelihood that resolution will occur.

Psychic Energy

Psychic energy is an important concept in the understanding of how the Id, superego, and ego interact culminating in overt and verbal behavior. Although it is difficult to postulate limits on the amount of psychic energy, consider the following example: Suppose your Id started generating homosexual impulses from your libidinal drive directed toward a close boy or girl friend. The Id does not discriminate between homosexual and heterosexual objects of sexual desire. If your upbringing has taught that homosexuality is intolerable, this rule is internalized in your superego. Therefore, it is up to the ego to protect you from knowing you are indeed attracted to your friend. It takes psychic energy to keep this Id impulse and potential conflict repressed. If it slipped through to your consciousness, the dissonance between what you had internalized as a child and your present self-image would create tremendous anxiety; in effect, pain to the ego. Since you do not wish to experience anxiety, the ego will utilize psychic energy to repress the impulse. If, however, you are at a stage of life where there are great demands on your store of psychic energy, there may not be enough to completely repress homosexual desires. More than usual amounts of conflict, stress, and fatigue can create situations where psychic energy levels are too low to repress Id impulses that have normally been kept unconscious. At these times, the ego's efforts to block or at least rechannel the Id's unacceptable desires may fail, and the ego will experience pain, that is, you will become anxious.

An Id impulse becomes a need. The need that is generated demands satisfaction. People are uncomfortable when a need is not satisfied, even if its origins remain unknown. Following the pleasure principle, we find pleasure when a drive is satisfied. However, when the need that comes out of the Id is not acceptable to the superego, it is up to the ego to step in and block or rechannel the impulse so that you can continue fulfilling your self-image. The skill with which the ego performs this task will determine how well you are able to function. If the ego tries to block too many impulses, an individual will use up what psychic energy is available and libidinal or aggressive desires will begin to slip through into the awareness, creating anxiety, or worse.

Thus, the ego keeps a lid on things by utilizing psychic energy to keep unacceptable impulses unconscious. The means by which this occurs is through a *defense mechanism*. These defense mechanisms are usually unconscious and their purpose is to protect the ego. Often, an awareness you are using a defense mechanism means it is no longer doing an effective job of protecting you from pain and anxiety. The use of defense mechanisms is not necessarily an unhealthy process. There are times when the ego needs protection and times when you need to face the conflicts Id impulses generate. For example, you might have learned that showing anger is unacceptable. As a child, when you dared to get mad you were punished. To survive you learned to repress anger and act as if you were accepting a difficult situation. And as far as you are aware, you have no idea that there is any anger in you since your ego is using the defense mechanism of repression, among others, to keep the aggressive impulses repressed. But as you get older and leave the family, it is possible to get into situations that make you very angry. With the anger drive heightened and aggressive impulses stronger than ever, it will take more and more psychic energy to repress or rechannel them. It may even get to the point that you are immobilized because so much psychic energy is being used to keep the anger unconscious. It is likely anger will come through indirectly, as in passive aggression or depression. Repressing anger impulses during childhood helped you get through the family experience with a minimum of pain. But as an adult the process may become dysfunctional depending on environmental demands. If such symptoms as chronic depression or passive aggression become serious, normal functioning could be impaired and therapy would be in order.

Ego Psychology gets its name because of its central focus on strengthening the ego in its ability to deal more effectively with reality/Id/superego conflicts. A strong ego has the ability to face and resolve some of these conflicts while using the least amount of psychic energy to control others. Therapy strengthens the ego's ability to cope with the interrelationship between the demands from the environment and the conflicts this generates between the Id and superego.

Defense Mechanisms

The way the ego protects us, or our consciousness, from becoming aware of threatening feelings that would provoke anxiety is through the use of defense mechanisms. They are also called *mental mechanisms*. Remember, when a defense mechanism is invoked, it is basically an unconscious process. Usually, if we realized it was being used, these defense mechanisms would no longer be able to protect the ego from the threatening emotional components attached to behavior motivated by Id impulses. There are over twenty basic defense mechanisms, but for our purposes we will discuss only the major ones.

Repression. Putting a thought or feeling from the conscious to the unconscious. For instance, a close friend seriously hurts you. When you begin to get angry, the superego dictates how unacceptable it is to be angry, so these impulses are pushed back or repressed back into the unconscious. What you may be aware of in this process is some initial irritation and how fast it went away. Many sexual feelings are also repressed. Sexual attraction to members of the same sex; to brothers and sisters-in-law; and between family members are normally repressed in the Western societies. One of the stereotypic sexual repressions that occurs in families is between a father and an adolescent daughter. Since it is absolutely taboo to even recognize that there is any possibility of sexual attraction between Dad and daughter, these feelings are kept firmly in the unconscious. However, since it is entirely possible that daughter is sexually attractive, and Dad is an attractive man, it would also naturally follow that if they met on the street as strangers they would at least give each other an appraising eye. Nature wanted to be sure that the species was propragated! However, between father and daughter, such thinking and feeling are not acceptable. What often happens after these impulses are successfully repressed is that other defense mechanisms are brought into play. Dad might use *projection* and be extremely angry with any boy who dared touch his daughter; the daughter might use *provacative behavior* and do her damnedest to find a boyfriend with whom she could act out, and be sure that Dad found out about it.

As you can see from this example, defense mechanisms work together to keep the ego from experiencing pain. Repression and projection are commonly used in conjunction with one of the others.

Denial. The ego is unable to deal with the reality of a situation, such as the death of a loved one or a sudden failure. For good mental health, denial should be only a temporary defense until the ego has garnered the necessary resources to effectively deal with the present reality. A simple example of denial is when someone mentions that an acquaintance has died. It is not uncommon for the response to be: "No!" Very soon after that, usually only seconds, we begin to accept the reality of the situation. However, if denial is used too long, one remains out of contact with reality, which of course is a serious problem.

Reaction formation. In utilizing this defense mechanism a person actually reflects the opposite of what the Id impulses are demanding, due to the ego's inability to tolerate the reality of the conflict. For instance, overprotection could be the result of a reaction formation for a mother who has feelings of rejection for her child. Since the superego rules out rejection of one's child, and the mother's ego must be protected from the pain of that reality, an exaggeration of the opposite extreme of the Id impulses develops. In this case the opposite reaction would be overprotection. What the mother is saying to herself and the world is, "How can you say I reject my child. Look at all I do for him."

Projection. One of the most frequently used defense mechanisms. You put a label on someone else without realizing that the label fits you. Blaming is one type of protection. "Well, this is all your fault, and if it hadn't been for you things would have turned out fine." Statements such as these which assign blame in a generalized kind of way are projections of feelings that people do not wish to face themselves, such as, "A lot of the way this situation turned out was my fault, and I feel guilty." Since the reality of taking responsibility for one's part in an unpleasant situation is often painful, projections are protective. Unfortunately, they may also inhibit problem resolution.

Isolation. Isolating the feeling from a task. This defense mechanism is not exactly what the term *isolation* implies. Actually isolating oneself from other people could certainly be a way of avoiding pain, but it is a conscious behavior. Isolation in the sense that the ego uses it to avoid pain is a way of separating thoughts and ideas from the feelings associated with them; separating a feeling from the task associated with it. In this way people can behave in a way that is not exactly congruent with their past behavior. For instance, if a doctor wished to operate on his or her mother, the only way he could do it without anxiety would be to separate the feelings about mother from surgical skills. Some people use this defense mechanism as a daily part of their lives. People who consistently separate sex and love are using isolation to allow them to have sex with a number of partners. It would be too painful to be in love with all of these partners, so the isolation defense mechanism separates the feeling of love from the sex act.

Displacement. The reattachment of a feeling to something other than the true situation. When you kick the dog instead of your wife or husband. Kids frequently use displacement when they cannot functionally express their anger at parents. They direct anger at their friends, objects, or other less threatening adults. Displacement is used when the object of the love or hate is far too risky to approach with honest feelings. Remember, since you often don't know this mental mechanism is being used at the time, it would seem that you really are angry with a friend and certainly not with someone who may be riskier to confront, such as a boss, spouse, parent, or lover.

Substitution. A rebound love affair is a simple example of substitution. When the pain of the breakup is too hard to face and the grief process too threatening to experience, then immediately finding another object of one's affections is a way to feel better. Because it is an unconscious process, it is very difficult to know whether you really do love the new person or are substituting him or her for what you lost. Overeating and smoking could also be viewed as a substitution for more basic gratification.

Rationalization. The intellectualization of a threatening feeling. Making excuses or explaining away failures. "Yes, I do understand that what you did to me was rotten. Of course I do not like what you did, but really now, will it do either of at this job, losing my income, having to declare bankruptcy, and putting my kids in the poorhouse. But I know that every cloud has a silver lining, and how would it help if I felt guilty?"

Undoing. Avoiding anxiety by participating in some ritual behavior which magically deals with the threat. "Step upon a crack, break your mother's back," is an old superstitious rhyme children sing as they walk along sidewalks. It can be a behavioral manifestation of undoing if the child participating in this game has unconscious feelings of hostility toward Mother. If these feelings are unacceptable, the refusal to step on cracks reaffirms to the child that there is no anger directed at mother.

Introjection or incorporation. The opposite of projection. People accept or incorporate something to keep from knowing what is really going on in their unconscious. For example, people can accept even more guilt instead of facing that they have anger to give to the people who are involved in the guilt-producing situation. Accepting degrading criticism is another form of introjection.

Identification. This is one of the major defense mechanisms. Its simplest manifestation is when we empathize with what is going on around us. When the sad part comes in a movie and the whole theater is in tears, identification is going on. When someone we barely know dies and we are really upset about it, the same process is likely going on. What is being defensed against in each case is facing how these situations personally affect our lives. Crying for someone else's pain can easily deflect from facing that their pain is also our pain, their death is also our fear of dying.

Conversion. Conversion is certainly one of the most interesting and intricate defenses, always used in conjection with other defense mechanisms. It is not one of the more common ones, but when it does occur we have to be awed by the power of the mind over body. A person unconsciously wishes for something to happen, for instance, he wants his invalid, overbearing mother to die. The event actually occurs and instead of facing the guilt and pain these unacceptable unconscious death wishes would evoke even after the fact, the feelings are converted into a physical symptom. These symptoms can vary widely, but are usually symbolic. In the case of the son who unconsciously wished his mother to die, he might wake and find that the arms with which he carried her around are paralyzed. You've probably seen television shows where somebody lost his or her sight after seeing something that he could not tolerate seeing. The unstated basis for this, and other conversions, is that it is less painful for the ego to deal with the symptom than with reality.

Provocative behavior. This defense mechanism is normally reserved for adolescents, but some people never grow up. Provocative behavior is simply provoking another person unconsciously so that you can retaliate against him or her. The feelings of hostility for that person are kept unconscious until they have been provoked, and then there is permission to ventilate hostility. It's a way of venting anger and other feelings without having to feel guilty.

The use of defense mechanisms is not a static process, but changes developmentally as people grow and their environment changes. Some of these mental mechanisms are used more in childhood as ways of resolving specific developmental problems. Once resolved, they are not needed to protect the ego, and new, more sophisticated defense mechanisms are learned. The use of defense mechanisms is obviously not cause for entering therapy. Only when there are behavioral symptoms of a problematic neurosis, or worse, a psychosis, is a serious examination of a person's defense mechanisms indicated.

Personality Development

It cannot be denied that Freud's work in personality development was a stroke of genius. In fact, even today it is the only theory that attempts to systematically tie a person's early conditioning with current behavior in a way that would suggest directions for therapeutic interventions.

There are five stages of development that are basic to Freudian personality theory: the *oral, anal, Oedipal, latency,* and *adolescence* (genital) stages. Each of these stages has at least one basic conflict for a person to resolve in order to successfully pass on to the next stage. For those who do not resolve each conflict successfully, a fixation will occur that will have great impact on an adult's personality and level of functioning. In general, a baby starts with its Id. The ego develops very early when the child begins to stop crying with the expectation of food and nurturing. The superego develops through the process of identification, around six or seven years of age, as a child's way out of the Oedipal stage.

The oral stage. How many times have you heard people joke that someone has an oral fixation when they smoke or eat too much? While this is popularly known as an oral fixation, it is more correctly a residual of the oral stage. Most of us were able to resolve the problems of this stage and move on. In the oral dependent stage the child demands that its needs be met. The mother (and father in some families) is important since she must be on hand to gratify the baby's hunger. A child at this stage is working purely on the pleasure principle. "I'm here and I want what I want when I want it, and everybody is here to make sure I get what I need." When the baby gets teeth the oral sadistic stage starts with the same premises as the oral dependent stage but with the added advantage of being able to bite on things and people.

Infants partly get to know their world through their mouths. The first thing very young children will do if they get near an object is to put it to their mouths. Since this is the means of eating, it does seem a reasonable exploratory behavior. But very quickly children are confronted with the fact that their environment does not seem to be meeting all of their needs. Either the child begins to make some adjustments with the environment, with parental help, or the ego will become fixated at us any good for me to get angry?" Or, "I know I should be feeling guilty for failing this stage of development. The basic problem young children have to solve at the oral stage is to begin giving up the pleasure principle and dependency and begin to experience object love. Perhaps it would be more accurate to say the resolution involves realizing others exist and certain attachments can be made. Love is probably learned later as a more sophisticated ego function. An adult fixated at the oral stage as a child would tend to be overly dependent and demanding.

The anal stage.   At about the age of two or three years, a child enters the anal stage, which is frequently associated with toilet training. There are a variety of issues or problems that confront a little boy or girl when Mom and Dad begin trying to communicate how important it is to put their urine and feces into the proper place. This issue is highly representative of the child's major concern for handling parental demands, rules, and the concept of right and wrong. Certainly these developmental problems don't have to center around whether the potty is used appropriately or not. Yet the process of elimination is such a primary instinctual need, it is likely that toilet training is a very basic and central way that most children act out the developmental issues of this stage. The focus is centered on the dynamics of toilet training because a child is being asked to control an instinctual physiological process for the first time in its life, and it is the parents who are making the demand.

When Mom and Dad begin toilet training, a child begins to realize most clearly that it is possible to do something wrong or right in the parents' eyes. There is a natural resistance, both physiological and psychological, to holding it in until a toilet is in view. Children are filled with ambivalence at this point. On one hand they want to please the parents; on the other hand they want to let go when the urge comes along. Giving up part of oneself is also a major issue. In addition, it is at this stage that love and hate for your parents is experienced with all the resulting confusion these two polar feelings can bring when they are felt toward the same person. Feeling hate for someone you have loved and depended upon for so long is a new and difficult experience.

The resolution of the anal stage is for a little boy or girl to learn to conform. Toilet training is finished along with the setting of limits by the parents on a wide number of issues. Learning to follow rules is often a painful process, to which many of us can attest even in our adulthood. It is mixed with threats and punishment; the wish to please and the need to maintain personal integrity; the integration of love-hate feelings so that we can feel degrees of both love and hate for the same person and not be scared by the experience. In addition, children learn to separate the concepts of right and wrong to complete the process of moving past the anal stage. These are tremendous tasks for little tykes, but it is at the anal stage that we are confronted with these problems and search for the solutions. The degree to which our parents can teach us how to perform these problem-solving behaviors will go a long way in building the foundation for a strong ego as an adult.

Being fixated at the anal stage is called being *anal retentive*. It literally means refusing to give up your feces to your parents and manifests itself in being constipated. A person fixated at the anal stage would save and collect things, be resistant to throwing anything away, not be too giving of him or herself and be rather self-centered. Other manifestations could include ambivalence about relationships, compulsive behavior patterns, and rigidity in moral and personal beliefs.

The Oedipal stage. One of the most difficult stages of development to understand is the Oedipal stage of development. Popularized in literature, Shakespeare's *Hamlet* for example, some people question its validity and suggest that Freud was biased by the culture in which he lived. It is often a subtle phenomenon where a child and the same-sexed parent seem to be competing for the love of the opposite-sexed parent. Since it is unusual for this kind of competition to be explicit, the behaviors of the family members have to be interpreted in the light of the basic Oedipal needs that surface. Furthermore, there is a clear tendency to channel the issues of the Oedipal period through the eyes of a male-dominated society. For instance, Freud believed that penis envy was a natural part of a little girl's psychology during this stage and that girls could not go the the next stage until penis envy was resolved. Thus while boys did not have to deal with penis envy, girls had the added burden of dealing with wanting to be a boy before they dealt with the same kind of concerns that their brothers had.

The Oedipal conflict (for boys) or the Electra conflict (for girls) usually begins before school age and is often resolved by the time a child is attending school. As children become more aware of the differences between boys and girls, and thus of their own sex organs, their attention is focused on the dynamics between their parents and themselves. This awakening of sexual identification combined with the close ties that children form with the parents, especially the opposite-sexed one, creates the Oedipal and Electra conflicts. The Id is generating impulses telling the children that their relationship with one parent is somehow threatened by the other; a boy feels that his father is coming between him and his mother; a girl feels the mother is coming between her and her father. These conflicts can create real tension in a household, with children throwing tantrums, being oppositional, and parents fighting about what is the most appropriate way to deal with the child. Unless these conflicts are resolved, the triangle created by the Oedipal stage can last a lifetime with children learning the techniques to, in a sense, divide and conquer their parents. This manifests itself with alliances being developed between children and one of the parents against the other.

The way out of this potential problem for a child requires that the parents do some important modeling and teaching. Dynamically, it is at this point in a child's life that the superego is developed to the extent that it can protect the ego (the conscious) from the need to be sexually involved with the opposite-sexed parent. In most families children learn that the love they need from one parent is not threatened by the other. But superegos do not just appear. They are borrowed and then incorporated. It is the parents who do the giving of their superegos to the child through the important process called *identification*. By identifying with the same-sexed parent, a little boy or girl can successfully begin the process of resolving the

Oedipal or Electral conflict. If the father or mother, as the case may be, has a reasonably sound superego, then the children will adopt values and rules that will help them form close relationships and teach them how to get along with people in general. A child also learns through identification with a parent's superego what social and moral values are acceptable and those that are not.

If, however, parental models for a child are not conducive for learning how to resolve the Oedipal or Electral dynamic, the superegos of the parents being too weak, then the child will not effectively resolve this conflict. People fixated at this stage will have an Oedipal or Electra complex. A boy who is fixated at this stage might perceive his father as a castration threat. A girl might continue penis envy and never get to the issue of making a strong identification with her mother. Also, according to the theory, fixation at this stage could result in confusion concerning one's sexual identity as an adult.

Complete resolution of the Oedipal or Electra conflict probably never occurs because of the complexity of the dynamics involved. But with the formation of the superego, a demand is made that the child identify with the same-sexed parent more strongly, which is necessary for a clear sense of one's sexual identity. However, play with peers is sanctioned. Thus young boys play with boys and girls play with girls. And so it stays until nature tells them that boys and girls need each other for some other very important functions.

The latency stage.   For the next six or seven years children enter into what is called the *latency stage*. The name is what it implies: a latent or a quiet period where sexual desires are not an important issue. Latency occurs between two exciting times, the Oedipal-Electra and adolescent periods. However, some important growth does indeed go on during this time. Character formation, or the balancing between internal and external demands, begins its development here. And the more varied use of defense mechanisms also gets a lot of practice.

It is possible to become fixated in the latency stage. If children are not allowed the time and space to develop their character, and to practice using different and more sophisticated defense mechanisms, an asexual character personality can develop.

Adolescence and puberty—The genital phase.   Nobody who is reading this book needs to be told too much about this period, or about the "stürm and stress" many of us went through. Unlike the earlier stages, we were aware enough of ourselves and others to remember the dynamics of our growth from a child to a young adult, and the new feelings and stresses we experienced as we became aware of our sexuality.

The broad issues that confront an adolescent as puberty commences are sexual impulses and developing independence. In many ways it is the most confusing part of our lives and the most difficult to understand while we are going through it. On one hand we love and are dependent on our parents, but on the other hand we need to declare our independence from them. We physically experience that our bodies are ready to take on adult functions, but society and our own insecurities inhibit that role.

At this stage the unfinished business of the earlier Oedipal-Electra periods come thundering up to confront us. We scrutinize our sexual identification with microscopes, looking for any abnormality that makes us different. Finding one can be a crisis that needs to be resolved immediately. Adolescent boys and girls are very quick to pick up on any homosexual behavior and demand conformity or exclusion. They are constantly examining their interest in the opposite sex and trying to balance it with other concerns such as school and careers.

The Id is in full sway, generating all kinds of new sexual and aggressive impulses arising from needs never experienced before. The ego is being kept busy full time trying to control all of the impulses that can't be handled, and trying to sort out new realities that environmental demands put on young adults. Lots of psychic energy is being utilized that went for other things during latency. One of the tremendous difficulties that adolescents face now is that they can no longer directly use their parents' superegos to face the new problems created by the Id. That would mean staying in the dependent role, which is anathema at this point. Yet here is the one time in their lives when the superego is needed more than ever. The way the adolescents resolve this problem is by identifying their own superegos and differentiating them from their parents'. This process can be painful for both parties. The parents of course have an investment in seeing their lives conducted according to their rules and values. If their children violate these it may bring up issues that their egos are not prepared to handle. The adolescent's experimentation with new rules and values can leave him or her just as unprotected. Yet, in the context of new independence from parents, there is still a very real need for their guidance. Since teenagers can no longer go to parents, peers take on a whole new meaning to them. Peer pressure is also used to help control impulses, sometimes successfully and sometimes not.

As if these struggles are not enough, there is a very important reorientation of an adolescent's self-image. When we were little we wished and dreamed about being big. At adolescence we became big and our self-image had to adjust to that fact. Fortunately, by this time young adults should have the mental apparatus to accomplish the task. Not only can they fantasize better than at any time in their lives (and they've got plenty to fantasize about) but self-awareness has never been better. This is one reason adolescents are so preoccupied about the physical changes in their bodies.

People probably never completely resolve the many issues that confront them in adolescence. In that sense all of us are still fixated on some adolescent concerns. But the major ones, those of developing independence, coming to grips with our sexual beings, and identifying a sense of our own superegos as separate from our parents', are critical to a healthy move into adulthood. While none of these issues will ever be finished perfectly, they need to be resolved enough so that we can function successfully without our parents or parental figures and can form intimate relationships that are emotionally and sexually satisfying to us. In fact, since the work of adolescence is so dependent on the successful resolution of previous stages, it is very likely that fixation in the genital stage also contains unfinished residuals of earlier stages of development.

There are later stages of development that come after adolescence. Life does go on into adulthood, parenthood, middle age, old age, and finally death. However, by the time a person passes into adulthood from adolescence, his or her personality is established. Life does not end with adolescence; the basic development of the personality does.

Neurosis and Psychosis—Assessment

What you will notice about Ego Psychology as far as we have gone is that the treatment technology is not yet clearly emerging. The personality theory does provide clues to how people get into emotional difficulties, but we still do not have a good understanding of how assessment is done in reaching a clinical diagnosis before treatment commences. A lot of time is spent on assessment during the initial interviews with a client. Regardless of the type of problem a client may have, there is a label for it. In order to put some organization to diagnostic work, clients are initially put into one of two major areas, with a few exceptions. These major categories are *neurosis* and *psychosis*. While psychosis is always considered pathological, or a mental illness, there is some serious disagreement about whether a number of neuroses are abnormal or not.

Neurosis. Neurotic people suffer. They are anxious, fearful, worry about things, are unhappy with their lives, themselves, and in a state of personal and interpersonal conflict. They tend to repress Id impulses, their basic needs, and instead respond to environmental demands. The neurotic method of coping is to regress to an earlier developmental stage where gratification was experienced. If you can't successfully cope with a present situation because of ineffective defense mechanisms and a weakened ego, then you can unconsciously regress back to an earlier stage where you did have a way of coping with the problem. This earlier period, while protective in one way, used a more infantile defense mechanism that is not as effective for adult problems. It also revives the conflicts of that stage. The price people pay for dealing with a problem by regressing is that their personality changes somewhat and there is considerable suffering. The ego is trying to satisfy the Id, the superego, and the reality of the present by the regression. It ends up that none of them is satisfied. The psychic energy used in trying to make the regression work leaves the ego so impoverished that the neurotic person ends up even less able to cope.

For example, a couple has a baby. After the excitement of the birth has worn off the husband begins to realize that he is not going to be the center of attention for his wife anymore. A man with a strong ego would become aware of his feelings of rejection, anger, and jealousy, and discuss the problem with his wife. Even so, a baby does put more demands on new parents and both will have to have the maturity and ego strengths to accept this new situation. If, however, the husband never really resolved the conflicts of his Oedipal period, the new baby could create a real crisis for him. His ego could not stand the competition for his wife and he might regress back to the stage where he faced this dilemma before. In this case, he would probably handle it as he did in his childhood. It is possible that the husband could start throwing tantrums, look elsewhere to get sexual needs met, or become aggressive with his wife and possibly even his child.

What is fascinating about neurotic people is they may know exactly how infantile their behavior is and still not be able to change it. They are helpless to control their inappropriate behavior even though they are aware of it as it is occurring. Although they have good awareness functioning they do not have the skills or the defense mechanisms to deal with the present problem because they never resolved the earlier conflict relating to it.

Psychosis. What distinguishes neurotic from psychotic people is that those individuals with neurotic symptoms are still aware of the realities around themselves, even if they feel helpless to change. People who are psychotic are not totally in touch with reality. Instead of trying to solve problems by regression, psychotics create a reality of their own repudiating their present awareness. Within this new framework of reality an attempt is then made to resolve the conflict.

An assessment leading to a psychotic diagnosis assumes that a person's ego has essentially been abandoned in the world of reality to some sort of fantasy that gratifies the Id. The personality disintegrates and a person's ability to relate to people is severely limited. The common behavioral symptoms include delusional thinking, hearing, seeing things that others do not perceive, and extreme aggressiveness or passivity, often coming quite unpredictably.

A third area of emotional maladjustment besides neurosis and psychosis is called a *character or personality disorder*. Personality disorders are usually not considered a mental illness, but that is not to say they are not a problem. People with such a maladjustment attempt to resolve internal conflicts between the Id and the superego by forcing external reality to conform to their needs, regardless of the consequences. The biggest problem in dealing with a personality disorder is that it is almost always not a problem to the one who has it, but it can be a pain in the neck to those who have to work and live with it. Because people with personality disorders usually don't perceive the problem, treatment is extremely difficult and often not possible. Treatment strategies generally try to show how far these clients fall short of their image and thus make them anxious about themselves. Hopefully they may then feel some motivation to change.

In summary, neurosis and psychosis develop when the present environment confronts people with problems they do not have the ego strengths to resolve. They are not using sufficient psychic energy or appropriate defense mechanisms to protect the ego, and neurotic or psychotic symptomatology emerges. However, while the onset of neurosis and psychosis are clearly tied to present stimuli, their causes are sown in our history, a combination of instinct, heredity, and the kind of parenting we received. Particularly for psychosis, no one is sure just how heredity, chemical imbalances, and environment interact to produce the seriously disturbing behavior associated with this diagnosis. But clearly, regardless of the ultimate biological determinants of neurosis and psychosis, early childhood learning greatly affects the ability of an adult to function effectively and form successful intimate relationships.

PRACTICE

The Role of the Therapist

Since Ego Psychology's roots are in psychoanalysis, there is a strong tendency for therapists to be nondirective. Instead of giving advice, they might use active-listening techniques, which include restating what clients have said, reflecting on their feelings, and empathizing.

While nondirectiveness may be one of the themes of the therapist's role, another is the great importance of the client-therapist relationship. It can be said, without too much reservation, that the focus on developing a good relationship is central to helping clients constructively change their behavior. Without it, not much will happen in therapy. This relationship is not necessarily a reciprocal one. Therapists do not generally attempt to make friends with clients, nor do they generally make it a habit to share their personal lives, unless there is some clear therapeutic reason to do so. Rather, therapists using Ego Psychology tend to be supportive and nurturing. It is very common for clients to perceive therapists as being in a parental role. As we shall see, this dynamic, which is really transference, is one of the cornerstones in the technology of Ego Psychology treatment.

The Ego Psychology Treatment Process

The greatest difficulty in studying Ego Psychology is in specifically defining its technology of treatment. A basic goal is to support and strengthen clients' egos so that they can function and cope more effectively. There are some important components of treatment that are typical of therapy, particularly with neurotics. First, therapists should expect that clients will try to manipulate the situation. As this occurs, therapists begin to support clients' talking; help them partialize their problems; reflect their feelings and show empathy; and offer support whenever possible and appropriate. Doing these kinds of things will by themselves not be the curative elements of the therapy. Therapists are after bigger game. There are three basic parts to the cure in Ego Psychology therapy. The first, as already mentioned, is the support and strengthening of the ego; the second comes through the development of insight into problems; the third is called the *corrective emotional experience* and involves the reexperiencing of an unresolved conflict from childhood.

If these goals and treatment strategies sound ambiguous, it is because it is very difficult in Ego Psychology to define terms behaviorally. Unless therapists are careful, they will use reification, circular reasoning, to describe the current level of client functioning and what they do to help. For example, Sam is chronically depressed, therefore he has low ego strengths. Why is Sam depressed? Because he has low ego strengths. How do we know he has low ego strengths? Because he is depressed. This kind of reasoning can play havoc with trying to understand how Ego Psychology therapy works, and it should be avoided.

Yet, even at best, it is difficult to describe client behavior using such labels as ego strength, superego, Id, psychic energy, defense mechanisms, and self-image. This difficulty lends itself to rather diverse descriptions of what exactly therapists do to support client change, even though there is general agreement in goals and philosophy. There is also no general consensus concerning a systematic treatment process in Ego Psychology, as we saw to some degree in the other therapies. However, this is not to say that there are no common therapist behaviors across the field. There are indeed. It is just not possible to put them in as sequential an order beyond the first stages of treatment. Rather, the basic treatment techniques in Ego Pyschology therapy are concurrent in their application and development and build together for a client cure. See Figure 4-1.

Assessment. As therapists initially engage clients in telling their stories, the major task is to watch and listen carefully. Not only will the type of problems clients present be significant in assessment but the dynamics of the forming client-therapist relationship are also important. How clients present themselves, what they apparently want from therapists, and their general demeanor are rich sources of potential information. At this stage it is helpful if therapists begin ascertaining the clients' present ability to cope and their current level of functioning. In addition, therapists use observable behaviors to make initial hypotheses about which defense mechanisms are being used, and what stage of personality development the method of dealing with the present conflict represents. While there are many clinical labels that

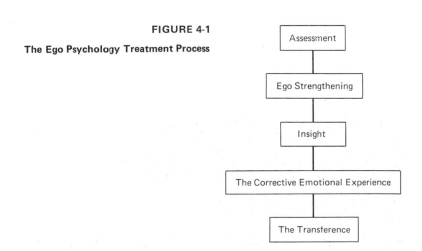

FIGURE 4-1

The Ego Psychology Treatment Process

Assessment

Ego Strengthening

Insight

The Corrective Emotional Experience

The Transference

can come out of assessment, the most important discrimination to be made is between a neurotic and psychotic diagnosis. Generally, neurosis is amenable to outpatient treatment, while psychosis needs much more therapy than the normal once-a-week therapist contact. Additional therapy, hospitalization, and/or chemotherapy would also be indicated.

Ego strengthening. Having a strong ego when facing conflict is of course desirable. Strong egos can not only tolerate new stresses without falling apart but they can better perceive options for problem solving. Therapists help clients strengthen egos in a number of ways: first, they offer support. As I mentioned earlier, active listening skills are important in this regard. Second, they help clients partialize problems into more reasonable "chunks." Often, a problem seems so insurmountable we are overwhelmed by its enormity. We become paralyzed into immobility, and more anxious the more immobile we become. By breaking the problem into solvable parts, clients can see the possibility of resolving at least one piece of the problem. The ego is thus supported and can use its available energy to begin work. A third way therapists work to strengthen egos is by helping clients improve their self-image. Therapists aid in this process by attending to positive behavior and making sure clients do the same. And fourth, by structuring a safe and therapeutic atmosphere where confidentiality is insured and rules are consistent, clients know they have at least one haven where they can talk freely and be dealt with fairly. Since some clients come from situations where they are reacting irrationally to very inconsistent relationships, a predictable therapeutic relationship can be very supportive to the ego.

There are of course many other ways people support each other and egos are strengthened in therapy. The basic goal throughout all of this work is for clients to feel better about themselves while they energize their own resources to problem solve.

Insight. Insight is an integral part of Ego Psychology therapy. While not universally emphasized, most therapists of the Ego Psychology persuasion would agree that as clients develop insight into their problems, they are often better able to resolve them. If people become aware of the original conflicts that are related to their present difficulties, just that realization itself may considerably dissipate anxiety and free up psychic energy.

Consider a simple example. A little boy is spending his first night solo in his backyard tent. He hears a strange, scary, hooting sound and runs to find Mom and Dad for protection. If he has had any experience with owls before, by seeing them in the zoo or on television, then just an explanation can help him make the connection between his present experience and his past. This connection, or insight, could reduce his anxiety and allow him to return to his tent. Granted, the little boy might still be uncomfortable when he heard the owl again, but this time he would know more about what caused his fear and thus would have more tools to cope and reassure himself. In the same way, when we are able to see what historical forces and prior situations are impacting on the motivation for our present behavior, we can experience a reduction in anxiety. As with the little boy and the owl, connecting our past with the present may give us more information and help us decide where to direct our resources for problem solving.

People do not necessarily need professional help to get insight into their problems. We often discover what is controlling our behavior through normal life experiences. However, therapists can help insight along by asking questions directed at making connections between the present and the past, such as, "Does this situation seem familiar to you?" or, "Who does this remind you of?" In addition, when the connections are so obvious that they beg to be discovered, it is certainly reasonable for therapists to mention what they see or interpret.

There is no question that insight alone is not a therapeutic panacea. However, when used in conjection with the other Ego Psychology techniques, it can be a supportive tool in helping people come to grips with problems they are dealing with. Most therapists have had experiences where clients have gotten insight and were immediately able to resolve a problem. Once the fog of uncertainty and fear is lifted by making some important connections, there are people who are able to apply existing problem-solving skills and effectively cope without further help.

The corrective emotional experience. In conjunction with insight, the Corrective Emotional Experience is a fundamental process by which people change how they feel and behave in problem situations. Essentially, the techniques supporting this process lead to the reexperiencing of an historical scene, usually from childhood, with its original affect. By facing the situation again in the present, one may be able to behave differently and let repressed feelings flow. This is not necessarily a role play or structured reenactment. Just thinking and talking about early experiences can bring back original affect from early-childhood scenes. But this time, it is an adult with a stronger ego who is facing the situation. The experience is corrective in the sense that people can reexperience a past scene releasing repressed feelings and free up psychic energy to focus on resolving their present conflicts.

For example, if during the anal stage you were forced to repress the anger you felt when parents demanded conformity, it is possible to remember scenes connected with these dynamics and, as an adult, ventilate that unexpressed anger. Theoretically, all these years you have been using psychic energy to repress anger or displace it to someone else. By returning to the original repression experiences, and now using a stronger adult ego to face the expression of Id impulses, the need to repress so much anger may no longer be necessary. Psychic energy will be freed for solving present relationship problems.

There is also a cathartic response connected to the Corrective Emotional Experience. Catharsis is more a phenomenon in Ego Psychology than it is a technique. It is the release of pent-up emotions, often like a dam breaking, causing a flood. A catharsis in and of itself is of limited value over time unless it occurs concurrent with with a Corrective Emotional Experience. A true Corrective Emotional Experience with its cathartic release of repressed feelings will lead to some restructuring of a person's personality and important changes in his or her pattern of relationships.

Let's look at a clinical example. Mike has been working on his inability to keep intimate relationships with men or women. He is successful in his career as a businessman, but lonely otherwise. He has been in therapy for about six months and has been spending more and more time getting in touch with feelings about his upbringing. He has recently had the insight that his inability to be vulnerable with people is one way he keeps people distant. We will pick up the session as he is talking about his new insight:

MIKE: I'm not completely sure why people want you to be vulnerable before they will love you.

THERAPIST: Has that been your experience?

MIKE: Well, my former girl friend kept saying she would do anything if she could make me cry.

THERAPIST: Why don't you cry?

MIKE: I want to sometimes, and I know that if I did I would probably feel better, but I just can't.

THERAPIST: Why not?

MIKE: Oh, I know the traditional reasons. My mother wanted me to be strong and kept telling me that if I let myself be weak, I'd end up like my father, who was an emotional cripple. I'm sure that's the way it happened, but it doesn't do me any good to know that.

THERAPIST: If that's the reason, how do you feel about it?

MIKE: Look God damn it! I don't know how I feel. Why do you keep asking me how I feel when I don't know? (pause) Oh, God, I'm sorry for blowing up.

THERAPIST: (softly) You can be angry with me, Mike.

MIKE: (tears in eyes) No, I can't. I just can't.

THERAPIST: Who are you talking to, Mike?

MIKE: (pause) To you. (another pause) No, my mother. (another pause with tears now streaming down Mike's face) Oh, Mom, why wouldn't you let me feel the way I wanted to? You spent so much time worrying that I'd turn out like Daddy that you never let me feel; you never wanted to listen to how I felt. Didn't you ever want to know me? At least I could get close to Daddy, but never to you. (Mike is really sobbing now)

THERAPIST: (gives Mike some tissues—there is a five-minute pause while Mike cries)

MIKE: (composed now) Well, Mother must be so proud of me, I turned out to be just like her.

THERAPIST: Not just like her, Mike, You're letting yourself be vulnerable now in front of me. (pause) I hestitate to ask you again, but how do you feel?

MIKE: (laughing) Better now. I think I needed to get that out.

The dynamic here that supported Mike's Corrective Emotional Experience and catharsis was his transference with the therapist. A transference often helps set the stage for the Corrective Emotional Experience. In any case, Mike was able to release years of grief, tears, and sadness about how lonely he felt growing up with his mother. By going back to the source, so to speak, and releasing the pent-up feelings, Mike's psychic energy being utilized for that repression was in the process of being freed for other conflict resolution.

The transference. As we saw in the previous example, the transference that develops between the client and therapist is often used in conjunction with the Corrective Emotional Experience. It would not be fair to say that all Ego Psychology therapists practice in such as way as to foster and support clients in developing a strong transference. After all, given half a chance, many clients will do much of that work all by themselves! But one could say that Ego Psychology therapists take advantage of the phenomenon when it occurs. And you shouldn't be surprised, either, if you see therapists actively fostering a transference by being more inaccessible, full of authority, nurturing, or parental at times. These are some of the ways therapists set the stage for a transference to occur, assuming there is a client who is amenable.

There is no question in Ego Psychology that transferences are functions of clients' parenting history. The transference will depend not only on how much they project expectations on their therapists based on early-childhood experiences, but also how powerfully the therapy situation simulates the parent-child dynamic. In this regard therapists obviously have some control. Working through transferences is often connected with a Corrective Emotional Experience. However, as clients act out their historical parent-child dynamics in the present, therapists can help them use their adult egos to discriminate the differences between their projections and the present realities of the therapeutic relationship. Facing realtity is always supportive to problem solving.

Termination Criteria

Theoretically, clients are cured when they are successfully coping with the problems in their lives, have improved their self-image, increased their ego strengths, and are using more sophisticated defense mechanisms. However, since these goals are all rather subjective, it can be difficult to describe termination solely based on these criteria. Rather, therapists, and to some extent clients, too, judge how present behavior symbolizes the meeting of these theoretical goals. Certainly, one of the keys to successful termination is the absence of symptomatic behavior, such as anxiety, depression, or obsessive-compulsive behaviors. And evidence that clients are functioning more effectively in personal and professional relationships is a good sign, too. In addition to these more obvious criteria, therapists must also be assured that client symptoms are not just alleviated but the underlying causes of problems have been successfully dealt with, too. This inevitably means that there should be some evidence that clients have faced and successfully overcome some of the dynamics of their history. Insight, working through a transference, and/or going through a Corrective Emotional Experience would be good indications in this regard. Unless there is evidence that underlying issues have been dealt with in the context of a decrease in behavioral symptoms, there is every reason to believe that the same problems will reoccur, or new problems will develop based on the same themes, which in Ego Psychology is called *regression* and *symptom substitution*, respectively.

The Therapist's Response to Resistance

Client resistance is based on what is perceived as threatening to the ego. Therapists need to set up an atmosphere which reduces that threat. The basic strategy to accomplish this is to accept clients for what they are, which includes a receptiveness and responsiveness to their feelings. In addition, helping clients acknowledge their resistance and gaining insight into its origins from the past will also support overcoming it. Essentially, clients' resistance in Ego Psychology is a phenomenon to be overcome when the ego is strong enough to face the issues underlying the resistances.

The Therapist's Response to Transference and Countertransference

We have already discussed how therapists using Ego Psychology react to and utilize the transference relationship. Their use of the countertransference phenomenon is quite a different matter. In clinical training, attention is paid to the ways therapists project onto clients based on their past, and how to compensate for it. First, it is recognized that the more self-awareness therapists have, and the more they have worked through the issues of their own psychological development, the better they will be able to help clients. One by-product of having a strong mature ego will be the ability to recognize a countertransference and not allow it to manifest itself behaviorally in nontherapeutic ways. In general, these therapist struggles are not directly shared with clients who may not even know that a countertransference is going on. Yet, if therapists trust their feelings, they can share some of their internal struggle if deemed therapeutic. For example, if a client is successfully baiting the therapist, who is overreacting with anger, he or she could say, "You know, I am having a hard time being with you today because you seem so hostile." Clients will generally be asked to reflect on their own behavior when therapists become aware of a countertransference.

SUMMARY

The treatment of psychosis is one area we did not really deal with. Although the same general treatment strategy discussed here is used, therapists are saddled with the additional burden of facing a person whose perceptions of reality and ability to talk may be impaired. As with all of the verbal therapies, those that rely heavily on talking, Ego Psychology is limited in its ability to predictably help psychotic people.

Ego Psychology's great strength is in its theoretical hypotheses concerning the development and motivation of human behavior. It is more of an intrapsychic approach to problem solving valuing historical determinants. The practice of Ego Psychology is diverse, but it is possible to describe the general treatment strategies used. When all is said and done, the foundation and practice of Ego Psychology has had a profound effect on psychotherapy, and needs to be, in my opinion, incorporated into any serious study of the field.

REFERENCES

BLANCK, G., and R. BLANCK, *Ego Psychology: Theory and Practice*. New York: Columbia University Press, 1974.

FREUD, S. *An Outline of Psycho-Analysis* (revised and translated by J. Strachey). New York: W. W. Norton & Co., Inc., 1969.

———. *The Ego and the Id* (revised by J. Strachey). New York: W. W. Norton & Co., Inc., 1962.

HARTMANN, H. *Ego Psychology and the Problem of Adaptation*. New York: International University Press, 1958.

———. *Essays on Ego Psychology*. New York: International University Press, 1964.

HOLLIS, F. *Casework—A Psychosocial Therapy*. New York: Random House, 1972.

JOSSELYN, I. *Psychosocial Development of Children*. New York: Family Service Association of America, 1977.

PARAD, H. J. and R. R. MILLER (eds). *Ego Oriented Casework*. New York: Family Service Association of America, 1963.

PERLMAN, H. H. *Social Casework—A Problem-Solving Process*. Chicago: University of Chicago Press, 1957.

POLANSKY, N. A. *Ego Psychology and Communication: Theory for the Interview*. New York: Atherton, 1971.

REFERENCE JOURNALS

American Psychoanalytic Association Journal. Published by International Universities Press, Inc., New York. Vol. 1, #1: 1953.

Social Casework: The Journal of Contemporary Social Work. Published by Family Service Association of America, New York. Vol. 1, #1: 1920.

CHAPTER FIVE
BEHAVIOR THERAPY
The Search for a Therapeutic Rosetta Stone

When you think of integrating any two theories of psychotherapy, much less four, it is necessary to find some thread of continuity between them. On the surface, therapies may look irreconcilably different. One deals in history, one in the present, one in games, and another in consequences. Most often, attempts to accentuate the similarities between psychotherapies are like trying to mix oil and vinegar. They mix when you shake, but left alone they separate again.

At this juncture in our primitive understanding of human behavior it is not possible to completely integrate the major theories of psychotherapy. The theories of Freud are basically *not* compatible with those of Skinner; Gestalt and TA, while they might be compatible in places, have philosophical gulfs so wide they beg for separate quarters. The best place to start attempting to integrate psychotherapy is emphasizing practice rather than theory. It is what therapists *do* that joins them as brothers and sisters. The trick is in deciding what basic concepts are key to behavior change and what therapist behaviors are active in bringing these key concepts to life. The most reasonable conclusion to draw at this stage of the game is that all of the major psychological theories have some piece of these key concepts.

I am going to make a number of assumptions in order to build a foundation for integration:

1. There must be laws that govern human behavior. There are laws that govern all other aspects of science and it is an accepted view in the philosophy of science that laws exist.
2. If these laws exist, they must certainly be applicable to all animal life on earth even if differentially applied based on species differences and evolution. Humans are, after all, the highest form of animal life on the planet. Granted there

are very significant differences from humans' closest predecessors, but that shouldn't change the validity of the Laws of Behavior—just make them more complex in their application.

3. All of the four therapies under examination here utilize these Laws of Behavior in their practice and at least allude to them in their theoretical concepts. But since these psychologies are mutually exclusive to some degree they must also contain fallacies.

4. Effective therapists perform remarkably similar behaviors to promote behavior change in clients. They just describe what they do using different language and may believe in different philosophies of life. But regardless of what belief systems are espoused to be the most meaningful, the laws that govern human behavior remain the same.

In order to begin comparing our four practice approaches we must agree on a common language, and then on a common set of principles. No therapy has the market on adequately describing why and how people change. In fact, the best explanations would probably take a little of each—a little reinforcer here, a game there, an insight, and a few resistances. Unfortunately, when we mix theories, the logical continuity of practice as well as theory goes down the drain, not unlike trying to make a new language out of English, French, and German. We are stuck with choosing one of the therapies and using it as a basis for comparing all the others if we are to come up with an integrated approach, a therapeutic Rosetta Stone, if you will.

For better and for worse I will choose the behavioral approach as the basic foundation from which to look at Gestalt, TA, and Ego Psychology. As a practicing Gestalt therapist I am more comfortable with Gestalt, but there are compelling reasons why only behavioral theory and practice will do. Behavior Therapy is the most scientific approach to behavior change in the current psychological marketplace. Its basic premises have been heavily researched on animals and humans; its terms are behaviorally specific, and its treatment procedures can be better replicated than those from any other theory. Psychotherapy is not only a science but an art as well, and that is one of its greatest contemporary struggles. There is too much art and not enough science. If we must make some sense about why and how people change, there must be an orderly method to help us in these discoveries. While some might consider Behavior Therapy comparatively simplistic in its application, the scientific method is infused into its practice. The basic question that all behaviorists ask is, "What am I specifically doing that is affecting how my client behaves and how am I going to know?"

Another reason Behavior Therapy can be considered a therapeutic Rosetta Stone is that the basic principles underlying its practice are equally applicable to all types of human problems, and are applicable to the animal kingdom as well. Try training your dog using Ego Psychology; or teaching an elephant to pick up trees using Gestalt.

The biggest factor in favor of the behavioral approach is that you can describe its therapeutic techniques and procedures with relative clarity. This is a tremendous advantage when therapists wish to communicate with one another. This is not to say that Behavior Therapy is better or any more effective than any of the others. There is no *comprehensive* data base supporting the claim that any therapy is generally more effective than another. However, since each therapy probably has some advantages, it makes good sense to use one of the strengths of Behavior Therapy, its power to make therapeutic behavior relatively clear, to help us understand the strengths of Gestalt, TA, and Ego Psychology. The behavioral approach will do just fine as long as we realize that we are using it as a tool and *not* as THE truth.

> God grant us the serenity to accept the things we cannot change,
> The courage to change the things we can,
> And the wisdom to know the difference.

I will begin our integrative journey with a prayer, not so much for support in insuring a favorable outcome, although I accept help from all quarters, but to suggest a format for analyzing the ultimate outcome of therapy. It is certainly true that there are many very complex phenomena occuring between therapist and client before either can call the experience a success or failure. In the first section of this book we have touched on many of these, and as I compare and contrast the four therapies toward an integration we will look at them again using different perspectives. However, I believe that all therapeutic interventions can be classified by their ultimate strategy for behavior change: 1) they teach people to be assertive, or to directly act on their environment to change the things they can; or 2) they teach people to relax. come to peace with themselves, and accept the things they cannot change.

It is of course a simplification to suggest that the techniques and procedures involved in Behavior Therapy, TA, Gestalt, and Ego Psychology are nothing more than assertive or relaxation training. But regardless of what complex cognitive and verbal therapeutic pathways each therapy purports to be part of its curative elements, I believe that all of the actual techniques are geared toward just two logical problem-solving outcomes: clients will either attempt to modify the situations and people who are part of their problems, which we will call *assertive behavior*; or they will have to learn to cognitively accept what they cannot change. True acceptance always ultimately involves relaxing in the face of anxiety-producing situations, and we shall call this *acceptance behavior*.

By looking at therapeutic procedures as ultimately directed toward learning assertive and acceptance behavior, we may compare our four therapies in some very interesting ways. Each has its own unique assertive training models for both overt and covert behavior, including assertions toward internal thought processes. In addition, we will see that teaching people to relax and accept what they cannot change takes many forms, from systematic desensitization to reenacting internal dialogues in double chairs. Please do not assume as we journey on that the strategies involving assertive and acceptance training need to be performed as in Behavior Therapy because I am using its terminology and principles as a practice Rosetta Stone. On the contrary, Gestalt, TA, and Ego Psychology have much to teach us about how we can creatively help people become more assertive and less anxious.

Let's look at some examples to demonstrate how treatment strategies ultimately move toward teaching assertiveness or acceptance. Starting simply: Consider a phobic fear of spiders, a single stimulus event. The spider is there, facing you, just a few feet away. You are experiencing fear, anxiety, muscle tension, and do not wish to continue this experience. You have two basic alternatives to reduce anxiety:

1. You can assert yourself which involves physical motion and move away from the spider, or perhaps go toward it and squish it with your foot.
2. You can relax in the presence of the spider so that you are no longer anxious, which is what people do who are not normally afraid of spiders.

There are of course other assertive strategies, such as calling for someone to remove the spider, and many tactics you could go through to relax yourself, such as getting physical support (protection) in the spider's presence. But no matter what you do, you will either change the stimulus situation until you are satisfied or accept the stimulus situation as it is and change yourself, which ultimately means you will relax. And of course what is probably most common with any problem is learning a little of each—assertions and acceptance.

It is not often that we find a problem with a nice singular stimulus like a spider. Most problems are far more complex, but the same alternatives exist. For example, consider the following more complex marital problem. The husband wants his wife to stay at home; the wife wants to have a career of her own. There are, of course, many issues at stake in this marital conflict, but they will all boil down to both spouses' ability to assert themselves, or learn to accept the status quo in the face of a situation that they feel cannot be modified. The husband may try his damnedest to manipulate his wife into staying home (assertiveness), and failing that, will have to learn to accept his new reality, assuming they stay together. The wife will try manipulating her husband so she can start a career, or will have to learn to relax and accept her role as housewife if she wishes to have any peace with herself and comfort in her marriage. Of course either of them could assert themselves by leaving if they don't get their way. This is called divorce. Negotiation and compromise make the solutions less polar, but still will have elements of assertiveness and acceptance for both parties.

This marital situation can be viewed even more psychologically. Suppose the husband finally agrees to his wife's starting on a career, but is still unhappy about it. What kind of stimulus will he have to relax in the presence of, or assert himself toward? Depending on your psychological point of view, it could be a parental injunction (TA), unfinished business with someone (Gestalt), a developmental stage involving parents where he got stuck in his childhood (Ego Psychology), or a reinforcement contingency where someone is supporting his present discomfort (Behavior Therapy). Clearly, as we shall see, one pathway to relaxation and acceptance involves the cognitive domain. However, in every case, whether you attribute his problem to interpersonal, parental, or internal variables, it will always boil down to some stimulus situation that needs to be changed through assertiveness or accepted, ultimately involving relaxation. Those therapies that believe events occurring long ago are the key to here-and-now behavior change creatively distill out these situations for clients to clearly experience in the here and now. Even Ego Psychology, the great-granddaddy of covert historical introspection, still brings these stimuli to the present to be acted on by assertiveness and acceptance through the transference and corrective emotional experience.

Even though I am suggesting that assertive and acceptance training are integrally a part of the procedures and goals of psychotherapy, there are obviously other more basic phenomena occurring. These include reinforcement, extinction, punishment, shaping, stimulus control, chaining, and modeling, which are the fundamental elements in all procedures. There is just too much basic research describing and demonstrating the effect of consequences on behavior to ignore the phenomena. Reinforcement, extinction, and punishment come as close to Laws of Behavior as is possible at this stage of our ignorance. It does appear that, instinctive behavior aside, no behavior will occur unless it is reinforced. This may present problems for some psychological theorists, but to most it can be readily accepted as long as we stay with rats, bar presses, and food pellets. When we get to the complexity of human behavior, understanding what controls client problems and how people change becomes more difficult, especially if all that is in your theoretical arsenal is reinforcement theory. However, this does not take away from the power of the concept. The Behavioral Laws, when taken together, help explain phenomena at all levels of complexity.

It is my contention that aside from the influence of heredity, behavior *must* be controlled by its antecedents and consequences. No behavior will occur or be maintained unless it is *reinforced* on some schedule of reinforcement. Logic supports the idea; research supports the idea; the phenomena cut across the animal kingdom. It is therefore incumbent on all clinical practitioners to adjust their thinking to this present state of knowledge. As we shall see, this is not as difficult to do as prevailing psychological philosophies might seem to dictate. We must also make a place for the *Laws of Classical Conditioning* and their relationship to instinctual behavior. This is especially true when we look at the interplay between physiological events and their effect on our covert and overt operant behavior, such as the impact of anxiety on operant behavior.

Extinction, one of the major operant consequences, is another phenomenon we simply can't ignore. All therapies talk about the pain of change, the difficulty in dealing with changing realities, and how new behavior needs to take the place of less functional habits. Pain and anxiety seem to be an almost universal experience when something important to us is suddenly taken away. Again, based on the present state of the science and art, we must look at what we do in therapy in light of the extinction effect in order to better understand the pain of change and how behavior changes. The concept of *punishment* represents the third consequence that impacts on our behavior. Aversive stimuli, particularly, when used in punishment contingencies or as part of *negative reinforcement* are also very important in early learning experiences.

Most therapists and clients would agree that people modify their behavior patterns relatively slowly. The behavioral approach calls this process *shaping*. How this process works involves, if you will recall, the successive use of reinforcement and extinction (differential reinforcement) and the setting of short-term approximations that lead to a final goal. The question will be, as we go forth, not whether shaping occurs, but how. It does occur across all therapies, and often without either clients or therapists being specifically aware of the process.

There is also a large developing data base concerning how antecedents control our behavior: *stimulus control*. Since the power of antecedents, also called *cues* or *discriminative stimuli* (S^D), ultimately owes its strength to the laws governing consequences, I will add stimulus control to the phenomena that occur in all therapies. The process of *chaining*, which involves both stimulus control and consequences, will be helpful not only in explaining why behavior patterns are so similar time after time but also can add to understanding how the characteristic point of treatment intervention in different therapies affects therapy outcome. And last, but certainly not least, is *modeling*, which includes the process of *behavioral rehearsal*. We know the phenomenon is essential to learning. "Large chunk learning" is as important to growth as is shaping. Behavioral rehearsal, or role playing, allows us practice after observing a model.

The seven phenomena listed here from the behavioral approach (*see* Figure 5-1) are what will be called *behaviorally active elements* in the treatment of human behavior. The Laws of Classical Conditioning—the respondent S-R connection governing the antecedent control of behavior—also includes a number of behaviorally active elements, especially in their relationship to anxiety and relaxation. It is my contention that these elements, derived from the foundation of behavioral laws, must be woven into a therapist's treatment strategy in order to effectively support client change. This is not to say that these behaviorally active elements in the hands of Gestalt, TA, or Ego Psychology therapists will look anything like a behaviorist might say they should. The great gift that these other therapies have to give us is the wonderful, creative, and unique ways that behaviorally active elements can be applied.

FIGURE 5-1

The seven basic operant behaviorally active elements

1. Reinforcement
2. Extinction
3. Punishment
4. Shaping
5. Chaining
6. Stimulus Control
7. Modeling and Behavioral Rehearsal

Likewise, *acceptance and assertive training* procedures, the much more complex culmination of all therapeutic techniques, may not look anything like what they do in a behaviorist's hands. On the contrary, as we shall see, these two procedures are cloaked in very useful wrappings when they are delivered in other therapies.

Although I have been singing the praises of Behavior Therapy as an integrative tool, this is not to say it has no limitation as a therapy. It does indeed. Behavior Therapy's attempt to follow the scientific method creates a number of problems for therapists: first, not only is it necessary to carefully structure behavioral research but therapists are taught that each client and each practice act are miniexperimental studies, single-organism research designs. While this approach obviously has advantages, it also highly structures the therapeutic setting, leaving less room for the serendipity, creative, spur-of-the-moment therapist behaviors so common to other therapies.

In addition, behaviorists must define independent and dependent variables of therapy in observable terms. While this scientific demand makes for clearer indications of client outcome than in other therapies, it essentially limits the parameters of intervention and outcome to observable events. This puts severe strains on the ability of behaviorists to work in the cognitive domain. Yet, there are many Cognitive Behaviorists who are making the attempt, since it is obvious that internal events impact interactively on overt behavior. Their problem is that they have to basically rely on client verbal reports describing internal covert behavior, which are less reliable than overt behavior. While Cognitive Behaviorists are working diligently to overcome these weighty methodological problems, dealing with the cognitive area in Behavior Therapy is in its relative infancy.

Another area where Behavior Therapy is constrained, I believe, is in the creative use of client history in the therapeutic setting. Almost every therapy but the behavioral approach has an important place for historical events as part of its theory and practice. While clearly the past needs to be put into its proper perspective and connected to the present, it need not be ignored as having no therapeutic value, as I will demonstrate in later chapters.

As we go through Gestalt, TA, and Ego Psychology, I will initially look at each on a theoretical level to glean out what I consider to lead a *behaviorally active practice*. There is so much philosophy and so many unfounded assumptions in each psychological theory that we can begin determining what is truly functional. In addition, each of the theories leave important "holes" in understanding behavior and we must face their blind spots as well. Finally, and most important, I will suggest what techniques and procedures are generated by each theory that seem to have behavioral activity.

I must emphasize again that while it will be fun and interesting to compare how the behavioral laws fit into different psychological theories, the only true integration can be seen at the practice level of the four psychotherapies. Based on the assumptions I have established, it is my hypothesis that it is at the practice level the Behavioral Laws must be active for a therapy to be successful.

REFERENCES

DOLLARD, J., and N. MILLER, *Personality and Psychotherapy*. New York: McGraw-Hill, 1950.

GOLDSTEIN, A. P., K. HELLER, and L. B. SECHREST, *Psychotherapy and the Psychology of Behavior Change*. New York: John Wiley, 1966.

LAZARUS, A. A. *Behavior Therapy and Beyond*. New York: McGraw-Hill, 1971.

———. *Multi-Model Behavior Therapy*. New York: Springer Publishing Co., 1976.

MEICHENBAUM, D. H. *Cognitive Behavior Modification: An Integrative Approach*. New York: Plenum, 1977.

SHAFFER, J. B. P., and M. D. GALINSKY, *Models of Group Therapy and Sensitivity Training*. Englewood Cliffs, N.Y.: Prentice-Hall, 1974.

SKINNER, B. F. *Walden Two*. New York: Macmillan, 1962 (c1948).

SLOAN, R. B., *et al*. *Psychotherapy Versus Behavior Therapy*. Cambridge, Mass.: Harvard University Press, 1975.

WACHTEL, P. *Psychoanalysis and Behavior Therapy: Toward an Integration*. New York: Basic Books, 1977.

WANN, T. W. (ed.). *Behaviorism and Phenomenology*. Chicago: University of Chicago Press, 1964.

YALOM, I. D. *The Theory and Practice of Group Psychotherapy*. New York: Basic Books, 1975.

CHAPTER SIX
GESTALT THERAPY
A Behavioral Analysis

INTRODUCTION

As you will recall, Gestalt therapy raised a number of fundamental theoretical issues underlying its practice. These included the importance of the here and now, unfinished business, and personal responsibility. In addition, we must examine the validity of assuming people can be motivated by covert experiences about which they have no conscious awareness. An analysis of these issues will also serve as a foundation for the behavioral analysis of TA and Ego Psychology in the next chapters.

The Here and Now

Gestalt therapists are constantly asking clients to be aware of their here-and-now awareness in the therapeutic setting, including feelings and interpersonal dynamics. On the other hand, behaviorists are less concerned with the dynamics of the moment during a session but are more directed to the present environment in which the client lives. The Gestalt approach makes the assumption that all problems can be generalized as resistances to contact occurring in the here and now as well as in the environment. If it can be demonstrated that reinforcement contingencies controlling current problem behavior can be linked to more general behavior patterns, then attending to the here and now would indeed be behaviorally active. As we look more closely at resistances in Gestalt, I believe we will see it is possible to relate here-and-now behavior to what happens in the environment.

Unfinished Business

It is because of unfinished business that people are not able to go smoothly around the Awareness Cycle and thus get needs met. Some unfinished event from their history evokes resistances that get people stuck in the cycle. Unfinished business is nothing more than a concept representing a repeated historical contingency. Some important state of deprivation was left consistently unsatisfied. Perhaps a single critical incident, such as a death, occurred and a person was not allowed to satisfy a tremendously heightened state of deprivation. In either case, these situations have no meaning unless they are also represented in a person's current life. What makes the concept of unfinished business a potentially useful tool is that it ties together historical contingencies relating to present unmet needs. *Thus the past can be used to uncover the present*, rather than vice versa.

Clearly, we live our lives with many, many unmet needs; we live in a wide variety of deprivation states (the term *unmet needs* is synonymous with *deprivation states*). Most of the time we don't attend to these unmet needs because 1) they do not represent significant states of deprivation; 2) other needs are being met to some degree of satisfaction; and most significantly, 3) antecedents starting the chain of events that would heighten a particular state of deprivation do not often present themselves. Since one cannot consistently predict the behavior of others, antecedent stimuli are occasionally presented to us that set off an archaic chain of behaviors leading to the heightening of some deprivation state.

So by whatever name you wish to call the rose, we are dealing with heightened motivation in the here and now where people become aware they are not getting what they need, relating to some historical reinforcement contingency where they were in a similar state of deprivation. Gestalt does not concern itself with why you are not taking care of yourself but *how* you resist taking care of yourself now. Past history, then, is of interest in that it offers clues to the present controlling conditions of problem behavior, and in this respect it is potentially behaviorally active, especially for assessment purposes.

Personal Responsibility

The concept of *personal responsibility* as part of therapy probably originated more clearly with Gestalt, but is by no means owned by this approach. There are many contemporary therapies—including what I call the *Rice Krispies therapies* because of their snap, crackle, and pop appeal—that use the idea we are responsible for our behavior. Gestalt therapists consistently attempt to condition their clients to view behavior as under personal control and thus accept responsibility for what they do. Is this a behaviorally active therapist approach?

It is likely that people who act in contingencies where they end up blaming their behavior on others do not easily modify their own behavior. The problem is not with defining your own state of unhappiness in terms of another's behavior. In fact that kind of assessment can be very exciting and important in discovering what will have to be done to reach your own goals. Remember, the definition of *self-control* in the behavioral approach is the ability to manipulate your antecedents and consequences in such a way as to get the behavior from yourself you desire. So assessing how people deliver cues and reinforcing consequences to you is important. Problems arise when we assume that only others must modify their behavior toward us and that we do not need to perform differently as well. Behavioral Laws suggest that if indeed everyone around us did change, our behavior would likely change, too. But by demanding others do the work, we are failing to realize that all of the participants in a system reciprocally reinforce each others' behavior. You have been supporting people to behave inappropriately toward you by being a functional reinforcer of their behavior. Therefore, by excluding yourself from the behavior-change process, you are making it much more difficult for others in your system to modify their behavior patterns.

People who haven't had a lick of psychology education have an intuitive sense of this dynamic. When people start blaming they usually catch hell back and nothing is resolved. The only way problems can get solved in a blaming system is for both participants to "fess up" to what they have been doing to make the situation as it is. They then need to negotiate how each will stop reinforcing the undesirable behaviors of the other, how they will change their own behavior, and make requests for behavior changes in each other.

The Gestalt approach suggests that we are responsible for our behavior no matter what the stimulus cue or the consequence. It often seems to facilitate problem solving if people take responsibility for their behavior. In this crazy world where so many things appear out of our control, it may be important to own responsibility for what we do. Whether it is ultimately true may not be as important a question as whether it makes for more meaningful solutions to human problems. I contend that in the *therapeutic environment* it is a functional concept in problem solving.

The Unconscious

The question of the existence and validity of an unconscious or subconscious level of behavior should really have been saved for the chapter on Ego Psychology. After all, that is where the concepts originated. But we must face them now because so much of Gestalt therapy is based on the assumption that behavior not in our conscious awareness strongly influences motivation. Ego Psychology defines two different levels below awareness: the *subconscious* is supposedly just below the level of awareness and is potentially available to consciousness; the *unconscious* is inaccessible to awareness. To simplify our present discussion, I will refer to both concepts as the unconscious.

I cannot deal behaviorally with a concept that is not amenable to defining observable dependent and independent variables. Therefore I will finesse the issue by asking a question: Is it possible that there are measurable physical and physiological responses that people do not report as part of their present experience and that can be empirically connected to the reinforcement contingencies that control behavior?

I will answer with a qualified yes, the qualification being that while I will support my contention with logic I cannot empirically do so at this point. Yet, something is gained by putting the problem in behaviorally specific terms and applying the Behavioral Laws to it.

I believe that a chain of stimuli are conditioned in the motor and physiological behaviors of the body, which when started do not reach our awareness until the stimulus intensity reaches a "conscious" or awareness point. This idea is not unlike the phenomena of subliminal stimuli in Classical Conditioning: they are measurable, but do not produce an overt response. In addition, this chain starting below the level of awareness may have enough negative reinforcers connected with it that it frequently starts and is completed, never reaching awareness. There are a number of examples with overt behavior where this hypothesis can be made clearer.

Let us assume that you have a phobic fear of large dogs. When one presents itself, you make an escape response, run away. The running away removes the aversive stimulus and thus your running is negatively reinforced. On your way to school or work each day you walk a path along a row of backyards. Your fear was originally developed when one day a large Saint Bernard came bounding up to one of the fences, scaring you into running away. Associated with being scared was not only the sight of the dog but all of the yards, fences, trees, houses of various kinds, what you happened to be thinking about just before Rover showed up, and many other associated stimuli. If for some reason you were forced to continue this same path to work or school, a chain would begin to be conditioned. The fear would begin to develop first as you get closer to the yards; later it might begin as soon as you left your house; or even when you went to bed the night before. The chain would be elongated and augmented with other stimuli and symbols, depending on the intensity of the fear, and the frequency of the repeated pattern of behavior.

Children, especially, are exposed to many fearful stimuli in repetitive kinds of interactions with parents, teachers, and other children. When this occurs we begin developing avoidance behaviors that help us run away from the large dogs of the world, long before they are on the scene. The cues beginning the historical chain might be very subtle, or at least very hard to connect to the original fearful stimuli—the large dog, for instance. Once the option was presented, you would probably start avoiding the path by the backyards. If the contingency was very well conditioned, you might even avoid walking and drive instead. In any case, every once in a while as you meandered through life, stimuli would be presented that would make you feel uneasy and you wouldn't quite know why. This is a very common experience for all of us. If we were perfect computers we could keep a file on all of the many stimuli and behaviors associated with each fear experience. Since we are not, our conscious minds may not remember, but some part of our memory does and cues anxiety reaction in the muscles and glands of our bodies. We react with anxiety even though we may have no awareness as to why, the cues being too far removed from the original fear experience to make simple connections possible. And since our organisms do not happily tolerate anxiety for long, we will usually make some kind of avoidance response to lessen it. Often the avoidance response is firmly conditioned and occurs without much if any awareness. For instance, at a party we might come upon a conversation about dog breeding and drift away elsewhere. Later, if asked why we didn't spend much time with that particular group of people, we could conceivably come up with reasons that had nothing to do with their topic of conversation. Rather we might say that we just didn't have time to speak to everyone, or didn't like the looks of the people.

The avoidance of subtle cues associated with aversive experiences is not uncommon. If it is possible in our overt behavior, why shouldn't it be possible with our covert behavior? Certain thoughts, concepts, images, or fantasies might be associated with unpleasant experiences and would be avoided by thinking about something else, that something else being negatively reinforced just as the running from the dog was.

However, the key to this phenomenon is that while there may be no cognitive awareness connected to these avoidance responses, our bodies *always* react with measurable behaviors. It is Gestalt's contention that it is always possible to help people attend to these body responses, such as muscle tension and habitual mannerisms, and demonstrate how these "unconscious" behaviors are functional parts of behavior chains, keeping people from getting what they want.

As we get further into analyzing Gestalt techniques, I believe that I make a convincing case for considering that avoidance conditioning occurs covertly and that it is a potentially measurable event. Unconscious stimuli are likely an integral part of the complex behavior chains which weave in and out of overt, verbal, covert, and physiological response classes. Using this perspective, I believe we may ascribe behavioral activity to techniques that attempt to connect potentially measurable responses not in our present awareness to more obvious observable behavior.

THE TREATMENT PROCESS

The Awareness Cycle

When Gestalt therapists work with clients, they are guided by the Awareness Cycle. This guide, however loose it may be, is represented in their behaviors with clients. For instance, it is important for clients to know what they want for themselves and from their therapists. The awareness stage of the cycle is operational here. If a client is stuck at the action stage, as indicated by anxiety or confusion, the therapist will help heighten these feelings. In the same way, being stuck at the contact or withdrawal stages acts as a signpost, with its own accompanying behaviors to guide theme development and experiments.

Since *motivation* is behaviorally defined as a state of deprivation, it may be useful to look at the Awareness Cycle as a behaviorally specific representation of the deprivation process. Given this kind of behavioral specificity, it may also be useful to hypothesize how each step in a deprivation cycle might affect the power of reinforcers. I believe that the Awareness Cycle, and the concept of learned resistance behaviors at each stage, is a reasonable model from which to work. As we shall see, it is not entirely well founded, but in a vacuum of other behaviorally specific models delineating a step-by-step process of the deprivation experience, it will do for now.

If you will recall, the Gestalt treatment process included:

1. Awareness
2. Data Collection
3. Theme Development
4. Experiment
5. Feedback
6. Integration

Therapist behavior was guided by these steps, using the Awareness Cycle as a reference. Thus, we will examine practice in each step of the treatment process, looking for behaviorally active techniques and procedures. Much of what is discussed in this chapter will be applicable to the practice of TA and Ego Psychology, since all three are relatives, however distant. For example, therapists in all three therapies commonly ask clients, "What are you feeling?" The behavioral analysis of this question in Gestalt will obviously have a bearing on the others.

Awareness

All work in Gestalt starts with the therapists asking what clients want to do and what they are feeling. It is the central thrust of the initial work and carries throughout the whole experience. From a Gestalt viewpoint you cannot know what you want until you know what you are feeling; you cannot get what you want until you can take that feeling and utilize the energy it generates to make contact with yourself and others. It is my contention that *feelings represent states of deprivation and thus act as motivating cues*. However, just because the cue is perceived may not be enough. An appropriate behavior chain may have to be linked to the feeling cue through behavioral rehearsals and practice to help clients get their needs met.

This idea is not foreign to the Laws of Behavior. Confusion is generated only because some practitioners are not always comfortable in working with feelings as behavioral cues for more complex chains of behavior. Feelings are not always observable and not easily measured in their complexity. But if one grants the assumption that all feelings involve the muscular structure, among other measurable physiological responses, then we can easily consider how feelings cue behavior chains and act to motivate their occurrence.

Furthermore, it is a Behavioral Law that motivation is defined by states of deprivation. Every organism must assess its current deprivation states by experiencing internal sensations. I contend that the human race has labeled these internal deprivation cues as feelings, which establish motivation for behavior leading to a consequence to satisfy this "deprivation state-feeling" cue.

Finally, because of the tremendous complexity of both Classical and Operant Conditioning, we should expect a wide physiological and psychological variation in

how each person reports any feeling, and just as wide a variation in the kinds of consequences that have been experienced to satisfy the deprivations that each feeling
represents. There are generalizations that can be made about these deprivations and
consequences, but we must always remember individual differences. As a working
hypothesis, let's take five of the major feeling response classes and see what generalizations concerning deprivation they might suggest.

1. *Anger* (frustration, irritation, annoyance). When people experience anger they
    are making a self-report that something is bothering or hurting them and they
    wish it would cease. It is a motivating cue to make attempts to either remove
    the aversive stimulus or remove oneself from it. Since the internal sensations
    of anger are usually unpleasant, involving high energy and muscle tension, the
    behaviors that act to resolve or lower anger, no matter how functional for
    problem solving, will likely be powerful negative reinforcers.
2. *Sadness*. This feeling represents a deprivation that motivates requests for sup-
    port from oneself and others. Its onset always includes the withdrawal of an
    important source of reinforcement and cues the attempts to find alternative
    sources of support.
3. *Hurt*. People probably use this term to describe a wide variety of internal sen-
    sations. The experience of being hurt psychologically is different from the
    hurt of physical pain. The term likely gets its meaning more from the symbol-
    ism surrounding its onset as well as the internal sensations, which are very un-
    comfortable. People who report hurt are symbolically "hit" with situations
    they find aversive or the withdrawal of important sources of reinforcement.
    This feeling experience is a deprivation state that motivates withdrawal from
    an aversive stimulus, or a request for the return of a reinforcer. This takes a
    number of forms, including requests for protection, as well as escape behavior.
4. *Fear* (scared, anxious). In the same vein as *hurt*, fear and anxiety represent a
    state of deprivation for the negative reinforcer resulting from escape behavior.
    It can also, of course, motivate requests for support and protection.
5. *Happy* (glad, satisfied). Depending on one's conditioning history, feeling
    happy could be a state of deprivation for interactional reinforcers such as
    sharing good news, getting praise, and so forth. It could also motivate with-
    drawal, as in the case of enjoying "self-satisfaction."

Clearly, people learn to label their internal sensations through a combination
of modeling and personal experience. And it is likely that some feelings frequently
occur in tandem, such as anger and hurt, making discriminations even more difficult.
The chains of behavior tied to these feelings-deprivation state cues are obviously idiosyncratically conditioned as well. One person learns to run from fearful stimuli;
another learns to attack.

There is no value in simply helping people identify what they are feeling as an
isolated event. However, if we view feelings as information about current states of
deprivation, then their identification becomes an initial behaviorally active step in
the assessment of what assertive behaviors are necessary to modify the environment
to get needs met, or in accepting that deprivation states will not be satisfied and
seeking alternative means of support. The Gestalt emphasis on unfinished business

and what you are feeling now is a relatively systematic attempt to heighten one's present deprivation state so that it can be attended to immediately. Taken in the light that feelings are important cues for discovering states of deprivation, it becomes a behaviorally active process for a Gestalt therapist to help clients know and label what they are feeling.

Feelings play yet another role in Gestalt therapy, suggesting a further behaviorally active element. When clients report a here-and-now feeling experience, they are giving clues to historical contingencies essentially identical to those controlling current behavior. For example if a client is typically shy in social situations and feels anxious, these present feelings are clues to the reinforcement contingencies in social situations under which he or she was trained as a child, which Gestalt labels "unfinished business." Both Gestalt and Behavior theory agree that this data from the past, while interesting, is not necessarily useful to intervention for present problems. However, if feelings are a tie to the contingencies of childhood, which are being acted out in the present as well, it would mean that therapists have two possible sources to assess the controlling conditions for current problem behavior: the past and the present.

This dual approach for assessment offers therapists a number of advantages. First, some clients and therapists prefer to deal with past relationships. Good assessment information would still be obtained if what was learned was specifically tied to the present. Second, there are times when clients just do not report good environmental data. If they are willing to talk about past situations and how they felt about them, the assessment process can still proceed. Third, and most obvious, if feelings related to problems are exhibited with the therapist, there will be an opportunity to see in the here and now exactly how the contingencies operate. Gestalt therapists consistently reinforce clients for tying their background or historical experiences into the present. They talk about how unfinished business keeps people from getting their needs met now. I would rather suggest *historical behavior patterns are essentially identical to present ones* and can support a good assessment of current controlling conditions.

In summary, the value of reinforcing clients for reporting what they feel is threefold: 1) it allows clients to clarify current states of deprivation, thus enhancing motivation; 2) feelings are clues to past conditioning history which can help in the assessment of current controlling conditions; and 3) the expression of here-and-now feeling states enables therapists to assess problem-related reinforcement contingencies firsthand in the treatment setting.

Data Collection and Theme Development

In the initial part of each session, Gestalt therapists report both what they see and hear as well as their own personal reactions. This behavior not only sensitizes clients to being more aware of themselves and others, which increases the possibility for better self-control, but it also sets the stage for theme development. The act of synthesizing and labeling the kind of work a client is doing is very important in

Gestalt and is one of the necessary precursors to the experiment. Choosing a theme is beyond the problem specification and goal setting occurring in the behavioral treatment process. It labels a much broader response class to the point that entire chains of behavior come under the theme umbrella.

As a theme is developed, Gestalt therapists are trying to encompass a whole pattern of behavior into a single symbol or phrase. The assumption is that there must be common response patterns and common chains of behavior cutting across a wide variety of problems for each client. While Gestalt does not entirely dictate what these generalized contingencies must be, it does suggest five of them in the resistances to contact. However, clients do have the opportunity to uniquely choose a label to summarize their own experiences, which takes into account those patterns not fitting completely with Gestalt's prepared resistance themes.

Because of the methodological nightmare in trying to synthesize and codify generalized chains of behavior, the behavioral approach is not ready to suggest a similar labeling system for normal problems. Yet, I believe there are valid common-response classes and contingencies of reinforcement that will be identified as the years of behavioral research go on. Interestingly enough, an analysis of the therapies examined here will show that each has attempted to develop a system of classifying patterns of problem behavior. Our task will be, then, not to judge the empirical validity of these labels, since there is yet no sound data base to do so, but to hypothetically decide whether the generalizations are reasonably congruent with the Behavioral Laws, and thus could generate behavioral activity with their use.

Experiment

It is in the experiment where the most productive and behaviorally active interventions occur. While the client is doing most of the work, the therapist helps design the experiment, keeps it on track, watches dynamics like a hawk, and may even be an active participant. Gestalt therapists use so much technology in this experiment phase of the treatment process that I will discuss the major techniques separately. First we will cover the double chair and associated techniques; then we will discuss how Gestalt therapists help clients heighten resistances; and finally I will do a thorough analysis of the five Gestalt resistances to contact. If you will recall, most of what therapists do in the experiment is support clients in heightening their resistances and feelings. Of course, clients also practice new behaviors in this phase, which is of course behaviorally active, but these behavioral rehearsals usually come after some resistance or feeling has been heightened.

The double chair. The term *double chair* covers a multitude of techniques where clients end up personifying and speaking for some symbolic part of themselves. Among other things, this symbol may be a part of their bodies, another person, a feeling, an abstract idea, or any animate or inanimate object. I believe it can be demonstrated that there is a high degree of behavioral activity in the double-chair technique.

One of the most common examples of how therapists help clients know what they are feeling utilizes the personification of a part of a client's body where there is observable tension. Assuming that you, as a client, don't know what you are feeling, I would ask you to attend to wherever there is energy in your body—movement and muscle tension. In pure Gestalt fashion I would suggest you let the active or tense part of your body, a clenched fist, for instance, "speak" to you in one chair, and for you to respond in another chair as if you and that body part were really conversing. Behaviorally speaking, how can this help?

Humans, of all the animals, use symbols to communicate and think. Speech is word symbols put together into symbolic concepts. We are guided intellectually by how we communicate symbols to others and how we use them in our own thinking processes. There is every reason to believe that the covert thinking and imagery process, internal though it may be, is also under the control of antecedents and consequences, just as is overt behavior. Thoughts are covertly reinforced, extinguished, or punished. In addition, chains of thought occur which follow the chain rules. The extreme case of a chained thought is called *obsessive behavior*.

An example of how a symbolic thought comes under the laws of operant behavior would be as follows: Imagine that you have a recurring thought of, "Boy, am I stupid." This thought would likely be stimulated by some overt behavior such as a recurring response you consider a mistake. But like the overt response itself, the thought could only be maintained if it were being intermittently reinforced with some important consequence. And to complicate the phenomenon even further, the thought is likely accompanied by a feeling which involves muscular tension. Whether the thought comes first and is reinforced by the feeling, or the feeling comes first and is reinforced by the thought, is an interesting but mute concern for our purposes. Clearly they are inextricably tied together in a chain of behaviors, like the chicken and the egg. So you end up with antecedents and reinforcers jumping in and out of these three domains of behavior, all tied together in complex chains. It is only common sense to realize that overt behavior, thinking, and feeling are occurring at high rates during our every waking minute and that *all are involved in the reinforcement, extinction, and punishment of the other*. Therefore, the kind of thinking we do, which is done in symbols, can easily be accepted as part of exploring what antecedents and consequences are part of our behavior. By making use of these symbols, and finding new ones to encapsulate our experiences, the Gestalt therapist has a rich source of behavior from which to draw.

It is likely that in our previous experience we have not had a conversation with a clenched fist. But a fist can be a symbol, like a word, which represents something important. By examining this symbol and beginning a double-chair dialogue, you may find out what it represents. Even if your thinking processes are not "aware" of the tensions within you and what feeling label you characteristically assign to them, by attending to the muscles that are part of that tension, and making symbols out of them, you can meaningfully carry on a dialogue with a fist, tight stomach, swinging leg, or headache.

The human race's ability to symbolically represent its own experience is complex. In Gestalt we find that people can even make symbols of esoteric parts of themselves, such as the good and bad parts or the parts they like and don't like about themselves. Gestalt theory suggests we are made up of millions of unintegrated parts. I partly reinterpret this statement to mean that we tend to represent our experience in many differentiated symbols to which we have not yet assigned labels. A lot of what Gestalt therapists do is help us define the symbols that have meaning to our life experiences, and see how they help to explain the tremendous complexity of our relationship with the world, how they relate to our behavior, its antecedents, and its consequences—a kind of reductionism, if you please.

Another advantage of carrying on dialogues with symbols, especially when they are feelings, is that they put into words how feelings interact with an experience. For instance, we do not often know when we are covertly putting ourselves down. The only clue might be a momentary small knot of tension which we have learned to habitually ignore. By making that momentary tension into a symbol and carrying on a dialogue with it, we can put into words exactly what we are doing to ourselves, heightening this important experience. Thus, this fleeting feeling—a kind of shorthand message to the self—which, by the way, is a functional reinforcer for the overt behavior that preceeded it, can be put into the context of a clear, understandable contingency of reinforcement. We can then see how these feeling messages impact on our behavior—how they act as antecedents and reinforcers to some of the very behaviors that we wish to be rid of, including annoying thoughts and undesirable overt behaviors.

Using the double-chair technique with symbols allows another kind of analysis which more fully explains why therapies oriented to cognitive behavior can be effective. Let's take another Gestalt double-chair experiment as an example. Lisa, a successful young professional woman, is working on her discomfort with people in authority. The experiment will attempt to help Lisa heighten her resistance to changing her behavior when confronted with an authority figure.

Using the double chair, there are three possible domains for this experiment:

1. The present—Lisa could put an authority figure from her present environment in the chair and role play with him or her. This would be akin to a behavioral reenactment demonstrating in the here and now how she is presently reinforced for her discomfort. Another option would be to use the here-and-now relationship with the therapist, who is a likely authority figure for Lisa. In this case, the therapist could still use the double-chair technique, with himself symbolically in one chair and Lisa still playing both roles. And, of course, they could just be themselves and forego the symbolic chairs entirely.

2. The past—Lisa could put authority or parental figures from her past on the chair and have dialogues with them. Since the reinforcement contingencies controlling past relationships with authority figures are essentially similar to those in the present, bringing the past alive in the here and now is, as I have suggested before, behaviorally active.

3. Covert symbols—Lisa can put a "part" of herself in the double chair, personifying how she feels about herself, which is nothing more than what she says

to herself about herself. For example, assume Lisa symbolically puts the critical part of herself in one chair, which covertly treats her like most authority figures, and the rest of her in the other chair:

LISA: I don't like you much. You make me feel uncomfortable and get me into trouble.

CRITICAL PART: (Lisa switches chairs) Don't tell me about it. You sure do listen to me.

LISA: I know, but I don't like it. I don't like the fact that you are constantly looking over my shoulder waiting for me to make a mistake. I don't like it when you are ever ready with criticism but only give praise grudgingly. I don't like the fact that I'm so damned sensitive to the feedback you give me.

CRITICAL PART: Yeah, but I enjoy the power I have over you. You need me to watch out for you. Without me you wouldn't be as successful as you are now. So what if you don't like me. What matters is that you get the job done and my job is to make sure you do just that.

What we are seeing here, all interpretations aside, is the explication of a symbolic covert chain of behaviors being reenacted in the double chairs. It is my contention that without exception, *there is a separate covert symbolic representation of every problematic overt behavior pattern*. In addition, *the general contingencies controlling behavior in both domains are, for all practical purposes, the same*.

It was when Lisa was a child that criticism became a potent reinforcer for her, probably from one of her parents, who are the first authority figures for us all. When Mom or Dad criticized her, she "internalized" the behavior by repeating what they said to herself. Without powerful conflicting positive feedback, little Lisa believed what she was told about herself and it became her own critical self-evaluation. It should be no surprise that people with "negative self-images" come from environments that have viewed them in similar ways, and are often more critical of themselves than others are.

Remember, Lisa worked for reinforcement from her parents, such as it was. Therefore, if criticism is a functional reinforcer in Lisa's present relationships, it *must* be a powerful covert reinforcer for her as well. These internal negative evaluations act as secondary reinforcers that keep behavior chains rolling until overt negative criticism is delivered as a more primary reinforcer by people in important relationships. When Lisa has a dialogue with her critical self, we are actually seeing how the authority figure symbol in her, so to speak, fills in reinforcers to maintain the longer chain. Real authority figures eventually provide environmental reinforcement on an intermittent basis.

Working on modifying how Lisa treats herself is similar to dealing with the stimuli controlling her behavior with real authority figures. Thus, we see that Gestalt therapists can help clients get at the antecedent and reinforcing stimuli controlling their undesirable behavior in three ways: they work with client relationships in the present; they bring past relationships to life; and they help clients personify internal dialogues. Since all of these strategies bring to light some piece of a longer chain of behavior, helping clients modify selected response members in that chain should have some effect in breaking it. The long-term effects of any subsequent behavior change will depend upon where in the chain the behavior change occurred, and whether the final consequences of the chain were effectively dealt with.

To summarize, the double-chair technique of identifying and carrying on symbolic dialogues can have a number of very important behaviorally active functions. First, it is reasonable to hypothesize that since humans use symbols to communicate with others, they also use symbols to communicate with themselves. By identifying the symbols that are functionally part of problematic behavior chains, and putting them into words, it becomes clearer how they act as antecedent and reinforcing stimuli. Second, there is every reason to believe that covert behavior, including thoughts and feelings, are functional parts of complex chains of behavior where thoughts, feelings, and overt responses all play interactive antecedent and reinforcing roles. The modification of behavior in any one of these three broad response classes could impact on the others, following the chain rules described in the first chapter on Behavior Therapy. Chains could be broken by modifying thinking, feeling, or overt behavior. Therefore, techniques that help clients identify any stimuli, symbolic or otherwise, that are part of behavior chains they consider problematic, will increase their power to break those chains. Third, having symbolic dialogues with feeling behaviors, such as a clenched fist or a tight stomach, can heighten people's sense of deprivation. Clients who suddenly realize they are feeling angry will be more highly motivated to act, akin to what happens to a mildly hungry child suddenly exposed to a chocolate cake just out of the oven. The more we allow ourselves to experience our states of deprivation, the more motivated we will be to work. And fourth, the use of the double chair gives therapists access to the present, past, and covert domains, all of which present observable representations of how behavior problems are being reinforced in the environment. This kind of flexibility increases a therapist's power for assessment and intervention.

Resistances. We must applaud Gestalt for defining resistances in such a behaviorally specific way: saying no. Put in this context, we have an observable variable amenable to investigation. While the behavioral approach deals with the concept of motivation more than resistance, they are really two sides of the same coin. People who are resistant are not motivated, and vice versa. Therefore, both concepts are functionally based on states of deprivation. It is essential to assess people's nonperformance in terms of what reinforcers they are willing and not willing to work for. Clients are being reinforced for their present behavior patterns; there are no present alternative reinforcers for which they are willing to work. Thus, they are not motivated, and are resistant to change.

The technique of helping clients heighten their resistance to change plays two very important behaviorally active roles: first, it is an assessment technique where clients crystallize the contingencies maintaining present behavior. It is very frequently the case that people do not know to what or to whom they are saying no. Gestalt therapists help clients experience these contingencies by asking them to take responsibility for their refusal and exaggerate it. For example, clients who consistently say they don't know what they are feeling could be asked to respond to the therapist's request by saying, "I won't tell you what I am feeling no matter what you do." The therapist's response could be, "Well, I'm going to keep trying, even though I feel helpless in making you do something you don't want to do." Thus the operating contingency controlling the client's refusal to share feelings becomes clear. At this point either the therapist or the client can decide to break the chain by modifying his or her response.

The second function of heightening resistances is to increase states of deprivation and thus heighten motivation. If, as in the previous example, the client double chaired with tension in the neck, he would become even more aware of the pain in the neck, increasing his sense of deprivation. During the experiment he would have a heightened awareness of pain, and would thus be in a greater state of deprivation for some reinforcer. Since the most powerful functional reinforcer in the here and now is sitting right across from him, the therapist, it increases the probability that he will act to get his present need met, given his higher motivation. He might, for instance, share a little of his pain and even put a feeling label on it, calling it "hurt." It is up to the therapist to offer a functional reinforcer for this new and vulnerable verbal behavior or it will go the way of all extinguished responses.

Facing clients who are resistant to change and helping them increase their motivation are two of the greatest challenges for all practicing therapists, regardless of their theoretical persuasions. I believe that the Gestalt technique of heightening resistance represents an important behaviorally active advance in dealing with this difficult therapeutic problem. Heightening resistances uniquely takes advantage of the motivating impact that deprivation has on behavior, and clarifies the here-and-now consequences reinforcing clients' saying no as well.

The resistances to contact. Many Gestalt experiments ultimately boil down to one of five generalized contingencies that apparently keep people from effective problem solving. Introjection, projection, and retroflection, particularly, have some conceptual compatibility with other therapies. They address issues that are so pervasive in psychotherapy that I shall examine them more thoroughly, thereby doing analyses applicable to TA and Ego Psychology as well.

1. **Introjection.** Introjection had to do with our ability to say no to anything entering our organism, be it material or verbal. Introjects ended up cueing such behavior as values, attitudes, and general rules to live by. It also described a process by which we learn to take in information, feedback, and food. In both cases, when Gestalt therapists become aware clients are resisting contact by using introjects, they help clients heighten this experience so that the natural sense of disgust will surface.

A number of techniques are behaviorally active in the Gestalt practice of heightening the introjection experience. First, saying no is an obvious assertive-training issue. However, working with introjection in the Gestalt mode adds another important dimension. Often it becomes clear through the heightening of tension, symbols, or interactional dynamics that a person is following an archaic rule, acting as a cue, learned in the past and reinforced in the present environment. A disgust reaction is often concurrent with this recognition. The natural disgust reaction which comes from consistently doing something not healthy to one's organism is a power-ful fuel of motivation. Assertive energy emerges to reject old rules, values, and atti-tudes, and the people who are part of that present intermittent reinforcement system. A person says no to the archaic cues, setting off chains of undesirable behavior—stimulus control—and begins building new, more functional chains of behavior with new stimulus-cue rules.

For example, when little Mike is constantly told by his father that men are strong and don't cry, the statement initially acts as all parental attention does, to reinforce preceding behavior patterns. As Mike grows up, the message "men don't cry" begins acting as a cue as well as in a behavior chain generalizing to many other relationships (*see* discussion on Behavioral Chaining in first chapter). Thus, adults end up with covert statements about themselves that appear to be rational rules and self-judgments contributing to what is called our *self-esteem*. In reality, such state-ments are parts of chains used to reinforce old childhood behavior patterns and cue the formation of new ones.

If Mike presently found himself confronted with a very sad situation, such as the death of his wife or loss of his job, his "men don't cry" rule might no longer be functional, given his heightened state of deprivation. Even if he did not remember the rule, a Gestalt experiment heightening how he felt, or dialogues using present or past relationships, would probably remind him. The end point of this work would be the identificaton of who in Mike's present life was still reinforcing this rule. Mike's sense of disgust accompanying this recognition would likely lead him to make a more practical rule about crying, which would then cue a number of new chains of behavior affecting his self-evaluation and his judgments of other men as well.

The introjection style is also a learned response over many years. Some people are taught to accept most of what they are told, others are taught to discriminate before they accept new ideas. Again, even the teaching of how to accept rules or be-liefs about oneself is conditioned through reinforcement. Teaching a style of learning rather than a specific response is of course much more complex. But we all were conditioned to a particular learning style through trial and error, and modeling processes.

While therapist behavior with introjection seems to utilize assertive-training techniques, it adds richness to the process on some dimensions, and detracts on others. Since many clients have not labeled the rules controlling their behavior, help-ing them to identify these antecedent stimuli through heightening resistances is a useful stimulus-control technique. It crystallizes toward what and whom in the present environment they need to direct their assertive energies. In addition by enhancing the client's state of deprivation, usually through a disgust reaction, the motivation for assertive behavior is heightened as well. Therefore, working with introjections can include behaviorally active techniques for the management of assertive behavior toward both overt and cognitive stimuli.

On the other hand, therapist behavior around introjective resistances lacks clarity in the apparent disregard of systematic shaping. There is some conceptual basis for shaping in Gestalt, but its practice is not clear. Gestalt discusses the "grading up and grading down" of experiments, which would of course include those involving introjection. Grading up means that the experiment is too easy and needs to be made more challenging; grading down means that the experiment is too hard and needs to be made easier. In addition, one of the central issues in Gestalt is to make contact and get yourself support whenever trying anything new and difficult. This is nothing more than successive approximations and reinforcement in Gestalt clothing. But the support/reinforcement relationship gets confused when you hear Gestalt therapists saying that only the here and now is important; that reinforcement is less meaningful because reinforcers come after the present moment in the future. Part of the problem is a semantic one, but the place of reinforcement in Gestalt theory is a clouded issue. We know that Gestalt practice must involve reinforcement and shaping or nobody would change their behavior.

The clearest place for the inclusion of reinforcement in Gestalt is at the contact stage of the Awareness Cycle. Since contact comes directly after action, it is obviously the place where reinforcement occurs. When any action is repeatedly performed in a patterned way, it is the quality, degree, and kind of contact coming directly after it that reinforces the behavior. High and low contact is not analogous to reinforcer magnitude since low contact could be a powerful reinforcer and high contact the opposite. However, the implications of considering making contact the reinforcing experience are interesting.

According to Gestalt, attempts at making contact either fundamentally satisfy important needs or they don't. Those actions that lead to needs being met, or a decrease in deprivation, are obviously being reinforced by the kind of contact achieved. This is essentially what happens when any functional reinforcer is applied as a consequence to behavior. The probability that a particular action will occur again is increased. But what about all of those behaviors that apparently do not functionally meet apparent needs by avoiding reinforcing contact, including all of the resistances to contact?

From a behavioral point of view, using the Gestalt Awareness Cycle as a guide, *all* patterned behavior must end up with enough contact to reinforce it on an intermittent schedule. This means that any behaviors, even those that are used to avoid contact, are motivated by some state of deprivation and make enough reinforcing contact to keep them going. Chains of "unfinished business" and "resistance to contact" behaviors must be reinforced by some contact like any other behaviors if they are to be maintained. Whether the organism will experience significant satisfaction when a particular type of reinforcing contact is made may depend on what needs the person is aware of at the time. Clearly, contact is the place reinforcement fits conceptually into the Gestalt approach. It is not a comfortable fit. Yet, the fact that a therapy dealing primarily with the here and now leaves any theoretical opening for the inclusion of the Laws of Operant Behavior speaks well of it. Still, Gestalt could greatly benefit from a recognition of how operant consequences and shaping operate in the context of the Awareness Cycle and in actual practice.

On the other hand, assertive training as it now stands in Behavior Therapy could benefit from using "heightening" techniques from Gestalt as well as a clearer usage of present/past, covert/overt domains of behavior chains for assessing controlling conditions; and for helping us practice how to say no to people and thoughts that are part of problematic behavior patterns.

2. **Projection.** One of the hardest phenomena on which to get a behaviorally specific handle is what Gestalt and other therapies call *projection*. So much of what apparently occurs during projective behavior is not observable, making a behavioral analysis very difficult. However, I will attempt to describe in behaviorally specific terms what covert and overt behavior I believe controls therapists' usage of the concept. There seem to be three general types of behavior that are called projections in psychotherapy, defined not only by their response patterns but also by how much they are deemed appropriate in problem solving: 1) projecting feelings as in empathy; 2) projecting feelings as a resistance; and 3) projecting expectations.

a. *Empathy*. In general, people observe behavior, compare it with their own experience in similar stimulus situations, give a feeling label to what they see, and respond with what is called *empathy, understanding,* or *sympathy*. We "project" ourselves into others' shoes as if their experience were our own. Projection skills are not only important in therapy but as we shall see, they are also important to marriage, child rearing, normal human communication, and even survival of the species.

The ability to project is likely a learned response, with some people doing it better than others. Yet, the phenomenon is so universal that there must be some inherent contingencies that lead people to project. The modeling phenomenon offers some direction for a behavioral analysis. Why is it that many adults get sexually aroused when they see a sexy movie scene? They are not the direct recipients of the actual arousal stimuli at the time (usually). Yet the cues are familiar enough for them to respond similarly, but not exactly as if they were there. Their response is not the same in magnitude or duration, but it does correspond to the actual situation. In order to learn a huge amount of what we need for growing up we develop the skill of putting ourselves in someone else's shoes. Little children watch adults walk, imagine themselves doing it, and attempt to copy the behavior. This is basically the modeling procedure. Speech, walking, many fine and gross motor skills are learned through observing a model. Using imagery, children associate the same cues and consequences for their model as happening to them. Thus, if a child watches you step in a hole, twist your foot, and cry out in pain, you will model an important contingency. Watching you, the child may first experience fear after you fall, not as intense as your pain, but mimicking the response. Then he will imagine himself performing the same act and probably decide he does not want to experience the consequence he observed. Foot-putting-in-hole behavior will be punished. It should be of no surprise that after a little conditioning we respond to other people's cues and consequences almost as if they were our own. Furthermore, we learn a general contingency that the cues and consequences for others often relate to our own behavior.

In order for any child to survive, parents are forced to project. Babies cannot ask clearly for anything, so good parents use their normal projection skills to meet their needs. When baby cries, parents project it is hungry or bored or wet. When we get older and begin to give our parents corrective feedback about their projections on us, it helps to get our needs met better. There comes a time when parents' projections on us and our own sense of reality begin to differ markedly. This usually creates family conflict and is called *adolescence*. In any case, with all of this projecting going on, it is easy to see how it is modeled and reinforced. Therefore, the ability to project is born.

Look now at the top of Figure 6-1 and follow my hypothesis of how an empathetic projection operates behaviorally. Up to the point of Response 3 there is a simple cognitive process going on. Response 4 provides the actual physical feeling feedback that allows us to really put ourselves in another's shoes and experience to a limited extent what he or she might be feeling. One of the pioneers in modeling research, Albert Bandura (*see* References) has hypothesized that along with cognitive behavior, this "visceral" feedback we experience while observing others is one of the internal mediators that allows the modeling phenomenon to work. Our bodies *measurably* react along the dimensions of the feelings we perceive in others. From this internal physical and cognitive mediation, we label what we are experiencing and "project" it onto another, usually following the projection with a statement or a question. This is, incredibly enough, the first time in the projection response chain that we have an easily observable event. Empathetic projections get reinforced by other people's responses to them, although considering the number of times our projections are incorrect, the behavior pattern must be maintained on an intermittent schedule.

b. *Projection as a Resistance.* The traditional view of projection when it is used as a resistance goes beyond the ability to empathize. When being used to resist contact, people project their feelings onto others instead of acknowledging or owning the same feeling in themselves. Without much empirical evidence to back me up, I feel certain that the behaviors involved in the phenomenon called a *projection resistance* do occur, and they do act to make communication more difficult. Moreover, I believe that people work to fulfill these projections as well. Unfortunately, it is difficult to go beyond belief at this point because of the difficulty in experimentation with covert variables. However, a reasonable behavioral hypothesis can be constructed with the present state of the art so that we can begin exploring how Gestalt and other traditional therapies may have come upon an important behaviorally active phenomenon.

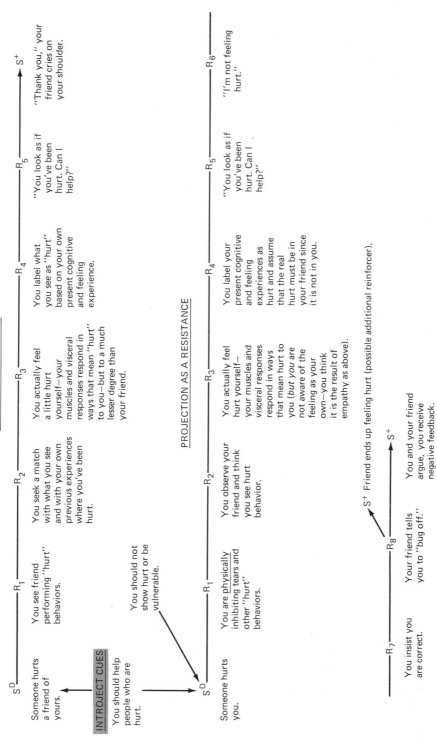

EMPATHIC PROJECTION

S^D — R_1 — R_2 — R_3 — R_4 — R_5 — S^+

S^D: Someone hurts a friend of yours.

R_1: You see friend performing "hurt" behaviors.

R_2: You seek a match with what you see and with your own previous experiences where you've been hurt.

R_3: You actually feel a little hurt yourself—your muscles and visceral responses respond in ways that mean "hurt" to you—but to a much lesser degree than your friend.

R_4: You label what you see as "hurt" based on your own present cognitive and feeling experience.

R_5: "You look as if you've been hurt. Can I help?"

S^+: "Thank you," your friend cries on your shoulder.

INTROJECT CUES

You should help people who are hurt.

You should not show hurt or be vulnerable.

PROJECTION AS A RESISTANCE

S^D — R_1 — R_2 — R_3 — R_4 — R_5 — R_6

S^D: Someone hurts you.

R_1: You are physically inhibiting tears and other "hurt" behaviors.

R_2: You observe your friend and think you see hurt behavior.

R_3: You actually feel hurt yourself—your muscles and visceral responses respond in ways that mean hurt to you (but you are not aware of the feeling as your own—you think it is the result of empathy as above).

R_4: You label your present cognitive and feeling experiences as hurt and assume that the real hurt must be in your friend since it is not in you.

R_5: "You look as if you've been hurt. Can I help?"

R_6: "I'm not feeling hurt."

R_7 — R_8 — S^+

R_7: You insist you are correct.

R_8: Your friend tells you to "bug off."

S^+: Friend ends up feeling hurt (possible additional reinforcer).

S^+: You and your friend argue, you receive negative feedback.

When a projection is being used as a resistance (*see* Figure 6-1), the basic differences between it and an empathic projection is first, a process of selection perception. Second, the situation or cue setting up the projection is impinging more directly on the "projector" than on someone else. There is no good behavioral way to specify selective perception except to say that it obviously exists. Gestalt suggests that our needs (states of deprivation) guide our perceptions. This is an intuitive notion. When we are hungry our perceptions will likely be guided to channels that will bring food. In the same way, if we are angry our perceptions will likely be guided to stimuli related to that experience. In a projection, our report of what we see may not completely correspond with the reality that others report. The label of our own present feeling state is not completely at a level of awareness, nor is there a clear perception of the cues impacting on us. Yet, our bodies are still reacting with muscle tension and other physiological reactions. Without cognitive awareness, an important state of deprivation is being heightened which represents the initial stages for all deprivation chains: the initiation of motor and physiological responses. Thus, when we look at the people around us it will be with selective perception that is significantly different from other people present who are not in similar deprivation states.

In order to make a reasonable hypothesis that attending to projections as a resistance can include some behavioral activity, I must develop a working behavioral model explaining how projections are conditioned. Gestalt says, and I agree, that all projections start with the process of introjection. Introjects are the foundation that projections build upon, or to use the behavioral nomenclature, at the beginning of every projection response chain there are at least one or more introject rules we are following. The final reinforcer for all projection behavior patterns reinforces a chain that started with an introject cue.

For example, when most of us were little we saw people, particularly our parents, helping us, each other, and selected others as well. We learned the rules of when and whom we were supposed to help and were reinforced for those behaviors. Some of us learned to feel empathy when we saw someone feeling sad; others were reinforced for ignoring it. For our purposes, let us assume that you learned the introject, "You should help people who are hurt." As you were growing up you tried to help people who were hurt and were reinforced for it on an intermittent schedule. And probably decreasing feelings of guilt as a negative reinforcer later helped maintain the introject. How does a projection come into this contingency? You can't really use the introject unless you have the ability to project hurt behaviors onto others. Many people who are hurt and who fall within your learned "helping boundaries" don't always announce they are needing help. You have to interpret their behavior and then put a feeling label on it. You use projective skills to do this. *The projection allows you to put the introject into operation.* The introject statement, "You should help people who are hurt," acted as a life rule cuing the projection. The whole chain is then reinforced, including the introject statement at the beginning, the projection in the middle, and the helping behaviors at the end. This is the simplest example of how a projection might be behaviorally analyzed. Let's get a little more complicated.

Assume that the same introject is operational as in the last example, but we have another strong introject as well: "*You* should not show hurt." In this case our hypothetical helper, whom we shall call Ruth, will still do her thing, as in the first example, but there will be an added dimension to her behavior. One way Ruth learned to deal with her own hurt and vulnerable feelings was to project them onto others. In that case what we would see is a situation where you and I would assume through our own use of projections that Ruth is hurt, but what she does is to ask others whether they are feeling hurt. In addition, if they say no, she would likely insist, perhaps in a nice way, that she knows them better than they know themselves.

Consider the process schematically for learning the introject rule, "I shouldn't show hurt," (*see* Figures 6-2 and 6-3). This is of course translated into specific inhibited overt behaviors, such as "I shouldn't cry, mope, have a long face," and so forth. There are attending covert behaviors as well, including muscle tension. As the internal experience of hurt is reinforced, she learns to inhibit the overt manifestations of the feeling. Figures 6-2 and 6-3 represent a possible differential reinforcement contingency.

However, there are times Ruth gets so hurt she has a crying need for immediate attention. But positive parental attention in hurtful situations usually comes only after it is clear to them that she is inhibiting herself. There are many times she wants her parents to comfort her when the hurt gets particularly hard to bear alone—as with any child. In lieu of positive parental attention when she feels so vulnerable, she will work for what she can get, which is negative attention in this case, as in Figure 6-2.

When Ruth became an adult she carried with her the same introject contingencies. Most of the time she could follow the rule to keep her hurt inside, earning intermittent reinforcement from herself and people who believed as she did. Every once in a while when she felt particularly vulnerable and hurt, she would fall back on the only way she knew to get comfort, such as it was: behave in a way that led to her being put down after showing her feelings, just as in the past. However, Ruth was very practiced at inhibiting tears by this time so that crying was not easy. So how is she to get negative attention for feeling really hurt if she cannot show how she feels? Through a projection. Remember, the negative attention she received as a child can act as a reinforcing consequence—something she works for when she is in a particularly high state of deprivation, associated with feeling very vulnerable and hurt.

FIGURE 6-2   Initial Introject Training Contingency

$$S^D \xrightarrow{\hspace{3cm}} R \xrightarrow{\hspace{3cm}} S^-$$

withdrawal of a reinforcer from child.	overt and covert hurt behaviors.	Negative Attention and Ignoring: negative statements by parents, such as shaming child and showing their disappointment.

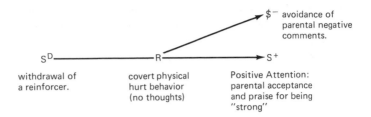

FIGURE 6-3   Final Introject Training Contingency

Notice in Figure 6-1 how similar are the cues for both the empathic projection and the projection used as a resistance. Both start with the "helping" introject; in both cases Ruth is actually experiencing subdued feelings of hurt—perhaps even consciously. But because of the "don't show hurt" introject, it is not easily possible for her to consider these subdued hurt feelings as her own. Since a projection chain is rolling, Ruth will continue to act on the projection just as if it were empathy. When she reaches the step where her friend refutes her perception, she can plug into the old and familiar chain of events that leads her to the same kind of attention she received as a child when she couldn't hold in her vulnerable feelings.

In addition, her friend may end up feeling much like Ruth originally thought: hurt. This also fulfills and reinforces the projection. But the most functional reinforcer for the projection is the negative feedback she gets, since she is reenacting a contingency of childhood telling her how to get attention when she is in this particularly heightened state of deprivation: feeling very hurt and vulnerable.

There are of course times that Ruth projects correctly—even when she is putting her own feelings onto someone else. People might even be thankful for her help. The thanks she receives is not much solace since she still ends up with her needs not directly taken care of. Helping others can give her only vicarious support at best. She is still left with the state of deprivation that her own hurt brings on.

The key to the behavioral analysis of projective resistances a la Gestalt is to realize that 1) the body is actually performing the feeling behavior even if there is no cognitive awareness of it; 2) the contingency that reinforced the central introject behind the projection is playing itself out in the here and now; and 3) the projection and the introject behaviors are being reinforced in the present environment—all three of these hypotheses could be empirically tested because part of what is occurring is observable and measurable.

We should remember that behavior can be reinforced by both positive and negative reinforcers simultaneously. It is likely that many introjects and projections are maintained by both kinds of consequences. For instance, the introject, "You should not be angry," could have been reinforced by parents' sitting down with a child and showing great concern and caring for the "infraction" he or she committed. Such a contingency might lead a child to getting angry for caring and concern and later to utilize a projection to achieve the same end.

c. *Projecting Expectations.* This kind of projection is relatively easy to describe. If you expect to fail a test, the question is whether the expectation is based on an historical pattern of failure or on your present reality. After all, you may know the material pretty well, but with an expectation to fail, that probability considerably increases.

When you project expectations, you are not only projecting a feeling but an opinion, attitude, or judgment. These are based on your prior experiences and may be a correct assessment of how things will be. In fact, one could make the case that all reinforcement, extinction, and punishment theory is based on the ability of animals to develop expectations about consequences through experience. The point Gestalt makes is that we do not always rationally interpret our experience by clearly discriminating the differences between the historical experiences and the potential of the present. If people have failed all their lives, the expectation that they will fail again is an entirely reasonable one. However, if the expectation of these failures is fed not only by history but by an introject dictating the outcome, then the projection tends to discount the present possibilities for success. For instance, the introject, "You shouldn't try too hard," could easily lead to the projection, "I won't be very successful in school." The introject may not be functional at all, but if internalized as a child, it could insure mediocre work as an adult. Or consider the introject, "You have to take care of yourself because nobody else will." This could be translated into the expectation, "When I get close to people they will eventually let me down." Again, it is the introject behind the projection as well as prior experience that lends credibility to the expectation, and will insure the fulfillment of the projection.

One of the most fascinating and insidious parts of a projection involves the reinforcing terminal behavior. People will go to great lengths to selectively perceive only those stimuli that will reinforce their projective behavior. It is amazing to observe. In a group of ten people there will always be some who are able and willing to reinforce almost any projection. If you have a projection that people generally don't like you, you are assured to find a willing soul or two to give that feedback. Of course the other eight won't count as much, even if some of them respond positively. One of the measurable behavioral manifestations of this selective perception is how much time and contact is given to those who said they didn't like you versus those who said they did. Typically in this case, much more talk time and eye contact is directed to the negative rather than positive people. Also you probably would not remember the frequency and content of positive comments but would recall the negative ones easily—another measurable cue that a projection is at work.

As you will recall, the basic way therapists interpret that a projection is being used is when clients respond in ways that do not seem appropriate to the present stimuli, an over or under feeling reaction, or do not accept corrective feedback. While these criteria are largely subjective, it very well may be possible to generate a consensus in any given situation that could suggest whether a person is over or underreacting and defensive. But what really saves Gestalt therapists' bacon, so to speak, in using their subjective judgments from such limited behavioral data is the rigid Gestalt belief system dictating that clients know themselves best. Thus, when therapists suggest that clients are over or underreacting, it is up to the clients to decide whether their therapists' perceptions are in any way congruent with their own personal experience.

Assuming that the client agrees he or she is reacting out of proportion to the demands of a given situation, Gestalt therapists will label the behavior as a projection and proceed to help the client "own" it. If the behavior is the projection of a feeling, therapists will ask people to heighten this resistance, exploring the possibility of whether they are feeling as they project others are. For instance, a simple experiment exaggerating an anger projection could be saying, "I'm not angry, but I know *you* are and I'm going to do everything I can to convince you that you're angry and I'm not." Another experiment that would be appropriate for either a projection of feelings or expectations would be to ask the client to heighten awareness functioning and carefully report in the here and now what is seen and heard. If after doing this, clients can be shown that their perceptions are not congruent with what others perceive in the present environment, then they must consider what internal stimuli are cuing their experiences.

Once a projection has been behaviorally defined in terms acceptable to the client, Gestalt therapists use two basic techniques to treat it. First, they help people discriminate the cues signaling their projection's onset. After this discrimination is learned, clients are asked to compare what they are seeing and hearing with other trusted people when the identified projection is operating. This tactic essentially extinguishes the reinforcer for the projection and puts the projection chain of behaviors under extinction. In the example with Ruth, schematized in Figure 6-1, consistently checking out her present reality with people she trusted could lead to the removal of both reinforcers in the projection chain: her friend fulfilling the projection by being hurt, and Ruth receiving negative attention.

The other technique Gestalt therapists use to get rid of projections is to break the chain near its beginning by helping clients modify the introject cue. This requires identifying these introjects through experiments, as we have already discussed. Again, in Ruth's case, discovering her introject, "You should not show hurt or be vulnerable," and changing it to a rule more functional to her present life would rob the projection chain of a way to get started.

The implications of using just one or the other of these techniques are interesting. If we just extinguish the reinforcer for the projection chain, it will eventually decrease the frequency of the behavior, but it takes some time for a long behavior chain to be totally extinguished. If you will recall, simple extinction alone was not recommended for a long chain of behavior. In this case, the introject cue at the beginning will still be operable to start the behavior chain, as the lengthy process of extinction goes on. Indeed, this is exactly what Gestalt theory says will happen, although of course not in these terms. In fact, Gestalt suggests that projections are never completely eradicated unless the introjects behind them are dealt with. I would contend, however, that any behavior consistently put under extinction will return to operant level. Therefore, what Gestalt therapists may be seeing is extinction being inconsistently applied, which is quite normal in the natural environment, or an operant level of the projection behavior after a successful extinction procedure.

When introjects alone are modified without addressing how people reinforce projections, the chain is broken in the middle with the end of it left intact. Since the client was receiving important reinforcement through the use of the projection chain, unless new reinforcers are substituted, the old projection will reoccur with the same introject cue (regression) or a new rule will get the chain going again (symptom substitution).

As with the identification and treatment of introjects, Gestalt tries to make a case that projections are one of the major response classes of behavior that cause psychological difficulties. Is this a viable concept? Frankly, at this point you will have to accept the whole response class mostly on faith. You have seen the difficulty I have had in defining a projection behaviorally, in working out a reasonable conditioning paradigm, and then attempting to describe how projections are maintained in the here and now. After all that, I am still in the position of having to accept on faith that projections as a human experience are ubiquitous, and that they do inhibit effective problem solving. It is not enough to say that most of the people doing psychotherapy, including many behaviorists, are aware of a behavioral set they call projections.

All I can say at this stage of our ignorance is that I believe, based mostly on experience, that projections are universal and that they can be problematical. If there really is a general response class of behaviors that can be identified as projections, and if through a behavioral analysis of them we see their history and maintenance such as what I have described here, then what Gestalt therapists do when they describe a projection is much more profound than simple awareness training and is behaviorally active. These techniques are working to modify an extremely powerful behavioral contingency that controls a person's ability to effectively problem solve over a wide variety of situations, and also significantly impacts on their basic perception skills.

It is my belief that there is a good deal of behavioral activity in the concept of the projection and the technology Gestalt therapists use in treating it. By continuing the process of behaviorally specifying what controls the therapeutic use of the term, we will be able to develop more effective means of empirically examining its validity.

3. **Retroflection.** As you will recall, retroflection is doing to yourself what you'd rather do to others; or doing for yourself what you'd rather have others do for you. From this somewhat confusing play on words comes a particularly important process that is referred to in many therapies under different rubrics. The doing "to yourself" part of the retroflective resistance is the most interesting from a behavioral point of view; the doing "for" retroflection is an obvious example of a particular introjection/projection chain of behaviors. In fact you will notice that introjects and projections are part of many of the Gestalt resistances and thus might be construed as more basic psychological processes.

One of the most common examples of a retroflection is depression. The traditional view of chronic depression is "anger turned inward," a perhaps satisfyingly graphic description of a complex behavior problem. This traditional definition also implies that people get depressed because they didn't get angry, and the solution for them is to learn how to do so. Unfortunately, the "feelings turned inward" explanation of a depression, or of any retroflection, for that matter, may contain a bit of truth, but is far too simplistic for a behavioral analysis.

The thread that seems to cut across all retroflections is a kind of masochism. We do perform negative behaviors directed at ourselves that range from simple aversive messages to physical self-abuse. This response class can be further broken down into problems occurring in two areas: psychosomatic, and cognitive/overt retroflections. While both may be connected in a behavior chain, one or the other is often foreground in therapy.

It should be of no surprise that the anxiety associated with chronic unresolved problems lead to psychosomatic symptoms. Our bodies do not tolerate well the heightened states of deprivation brought on by chronic anger, hurt, fear, or sadness. The question that must be addressed is not whether anxiety related diseases exist but whether we can treat them by asking clients to symbolically direct what they are doing to themselves to other people in their environment.

There is every reason to hypothesize that this intervention strategy is indeed behaviorally active. Anxiety is of course always functionally related to situations and the people that make them in the here and now. When people find themselves in serious states of deprivation they have two basic tacks to take: assertiveness or acceptance. No organism would naturally choose to tolerate high levels of discomfort for long without trying to manipulate its environment or itself to meet its needs. Yet, people do live with serious anxiety so there must be some psychological process immobilizing their problem-solving attempts.

Gestalt suggests that introjects inhibit people from asserting themselves. "Don't feel" introject rules, such as, "You shouldn't be angry," act to keep people from knowing and interpreting what they are feeling. This makes it very difficult to assess not only one's state of deprivation but also how people are supporting it. In addition, "don't act" introjects, such as, "You shouldn't hurt others," keep people from asserting themselves even when they know who is reinforcing their anxiety and how. When Gestalt therapists ask clients to symbolically direct a negative feeling outward, to another person, they are helping the clients confront the rules keeping them from asserting themselves. As you will recall, the basic assertive behaviors included the ability to express negative and positive feelings, make requests and demands, and say no. Teaching these three behaviors is always part of undoing a retroflection.

The second kind of negative retroflections, those occurring in the cognitive/overt areas, such as self-criticism and guilt, we have already discussed in some detail. It seems to be part of the human condition to symbolically kick oneself at times. And overtly showing such general retroflective behaviors as depression and guilt seem to have their operant level as well. The same principles and contingencies covering psychosomatic retroflections apply to these, and the treatment is essentially the same: *directing the negative statements we make about ourselves to those who are reinforcing them.*

This treatment strategy is not only completely compatible with behavioral theory and practice but it also creatively enhances it. Gestalt and Behavior Therapy both insist that people always act as part of a system and not in isolation. People who characteristically use negative retroflections have a strong tendency to believe their problems are mainly intrapersonal rather than interpersonal. Experimenting with undoing a retroflection by directing feelings and demands to others directly challenges the existing introject rules and the people reinforcing them while concurrently teaching assertive skills.

Of course, the empirical validation of the Gestalt approach to self-depreciation, psychosomatic symptoms, and self-inflicted injuries awaits us. We need to more carefully identify exactly what covert and overt behaviors are part of this response class, specify the environmental antecedents and reinforcers for this behavior, and monitor the outcome efficiency of using the more symbolic Gestalt approach versus, for instance, a straight behavioral assessment and assertive training. I believe it can be demonstrated that the Gestalt approach to retroflective behavior adds an important dimension to both the assessment and treatment of this common client problem.

4. **Deflection**. The next Gestalt resistance to contact we discussed was that of the deflection. Like its predecessor, it incorporates introjection and projection contingencies in its behavior chain. As you will recall, when we change the subject, we are deflecting; when we hold back tears, we are using our muscles to deflect from crying; when we go the long way around to avoid seeing someone, we are deflecting from making contact with them. The reinforcement contingencies controlling this type of behavior are fairly obvious. For example, the introject, "You should not cry," would lead to deflective behavior in sad situations. So far we have seen that we can take an introject and use it as a foundation to project, retroflect, and now deflect. It's as if once we have learned a rule to live by we need the instructions for carrying out that rule. It is very likely that we learn a variety of ways to follow each rule, and many times they work in concert with one another. Deflection is then another way of following introject rules.

Therapists label behavior a deflection when they observe a feeling or verbal response get sidetracked into another seemingly incongruent chain of behaviors. I have often seen clients start to cry or get angry, only to see the feeling die away. Gestalt therapists will not only ask what happened to the feeling but *how* did the client lose it. What muscles and thoughts did they use to keep from continuing with the behavior chain connected to the first feeling cues. Insofar as clients are requested to describe the behaviors they use to deflect from one experience to another, this approach could be behaviorally active. From my own clinical experience, I believe the deflective response class does reasonably describe a pervasive general behavior pattern. By asking clients to behaviorally specify how they are losing feelings, for instance, I am able to assess how these deflective behaviors are reinforced both by me and others in the natural environment. Treatment then includes assertive training to better express feelings and manipulate people to get needs met. In a common differential reinforcement paradigm, reinforcers for deflective behavior are extinguished while the expression of feelings and other assertive skills are reinforced.

As an exercise, start with the introject, "You should not be fearful." Develop a possible model for conditioning this introject and tie it in a chain of behaviors to a projection. Then further continue the chain to deflective behavior, with both positive and negative reinforcers at the end coming from other people who are close to our hypothetical client.

5. **Confluence.** The last resistance I mentioned in Gestalt was confluence. Despite the rather graphic demonstration in the Gestalt chapter of what confluence is, holding hands together until they get numb, a behavioral analysis of the phenomenon is very difficult. The definition had to do with a dissolution of boundaries between two people, a sameness, or collusion. The reason confluence eludes a behavioral description is that it is both vague and already a part of the other resistances we have discussed. When two or more people act together in a system to reciprocally reinforce each other's behavior patterns, we call it a *series of contingencies* and part of complex behavior chains. The fact that they repeat the patterns again and again is an obvious effect of conditioned behavior and needs no further clarification. The idea of people "meshing" their boundaries until they seem to act as one unit, either in a family or small group, is certainly an interesting simile. However, I do not believe that the concept of confluence adds to our understanding of what happens when people continue to reciprocally interact in the same chains of behavior over and over again.

The basic treatment strategy for confluence is to help people to define their boundaries as different and separate from others. While I feel confluence adds very little to identifying a clear response class, I believe that the Gestalt technique of helping people set boundaries is one of the most obvious behaviorally active intervention strategies. Actually, boundary setting occurs throughout the Gestalt treatment process and is by no means limited to confluence.

A *boundary* was defined behaviorally as being able to express what you will and won't tolerate, what you like and don't like, what you want and don't want, and to be able to describe how you are significantly different from others. Without any translation, these behaviors represent three of the basic assertive skills. In fact, when Gestalt therapists are helping clients establish better boundaries, the terminal goals are essentially similar to those in any assertive training session. However, Gestalt therapists would use the clients' resistance to asserting themselves in the initial stages of their treatment strategies, whereas a behaviorist might attempt to teach the assertive skills directly. For example, if a client was not able to tell the therapist what he or she liked or didn't like about his therapy, he would be encouraged in an experiment to heighten and clarify that resistance: "I won't tell you anything I don't like about my therapy and I won't tell you anything I don't like about you. All I will say is how much I like everything." As we discussed previously, by heightening the resistance, we have an in vivo example of the contingency-reinforcing nonassertive behaviors. The experiment may also heighten the client's state of deprivation, providing more motivation for learning assertive skills. By the time clients start practicing new assertive behaviors, the therapist techniques are essentially similar to what happens in the behavioral approach, though perhaps not as systematic.

During the *feedback* phase of treatment therapists and clients essentially evaluate the effects and impact of the experiment, which of course is potentially valuable. And giving clients time to *integrate* what they've learned, or take time out after therapeutic work, can't hurt either. However, before we leave this section, there are two relatively structured Gestalt experiences that are worthy of a behavioral analysis: dreamwork and polarities.

Dreamwork   While I feel confident about how the behavioral laws can be applied to most of the important Gestalt practices and concepts, nothing leaves me more uncertain than a behavioral analysis of dreams. The only saving grace for the Gestalt approach to dreamwork is that it is truly a single organism experimentally designed exercise for a therapist and client. A dream is described, symbols personified, and acted out. If the dream has any meaning to the client, swell. If what is learned augments the reaching of treatment goals, great. If not, the client goes on to bigger and better things. A good Gestalt therapist is not supposed to interpret dreams, only support the client's own interpretations of the dream experiment.

The biggest problem in working with dreams is that they are one of the ultimate covert images, supposedly being a symbolic representation of our experience. Not only are dreams covert and rely totally on verbal report but people often do not remember clearly what they dreamed. Thus, it is very difficult to get reliable variables to study dreamwork as a therapeutic tool. What cues and reinforces dreams is pure hypothesis, with very little empirical foundation for clinical work. But, as a scientist of behavior, I will not be deterred. Since dream behavior unquestionably occurs, it *must* therefore be ultimately reinforced if it is to continue occurring. There is no reason to expect that dream behavior is any different from any other type of human behavior. Therefore it must follow the Laws of Classical and Operant Conditioning. I must admit that while Gestalt's theoretical explanation of dreams leaves more questions than it answers, it does find a meaningful way to integrate the dream experience into the therapeutic process. So let us assume for the moment that dreams must follow the Behavioral Laws, that we know very little about their controlling conditions, and see what Gestalt may have to teach us about their use.

The Gestalt view of why dreams occur has to do with states of deprivation. They symbolically represent unmet needs in relation to issues in our lives that need attention. I like the idea that dreams are cued by some deprivation state, since all operant behavior seems to be motivated in this way. Why, then, don't we always remember our dreams, the assumption being that everyone dreams? The Gestalt answer, which is not very satisfying to the palate, is that people who don't remember their dreams are in some sense afraid to confront their present existence. Put *that* in behaviorally specific terms if you can.

A behavioral analysis of dreams uses models I have already developed. First, we think in symbols and images, inexorably tied to complex behavior chains, including overt behavior eventually reinforced in the environment. It is certainly possible that dreams are somehow woven into these chains. Second, when I did an analysis of the unconscious, I attempted to establish a behavioral model for the inclusion of symbolic imagery behavior occurring below present levels of awareness being negatively reinforced. Could it be that just after waking, the power of these negative reinforcers is sometimes momentarily lessened, allowing us to remember what is normally below awareness? What role does respondent conditioning play in dreams? It is entirely possible that dreams are controlled by an interaction between respondent and operant laws, much as are many anxiety related behaviors. However, there can be no question that dreams are related to the environment since it is from our experience that we get the material for our dreams.

TORNADO: I'm coming and I'm going to swirl you up.
CLIENT: No, you are not. I will get out of your path. There is no way you can hurt me.
TORNADO: But I am the most powerful weather force in nature and there is nothing you can do to stop me.
CLIENT: I may not be able to stop you, but I can make sure that I don't let you stop me.

In the discussion following his dreamwork, the client said he discovered that what the dream meant to him was an affirmation of a recent decision not to let himself be sidetracked from going to school after deciding to leave a very disruptive family life.

A research methodologist would go bananas with this example. We must trust on faith that the client was reporting and reenacting the dream accurately, and then reporting his interpretations free from influence of the therapist. Both variables are well nigh impossible to control. But as clinicians, and good therapists who believe that behavior is governed by laws, we must face that people do dream, and some people report finding meaning in their dreams after working on them a la Gestalt. Using the Laws of Behavior, I have developed a hypothesis about dreams and their therapeutic use. If you find serious gaps in it, as well you might, try applying the Laws of Behavior to dreams for yourself and see what you can come up with. It's a fascinating puzzle.

Whatever the source of dreams, the question of their usefulness in personal growth is left unanswered. Without a clear picture of their etiology, it becomes problematical to predict how they could enhance the therapeutic process except by some sort of faith in Gestalt theory. But let us consider for the moment this very tentative hypothesis: dreams are covert symbolic images interwoven into larger behavior chains under at least partial environmental operant control. This hypothesis may provide a plausible foundation for incorporating dreams into a behaviorally active therapeutic process. It has been the personal experiences of many Gestalt therapists and clients that when dream symbols are personified, *and* when interpretations are not imposed on the dreamer, then meaningful insights into both the contingencies controlling present-day behavior and current states of deprivation are discovered. And if clients are allowed to redesign their dreams after the initial reenactment, dreamwork provides creative imagery to practice new assertive behaviors as an approximation to handling more difficult situations in the environment.

Dreams can also act as confirmation of work already done or the heightening of satisfaction and happiness. I remember one dream I helped a person design. He set up a tornado coming at him on a highway with car wrecks strewn all over. But he felt impervious to it. Using the dreamwork as theater technique where different people are assigned each of the important symbols in a dream, this person set up his scene with people as wrecked cars, a highway, and one person as the tornado coming at him. He then went around his dream fragment, engaging in a dialogue with each person-symbol. His discussion with the highway was about how he was traveling down a road, not sure where he was going, but feeling comfortable in his journey nonetheless. He felt sorry for the cars which had already been wrecked by the tornado and gave them some first aid until tow trucks were on their way; the most interesting dialogue was with the tornado:

I believe that of all the techniques for integrating dreams into therapy, Gestalt offers the best approach for research. Because of Gestalt's emphasis on observable behavior and its refusal to interpret for clients, it would be possible to systematize the dreamwork procedure and develop measurable therapeutic dependent variables. The initial stages of research would obviously have to use single-organism designs, but that is what Gestalt therapists do anyway. Personally, I like including the Gestalt approach to dreams in my clinical work, even though I cannot firmly establish its behavioral activity. Its use with clients is fun, and apparently they have reinforced me when I've introduced this technique, or I wouldn't continue doing it. There is something to be said for having fun, especially in therapy.

Polarities   To be behaviorally specific about a polarity is not simple, since it describes not only an observable behavior but also implies an opposite tendency. It is of course impossible to measure a "tendency" unless it occurs at least occasionally. So where does that leave us, if not completely frustrated? The label probably has some value when a behavior problem fits, or can be made to fit, into considering polar extremes. For example, there are many behaviors that are conditioned as part of the polar sex differences, such as the ability to cry, be assertive, and grooming.

Gestalt suggests when children are being conditioned along polar dimensions many behaviors are tied together idiosyncratically that are not functional later in life. By symbolically putting these behavior patterns into an exaggerated behaviorally specific polarity, clients can reexamine them. For example, if crying is a natural expression of sadness, hurt, or fear, then men must be conditioned to perform some other behavior instead of crying. The feeling cues that would naturally lead to crying lead instead to muscle tension (anxiety). There are also covert introjects reminding them what behaviors are appropriate for men in this society. These reminders often are tied to other introjected stereotypes such as the beliefs that crying is weak, may cause loss of control, and perhaps worst of all, be feminine. These and other verbal self-reports are powerful positive and negative reinforcers for the behaviors that inhibit crying.

One technique a Gestalt therapist could use with a sad male client who would not cry is a double-chair experiment between two polar parts: "I won't cry" in one position and "I want to cry" in the other. What could happen in the ensuing dialogue is a heightening of the motivation to cry and reenactment of the contingencies reinforcing its inhibition. As we have previously discussed, these double-chair dialogues bring to life covert symbols and dynamics from the past, and are usually exact reenactments of how the behavior was learned, and the general contingencies controlling its present occurrence as well. In this example, we would be able to assess the history of what behaviors were tied to the sex role in early conditioning and what contingencies maintain them in present relationships.

Frankly, the use of polarities in Gestalt is more of a way to view a problem than it is a separate technology. To the extent that therapists use the other behaviorally active techniques already covered, behavior change could occur. Attempting to problem solve using this conceptual basis is certainly interesting but needs to be much better established as an inherently useful means to conceptualize problems. In any case, in both historical and contemporary times, looking at issues in polarities has been a common practice. Given Gestalt's unique way of incorporating this concept in psychotherapy, it may be worth further consideration.

Transference and Countertransference   There is no question that a careful behavioral analysis of transference and countertransference must be done in any thorough discussion of psychotherapy. I am going to leave the major discussion of this dynamic to the chapter on the behavioral analysis of Ego Psychology. Not only is transference more central to Ego Psychology than to Gestalt but it is also, after all, where the concept first came from. We have, however, in this chapter laid the behavioral groundwork for understanding how transference and countertransference develop through early-childhood conditioning and the projective process. What makes the Gestalt approach to these phenomena unique is how the transference and countertransference become like any other here-and-now contingency—something to be acknowledged, clarified, and acted on to make better contact. Suffice it to say now that in transference and countertransference behavior patterns there is a here-and-now reenactment of early-childhood contingencies that also represent part of the reinforcing contingencies maintaining current behavior.

Assertive Training in Gestalt

As you should have been able to ascertain by now, the teaching of assertive skills is pervasive throughout the practice of Gestalt. Every technique aims to help clients express what they feel, make demands and requests, or say no or yes. While the methodology is by no means as systematic as in the behavioral approach, it creatively uses history and covert variables in areas where most behaviorists would fear to tread.

I believe Gestalt therapy's greatest contribution to assertive training technology is in its use of the past and the double chair. Assertive skills can be assessed and practiced with people in long-past relationships, with esoteric covert symbols developed by the client, with people in the here and now including the therapist, and even with parts of the body.

Setting boundaries was one area where the teaching of assertive behavior in Gestalt paralleled the behavioral approach closely. However, along with the technique came the idea that assertions acted to protect the organism from being hurt and encroached upon. It has been my experience that clients readily understand how setting boundaries is a necessary protective mechanism for survival. Perhaps the concept is so basic to humans and the animal kingdom that people are able to more easily understand how assertive behavior is an important foundation of their relationships. In any case, I believe the idea is intriguing enough to justify further inquiry.

Teaching people to identify and assert themselves against dysfunctional introjects was another creative way that Gestalt therapy utilized assertive training. These rules acted as powerful antecedents of problematic behavior patterns; helping people say no to introject messages represented a significant means of breaking chains of behavior before they started.

And finally, the idea that retroflective behavior is the result, in a sense, of asserting oneself inwardly instead of outwardly to people in the environment is a novel and probably productive way for integrating the relationship of assertive behavior with such problems as depression and guilt.

Acceptance Training in Gestalt

You will notice that there has been very little mention of relaxation training in the Gestalt technology of treatment. This is not because it is not there. In fact, it is infused in every aspect of treatment, but under the guise of teaching clients to support themselves and get support from others. It is by no means as systematically done as in systematic desensitization. Yet, I believe that Gestalt therapists do as good a job as anyone in teaching us to relax in the face of our inability to manipulate the environment in meeting our needs. Learning to support yourself included, if you will recall, the ability to relax through breathing exercises, and to support our bodies physically. While I described the abdominal breathing method, it is by no means sacred. Some proponents of Gestalt teach yoga, meditation, or even relaxation exercises from Behavior Therapy. According to Gestalt, the point of all of these relaxation procedures is to free energy blocked in our muscles so it can be used in identifying our needs and getting these needs met. Be that as it may, therapists frequently ask clients to relax by whatever means they have been taught to gain better self-support.

In terms of getting support from others as it relates to learning to relax, clients will request or demand verbal or physical nurturing as well as empathy and understanding, all of which are likely somewhat incompatible with muscle tension.

Gestalt uses another basic psychological phenomenon to help clients finally bring about the true peace and muscle relaxation of acceptance. Remember, we are not talking about resignation, which implies giving up with reservations, resulting in continued muscle tension. People keep attempting to manipulate situations over which they have no control because their behavior is reinforced. If a client has repeatedly tried to get positive attention from his mother over many years, and bitterly complains about the failures, these attempts continue because there is some important reinforcing consequence being delivered on an intermittent schedule, perhaps in this case, negative attention. It is only when the reinforcer is withdrawn that nonfunctional repeat-attempt behavior will be extinguished. The muscle tension associated with this pattern of behavior will extinguish, too, and a new chain will be reinforced which is operationally defined as acceptance.

The behaviors defining what is called the *grief process* offer a good analogy for understanding how acceptance is conditioned operantly. When a person close to someone dies, he or she has lost a very powerful mediator of reinforcement. The natural process of extinction begins by following the extinction curve. If you will recall, there is usually an initial increase in emotional behavior before behavior slowly returns to prior operant levels. In the case of grief, people often experience sadness, depression, and anger before the loss is finally accepted. However, there are situations where people are not allowed to grieve, alternative behaviors to grief being reinforced instead. These chains could include refusing to acknowledge the loss or continually trying to replace it. Gestalt suggests that if grief is not allowed to follow its natural course, the tension gets stuck in the body, and is called *unfinished business*. More germane, I believe, is the frustration associated with the continual attempt to attain something unattainable. Frustration and muscle tension are inexorably related; one cannot be relaxed and frustrated at the same time.

When people will not accept their inability to change a situation to their satisfaction after long-term repeated attempts to do so, the finality of the loss has not been acknowledged. A death is usually a clear indication there will be no further reinforcers forthcoming. But in the case of our client who couldn't get his mom's positive attention after years of trying, the mediator of reinforcement is still around. Thus, in order for acceptance to occur when functional mediators of reinforcement are still present, two things must happen: 1) the inability to manipulate a situation in the present and in the near future must be acknowledged; 2) reinforcers for nonfunctional repeat-attempt chains of behavior must be extinguished and alternative chains and reinforcers developed to replace them. The frustration accompanying the repeated failures will be extinguished and the peace and muscle relaxation of acceptance will occur.

Gestalt uses the heightening technique to help people acknowledge their inability to manipulate after repeated attempts. Once it becomes evident to therapists how frustrated the client is, they can support the heightening of the pain, making it clearer how futile are the demands of the client on an apparently intractable environment. Heightening pain is another way of increasing motivation to change; the natural organismic response to continued pain is to choose alternatives to lessen it. The heightened pain should generate enough disgust or anger to confront the resistances to contact keeping the grief response from being finished up, that is, clients must confront the mediators of reinforcement maintaining their nonacceptance behavior. They will typically go through a grief process as the sense of loss is beginning to be accepted, including anger and depression at the unfairness of it all, and the sadness that losing something important brings on. However, the process is not finished up until clients make a firm boundary establishing exactly what they will and won't tolerate in relation to the people who refused to meet their demands.

Much of this work can be done using symbols and the double chair. The personification of past relationships or covert parts of oneself allows clients to reenact the contingencies controlling their inability to accept that which cannot be changed. Thus there are a wide variety of double-chair possibilities that could get the job done.

I believe Gestalt's basic strategy for developing acceptance is behaviorally active. It concerns me that Gestalt does not define the process in terms that easily relate to the Laws of Behavior. Yet there is an attempt to integrate the relaxation training occurring in learning to support oneself, such as deep breathing, with the ongoing process of therapy. The ability to relax in the face of adversity and accept that which cannot be changed can then be conditioned on two tacks: directly through self-support techniques, and indirectly through the heightening of resistances and supporting the grief process.

CONCLUSIONS

Now that we have completed a behavioral analysis of Gestalt therapy, how shall we evaluate it overall? There is obviously much in Gestalt technology and theory that can teach us a thing or two about expanding the horizons of a behaviorally active practice. But there was also an inherent fuzziness that made specifying its procedures and theoretical rationales extremely difficult at times. Gestalt is in some ways most ambitious. It not only attempts to describe a therapeutic process but provides a structure for people to struggle with the meaning of life as well. It's a big task for a science so young. Yet, people do seek meaning in their lives, so perhaps as behavioral scientists we should look upon these far-reaching goals with a degree of patience and appreciate the attempt.

It is through Gestalt we most clearly see the intriguing idea of looking at feelings as states of deprivation. The Awareness Cycle, which could be called the *motivation* or *deprivation cycle*, describes behaviorally how feelings and unique states of deprivation control our behavior. And Gestalt's use of heightening resistance as an assessment tool that increases motivation is a stroke of genius, in my opinion. In addition, the idea that symbols control our behavior, while not new, is given a clearer place in the assessment and treatment process. Gestalt suggests we use symbols not only for language but for feelings, thoughts, overt behavior, and entire contingencies of reinforcement.

We should not overlook the creative emphasis in Gestalt, either. While it is this very aspect that makes behavioral researchers squirm, it is also to be admired. Surely one day we will be able to empirically defend with some degree of confidence the serendipity integration of symbols, dreams, music, art, poetry, and dance into the human problem-solving process. These are, after all, very human experiences.

Another strength of Gestalt therapy is how it allows the weaving of present and past into an active here-and-now experience. The assumption is that present behaviors are under the control of here-and-now contingencies and reflect very closely the patterns of the past, particularly from childhood. This is an important contribution. Using here-and-now reenactments of the past can then become an exercise in assessment, clarification, and practicing new behaviors as old behavior chains are broken and new ones built. Furthermore, there is a clear implication in Gestalt, as seen through a behavioral analysis, that behavior is controlled through a complex combination of covert, overt, and physiological behavior chains. My hypotheses, derived from Gestalt practice, that we covertly carry out the same reinforcement contingencies as are seen in overt behavior is an important bridge in connecting our internal and external behavior.

One of the reasons I have been able to attempt to behaviorally integrate physical, physiological, cognitive, and overt behavior together is that Gestalt emphasizes the integration of the total organism. Of all the practice-based theories of psychotherapy, it tries to bring a unity, a "gestalt" if you will, to the psychotherapy experience. Organismic self-regulation is more than a theoretical construct—it is a term of respect for the power and integration of the human organism.

And finally, as you can see in many therapies, Gestalt makes an honest attempt to help people tie their specific problems to broader life issues. Put another way, there is an attempt to connect small response classes to broader behavioral contingencies that control not only the presenting problem but many other potentially dysfunctional behaviors as well. Gestalt, along with TA and Ego Psychology, has its own unique set of general contingencies that all problem behavior is supposed to fit into. For better or for worse, this attempt to codify and categorize behavior is a noble if often impossible task. However, the attempts should continue to be made, perhaps with less dogma, and all therapists should join in the quest. After all, although each person and situation is unique, there must be some general and important contingencies in life that cut across large groups of people.

One of the biggest problems in looking at Gestalt therapy was evident from the start of our Gestalt journey. The problem-solving methodology and theory is not as clear as it could be. Gestalt practice and theory varies far too widely from therapist to therapist, making empirical investigation a methodological nightmare. It is a tremendous problem for any psychology to have too much variation in it, to the point that one Gestalt therapist might not recognize the procedures of another, and worse, would come up with different theoretical interpretations of what they see and do. Gestalt's lack of standarization in its practice and theory is partly an outcome of the politics of Gestalt therapy, and mostly an inherent result of the very nature of the theory. In any case, it makes training and research more difficult.

Another difficulty with Gestalt is in its interpretation of the focus for problem behavior. All problems revolve around people's ability to know what they want and their ability to make contact. Often existential struggles become part of the problem-solving process sparked by a seemingly minor concern. For example, a client seeking help for a simple fear of spiders could be guided into identifying the spider as a symbol of some greater concern. Treatment would not only deal with how the client is failing in getting support from self and others but might also look at the spider as symbolic of some important unfinished business and inability to make contact. In essence, when you come into Gestalt therapy for a faucet, you end up buying the kitchen sink.

In contrast, a client arriving at a Behavior Therapist's door would tend to receive treatment only for the anxiety related to the spider stimulus. Any other issues associated with the fear of spiders would have to be specifically identified in order to be treated further. In this case, the client comes in for a faucet and receives a faucet.

Frankly, I do not like either polarity. It seems reasonable that many presenting problems are related to more central concerns. But that does not mean that therapy must always go for the psychological jugular any more than it must stay on specific presenting problems. Behavior Therapy has demonstrated reasonably well that presenting problems can be resolved to a client's satisfaction without dealing with broader concerns. Conversely, it is also likely that many presenting problems represent only the tip of an iceberg requiring broader treatment perspectives. I would wish a behaviorally active practice to allow for flexibility in defining the focus of a problem. Clearly, both approaches have value.

Of central concern, Gestalt tries to completely ignore respondent conditioning and the impact of operant consequences in its theory and in the explanation of its practice effects. Even though I was able to impose a behavioral analysis onto Gestalt therapist behavior, it was a difficult and sometimes impossible task. As you will hear me say again and again, we cannot ignore what is empirically known about human behavior just because it doesn't seem to fit into our present theory base. Yet the fact that I was able to impose the Behavioral Laws onto Gestalt practice as often as I did speaks well for the therapy. There seem to be quite a few behaviorally active techniques in its bag of tricks. It would do no basic harm to Gestalt to incorporate the Behavioral Laws into its framework.

CHAPTER SEVEN
TRANSACTIONAL
ANALYSIS
A Behavioral Analysis

INTRODUCTION

A behavioral analysis of TA is far simpler to do than with either Gestalt or Ego Psychology. Many of TA's basic concepts find their behavioral counterpart without significant translation. Some treatment techniques, too, are strikingly similar to those in Behavior Therapy. However, this is not to say that the practice of TA in totality follows the Behavioral Laws. Along with some very creative behaviorally active interventions we will find a number of rather vague concepts leading to treatment techniques upon which it would be difficult to build an empirical foundation.

THE TREATMENT PROCESS

If you will recall, the TA treatment strategy followed this general pattern:

1. Socialization Into TA Theory
2. Transactional Analysis
3. Script Analysis
4. Redecisions
5. Working Toward the Cure

Technically, therapists following TA theory used, among other things, contracting, behavioral rehearsal, identification of Parent, Adult, and Child transactions, modification of language, and a healthy dose of Gestalt, such as the double chair and the personification of symbols. As before, let us look at each step in the treatment process to assess behavioral activity.

Socialization into TA Theory

While of course not all TA therapists conduct formal pretherapy classes or workshops to indoctrinate the uninitiated, it is common. In my experience, TA makes the greatest systematic effort to teach clients a comprehensive psychological model. Too many psychotherapists do not share their theory base with clients except in very general ways or around specific presenting problem areas. Some theoretical foundations are too complex to be easily integrated into the therapy experience; and there are those who wish to emphasize the experiential rather than theoretical nature of therapy. Because clients often lack a sound theoretical knowledge base, therapy can seem to be surrounded by an almost mystical aura. Psychotherapy is a rare opportunity to teach people experientially and theoretically an area that is often neglected in schools and home. It is to TA's credit that it is easily taught to nonprofessionals and that clients are systematically exposed to a comprehensive theory of behavior as part of their therapy.

The Transactional Analysis

In order to analyze this assessment phase of treatment, we are forced to come to grips with the viability of TA's theoretical foundation. At this stage therapists are watching interactions, helping clients identify Parent, Adult, and Child transactions, games, and payoffs. Clients are often beginning to use the double chair as well for further game analysis. If there is any behavioral activity in this assessment behavior we must consider whether these key TA concepts are founded in the Behavioral Laws.

The Ego States   There are two issues to be addressed in an analysis of the Parent, Adult, and Child ego states: first, is it possible to reliably discriminate and identify each of them; second, are they psychologically important enough to consider? I believe that the answer to the first question is a qualified yes. The ego states are defined behaviorally, especially in the domain of verbal behavior. Statements using "should," "must," "have to," and words of praise and nurturing are fairly easy to identify and are called Parent behavior; statements of apparent facts are Adult behavior; and comments about feelings and wants are generally Child behavior. Nonverbal behavior, too, is supposed to occur in each ego state, and is of course more difficult to reliably code. However, there are some consistent postures and mannerisms attributed to each of the ego states, such as the wiggling, pointing finger associated with the Critical Parent; an erect, centered posture associated with the Adult; and a slouching posture often concurrent with crying, sadness, or depression in Child behavior.

Granting the assumption that it is possible to reliably identify behavior representative of each ego state, we are left with, "So what?" If TA had demonstrated beyond the shadow of all doubt that human behavior could be broken down into these three basic response classes, we would still be no further ahead in understanding the control of human behavior. You will notice, however, that the kinds of behavior occurring in each of these response classes is on the agenda in every therapy: making rules, praise and support, the ability to report perceived facts, dealing with feelings and wants. TA has used easily recognized metaphors that immediately allow clients to associate behavior with an historical reference from their own experiences. It was parents who first made rules to live by and gave support. Clients can usually remember themselves as children or at least are aware of the stereotypic child role, in which feelings and playfulness are so freely experienced. The ability to better perceive reality is associated with being an adult. TA uses these metaphors with an eye to developing a model of learning, where parents teach children and adults better perceive how to do this. This is exactly what was supposed to happen in all of our child-rearing experiences. Is it any wonder people can so easily plug into the TA model of learning?

I believe the PAC discriminations made in TA are reasonable, but certainly not exclusive. Since they are relatively well specified in observable behavior we may accept their validity for the moment and see where it might lead. However, we should not assume that these TA ego states are the only response classes possible. We have already seen how Gestalt divides up its world of human behavior and will soon examine the same issues in Ego Psychology. The question is not only whether a theory can successfully discriminate response classes; the question is also whether the discriminations are clear, reliable, and useful in the context of its model. TA's attempt is interesting and will, I believe, lead to the development of some effective and unique behaviorally active treatment interventions.

The Stroke and Time Structuring   The concept of the *stroke* makes for a simple translation to the law of reinforcement. It is to TA's credit that it has recognized the importance of consequences in the control of behavior. In many aspects the definition of a stroke is the same as a reinforcer. People are willing to work for both; states of deprivation increase people's desire to attain both; the final payoff or consequence is what controls the future occurrence of a behavior chain, or game. In fact, in one aspect TA clarifies the concept of reinforcing consequences. People are willing to work for positive and negative strokes, both of which are positive reinforcers. In Behavior Therapy we talk about positive and negative attention as being positive reinforcers. Negative attention is often confused with negative reinforcement or punishment. With the use of the stroke metaphor, it has been my experience that positive and negative attention is more easily perceived as a reinforcer.

It is perhaps the very simplicity of the stroke that makes using this metaphor for reinforcement an incomplete concept. First, the stroke deals mainly with that wide range of behaviors called *attention*, ranging from eye contact to physical abuse. Other kinds of reinforcers, while not necessarily ignored, are played down in favor of attentional ones, the assumption being that attention is necessary for survival. Be that as it may, there is too much known about the power of tangible reinforcers to systematically subjugate their use. Second, it is every unclear how the phenomenon of negative reinforcement fits into the concept of the stroke, as well as the true punishment contingency, and the very important process of extinction. Third, because of the emphasis on a generalized attentional reinforcer, the stroke, it is easy to be inexact in specifying it behaviorally, thus making it more difficult to manipulate latency, magnitude, duration, and the other factors that affect reinforcer effectiveness.

However, as far as the concept of the stroke goes, it obviously leads to behaviorally active practice. It strongly support the Laws of Operant Behavior and is essentially akin to positive reinforcement. We are going on without a firm theoretical support for negative reinforcement, extinction, or punishment, which leaves a large void. Yet, we shall see that just as with the systematic application of the concept of the stroke, TA develops some powerful and interesting techniques.

As you will recall, TA has delineated a broad series of response classes called *time structuring* in which strokes are exchanged. These included intimacy, games, pastimes, activities, rituals, and withdrawal, and were ordered by degree of stroking intensity. People are supposed to be able to move flexibly between these time structures, and especially be able to stop playing games and become intimate. While the concept is certainly interesting, I do not believe that it is a necessary part of a behaviorally active treatment strategy. It is impossible to measure stroking intensity from one way of structuring time to the next. Furthermore, I am not convinced that each of the time-structured response classes, assuming they could be reliably identified, is inclusive or important enough to use in problem-solving strategies.

I have committed the first of several heresies according to TA doctrine, but have not done any real damage to TA practice. We can still continue on the premise that changing the behavior defined in games is helpful in problem solving. And we can still define broad dynamic response classes with clients where they wish to improve their functioning. For instance, there is no reason that a client couldn't work on being more effective in pastiming or intimacy, as long as it was defined behaviorally for each situation.

Transactions   The transaction leads to a number of very interesting behaviorally active therapist behaviors, starting with assessment. Whereas Gestalt allows a wide variety of symbols to be used in assessing and working on problem interactions, TA ultimately synthesizes all symbols down to the basic Parent-Adult-Child metaphors. In addition, we have discussed in a number of places how chains of behavior weave in and out of the overt and covert domains. Neither Behavior Therapy nor Gestalt systematically specifies the parameters of how these internal and external dynamics occur and interact. One of the high points of TA occurs using the concepts of transactions and games to establish a model describing how covert and overt contingencies are played out and how they combine to enhance each other.

Call them what you will, TA has established three reasonably specific response classes, the Parent-Adult-Child, describing communication occurring at any point in time. The theory further suggests that a response from any one of these classes is often part of an historically conditioned pattern where the next behavior in a chain dictates a particular conditioned response from someone else. It adds clarity to use TA labels and metaphors: a response by one person from one of the Parent, Adult, or Child ego states is part of a conditioned pattern that is chained to another response from a second person's Parent, Adult, or Child ego state. Thus, a complementary transaction is one where the next behavior conditioned in a chain is alternately performed by one of two people. A crossed transaction occurs when one of the parties does not perform the next conditioned member of a chain and thus, in effect, begins an extinction process. If the next reinforcing behavior that would keep the chain rolling is not eventually forthcoming, that communication would indeed by extinguished.

In the early stages of assessment, TA therapists simply watch client transactions to see what kind of patterns develop between people. Since the behaviors in each of the ego states are fairly well specified, this is not too difficult with a little training. People will tend to continue interacting with those who offer the next conditioned reinforcers in their particular interactional chains of behavior. Thus there should be plenty of data to observe in any small group as people eventually find out who will engage in complementary transactions with them and who won't.

The double chair can be used as well for this assessment, starting with any symbols a client and therapist wish to use. Just as in Gestalt, a part of the body, feeling, or any person present or past can be put on the chairs. What makes TA quite different using this technique is that the therapist will always be looking for the PAC transaction patterns between whatever symbols are on the chairs, just as if the client were interacting with another person.

Working with transaction chains using the Parent-Adult-Child model allows imposing a structure on our covert as well as overt behavior. In my opinion, this is one of the areas in which TA has made a significant advance. For example, it is widely accepted in psychotherapy that the ability to support and reinforce oneself is important. TA offers a structured model for covert reinforcement training that is both natural and reasonably systematic, including such self-reinforcers as praise and reassurance. Covert self-reinforcement is structured into a Parent-Child transactional dialogue using the double chair. Almost every adult can fit into this dynamic as it is a natural function for parents to support children. Clients first practice in the double chair being a Nurturing Parent to the scared or anxious Child. They often have in their present behavioral repertoire the ability to nurture, support, and praise. It is a question of discriminating these two response classes, the Parent and Child, and using both skills to practice reinforcing oneself. In the case where clients do not have the appropriate support skills, they can be taught them. The next step is for the client to covertly practice the double chair Parent-Child dialogue, thus providing an effective model for learning to praise and support oneself.

The Parent position in the double chair makes the assessment of covert nurturing skill deficits possible, since the behavior is overtly reenacted. There are also many cases where clients clearly have nurturing skills but refuse to use them to support their anxious Child facing them in the opposite chair. I have seen many clients—even fellow therapists—who were very successful in taking care of other children and adults but would not take care of themselves as well as they took care of others. This contingency would also become evident in an overt Parent-Child dialogue. These situations call for assessing the contingencies controlling their inability to use nurturing skills covertly while demonstrating their use overtly with others. As we will see in the behavioral analysis of games, TA offers some guidance in this assessment task as well.

Games.   TA has made major contributions to enhancing a behaviorally active practice in psychotherapy with its development of the *game* concept. This is not to say that there are not problems with its application. TA has a tendency, I believe, to carry the idea beyond an empirically demonstrable point. However, the basis of the game is well founded in behavioral theory and thus deserves our serious consideration.

Games are first and foremost general chains of behavior occurring so frequently they can be labeled. They are made up of a series of transactions of varying lengths ending with an important payoff, or reinforcer. There is no question there are similar contingencies that have enough in common to lump them into contingency categories. The advantages of this for assessment and treatment are obvious: making a behavioral shorthand for assessing patterns of problem behavior, saving time, potentially increasing the efficiency of treatment, and developing better predictive prognoses. The problem with identifying these common contingencies is basically an empirical one. First, chains of behavior would have to be specified across clients and problems in such a way that therapists could reliably identify them. Second, these identified patterns would have to be consistently integrated into treatment in such a way that outcome could be correlated with chain identification. While it is conceivable to think of beginning this process at the present state of the art, the empirical demonstration of its clinical effectiveness is so far away, all a behavioral scientist can reasonably do is dream of what might be.

While behaviorists have been dreaming, TA has stepped where research methodologists have rarely tread. There are many pitfalls with such journeys, but we may glean fruitful directions for research and practice nonetheless. I believe that some of the TA games are common enough that they can be reasonably used without empirical validation *if* the members of the game-chain are behaviorally specified with each client. For example, it is my experience that the Kick Me game occurs with great frequency and almost every client I have ever seen could relate to it. If you will recall, the antecedents for games include a state of deprivation for attention (stroke deprivation) and an appropriate partner present. In Kick Me, the subject performs a behavior that historically has earned a negative or depreciating comment (or worse), which is one important final reinforcer for the chain. Most of the time people can relate similar contingencies in their own behavior patterns. Negative attention is such a pervasive reinforcer that it seems pretty safe to generalize this chain.

There is another concrete advantage to putting contingencies such as Kick Me into labeled categories with clients. Not only does it provide a metaphor for quick reference as treatment goes on but the game also implies that people are working for that kick payoff. When viewed in the light of stroke deprivation, clients usually realize some strokes are better than none, are able to understand the concept, and take responsibility for their role in the Kick Me game. Frankly, I find some clients can better relate to these metaphors than a more technical explanation using behavioral terminology.

Whenever we start trying to categorize chains of behavior from a theoretical rather than an empirical base there are bound to be serious problems. First, some of the categories may be too limited or conversely, cover too wide an area. For instance, the Uproar game includes a healthy fight ending with withdrawal. The immediate payoff is supposed to be avoidance of intimacy or sex, a negative reinforcement contingency. There are obviously many patterns of human behavior that include fights and withdrawal, but the apparent avoidance of an intimacy-sex payoff makes the category too narrow and interpretive.

Some of the games are so subtle in their operation and motivation they may continually elude good behavioral analyses. For example, the NIGYYSOB game, Now I've Got You, You Son of a Bitch, implies a motivation or state of deprivation that may not even be in the conscious awareness of the player. I would rather document chains without specifying probable intent, since that always involves interpretations. Not only do many TA games make undocumented assumptions about their intent but they frequently do not take into account therapists' ability to reliably assign observed behavior to the same games.

It is the experience of TA therapists, though, that categorizing behavior chains into games is often possible and helpful. Of course, much of what this involves is a teaching process where clients are exposed to the game concept and are encouraged to assign their own behavior into these standard categories—a kind of self-fulfilling prophecy. While this may be a serious weakness from an empirical point of view, it does not detract from the gallant theoretical and practice attempt to bring some order to very complex phenomena. I believe the use of games in TA demonstrates the value of categorizing and labeling chains of behavior. If we view TA's attempt as a beginning, and assign category labels with care, the concept can be a helpful adjunct to a behaviorally active practice.

There is another aspect to the game that deserves our attention. Each separate member of a game chain is a transactional Parent-Adult-Child response. The previous example of Kick Me showed how the game worked overtly. TA suggests that games have their symbolic covert counterparts as well. Thus, Kick Me can be played alone using covert Parent-Child symbols with a negative or depreciating comment delivered by the self. We saw this same idea in Gestalt as well, but TA imposes its much more systematic PAC model on the phenomenon. The chain can be played out covertly until the appropriate overt stimuli are present. As we have seen previously, TA provides an easily recognizable model for understanding how people put themselves down. Critical Parents in the present environment who deliver negative strokes to clients are working with the client to play out a reinforcement contingency from childhood. Clients can usually assimilate the idea that there is a covert Critical Parent response class in them as well, learned from actual parent models, that is the source of their critical self-statements. The double chair is an excellent way to demonstrate this dynamic. For instance, if you ask a client to discriminate the part of him or herself that makes mistakes on one chair, and the part that criticizes on the other, you will be amazed how closely the ensuing dialogue approximates an actual parent criticizing a child. What you will be seeing is a behavioral reenactment representing the games of how this client covertly criticizes him or herself. By using recognizable metaphors to describe what is essentially a covert-overt game-chain of behaviors, TA again uses its unique game model to systematize the behaviorally active assessment and treatment of covert behavior problems. I find the application of this concept very supportive for helping clients understand and modify the way they covertly treat themselves.

Script Analysis

It is with very great difficulty that I face a behavioral analysis of the script. I go into the task with the knowledge that I tread on sacred TA ground. Frankly, I have real problems with a good deal of script analysis, but at the core of the concept I believe there are some tantalizing ideas which may lead to behaviorally active therapist behavior.

Essentially, the script is a culmination of the outcomes of all of the games people play. In that sense, it is a broader categorization than the game and represents an even longer chain of behavior. Each game becomes a part of this massive pattern, resulting in a final payoff, ultimately reinforcing the whole very complex and elongated chain of events. TA uses the script to explain that people are ultimately out to prove something about themselves and their lives. As children we learn to accept basic script messages about ourselves and how our lives will be. These messages include, as you will recall, such statements as, "I will be a failure," "I am no good," "People will let you down." The games are used as the means by which the script prophecies are fulfilled, often taking many years before this happens.

It is obvious that humans are complex enough to develop patterns of behavior that repeat over relatively long periods of time. The question we must address, both clinically and empirically, is how long can a chain get and still be subject to modification in therapy? Clearly, the longer the chain the more difficult to establish a connection between intervention and outcome, the longer time allowing for much more contamination of experimental variables.

Some years ago I was consulting with a school for pregnant teenagers. It was the collective judgment of the professionals involved that many of these girls got pregnant as a way to act out anger toward their parents. As a behaviorist I had nightmares about assessing and treating the problem at that level, but I noticed that TA had no difficulty with such a broad contingency. Was it possible, I wondered, for adolescent sexual activity to be reinforced by negative attention, thus creating a clear message to the child about what would get a parent's goat? Furthermore, when I thought about the time it took for conception to occur, the nine months of pregnancy, and all the potential reinforcing family disruption that occurred along the way before and after the delivery of the baby, it became clearer to me why some of these young girls got pregnant more than once—not to mention all of the state and federal welfare benefits. Thus what I was faced with was the development of about a one-year chain of behaviors, intermittently reinforced along the way, culminating in a final and very tangible reinforcer at the end of the chain.

Then I began thinking about some of my clients who seemed to repeat patterns of behavior over many years, such as the man who during ten years' time had held more than twenty jobs and had entered therapy because he was depressed and tired of being unable to settle down. Think of how much energy went into finding jobs and then working to fail at them. Or the clients who went from one unsuccessful relationship to the next. Was it possible that there was some long-term reinforcer that fueled those smaller yet still fairly long chains of behavior?

TA suggests that indeed this is the case. It is the script message, specifically delivered by the self and from people in important relationships, that is the final consequence people are working so hard and long to achieve. For instance, if a person believes his heterosexual relationships will fail, and has been taught in childhood how to make them fail, he could spend a lifetime proving that projection along with reaffirming a negative self-image. The obvious problem with this analysis is the difficulty in demonstrating the cause-and-effect relationship of such messages. TA tries to save its bacon in this regard by not imposing these messages on clients but listening for them as transactions and games are observed and then supporting clients in finding their historical referents. Still, it's a sticky issue to tackle behaviorally.

What I like about the script concept is that it suggests very long chains with relatively concrete final reinforcers. People do appear to repeat long-term patterns of behavior. As behavioral scientists we must struggle with an empirically testable hypothesis to explain how such chains get conditioned and reinforced over so long a time. While TA's script analysis is intriguing and certainly offers important directions for research and practice, I can only assign tentative behavioral activity to its use. I feel the same about script analysis as I felt about the projection in Gestalt. I like the concepts personally and utilize them in my practice. However, in all honesty, both are based on so many assumptions that are impossible to currently empirically demonstrate that we must use them carefully. Frankly, what may be the most operational factor in what success I and others have had in performing script analyses is that clients have adopted this therapeutic belief system with its own internal logic. Script analysis is not an illogical concept and it fits very nicely within the general TA belief system. At worst I feel it does no harm; at best it may represent a logical extension of the behavior chain phenomenon.

Where I draw the line is in utilizing the TA life positions (I'm O.K., You're O.K., and so on), or when the script is described too generally, such as a winning or losing script. In both cases the terms are so general that they completely lose any chance for behavioral objectivity. At least a particular script message is relatively clear. Life positions and general script labels are so subjective that I believe it cannot be demonstrated they have any direct therapeutic value.

Redecision

According to TA there comes a time in the therapeutic process when clients make a basic redecision to stop playing games and change their scripts. Furthermore, this redecision resides in the Child ego state. Clients obviously make important decisions in therapy and life. TA suggests that along with the usual decision-making process, there is a crucial turning point in therapy, implying that from there on we should be able to observe a significant change in motivation and the rate of behavior change.

It is an interesting idea involving the concepts of resistance and motivation, and involves TA's approach to contracting. Many therapists have a sense that there is a turning point in therapy. I believe what they are perceiving is the culmination of a shaping process that finally begins to increase the frequency of those verbal and overt behaviors therapists wish to see. Since TA is after major life changes along with resolution of presenting problems, it has identified what it considers an important milestone in therapy as the point where the Child refuses to follow the script message anymore. This apparent breakthrough is at least observable, occurring either in discussion or in the double chair. Perhaps it is important to think there is some point where things turn around. I know that I often find satisfaction when I subjectively judge my clients have made important breakthroughs. It would be interesting to monitor whether there were any differences in the rate of dependent variable change before and after a clear client repudiation of a script message. There would be many methodological problems to overcome in such an investigation, but the attempts might be informative.

In any case, the TA redecision stage brings to the foreground the behaviorally active concepts of *motivation* and *resistance*. There is essentially no difference between the behavioral and TA definition of motivation. Both assume that motivation is best described as a state of deprivation for stroke reinforcers, reaffirming the interaction between us and our environment. As mentioned before, TA does emphasize the deprivation of attentional reinforcers, whereas the behavioral approach considers all reinforcing stimuli. But conceptually the similarities outweigh these differences.

As in Gestalt, TA has defined resistance as saying no, but within its unique PAC framework. It is the Child saying to the Parent, "I won't." In a more general sense, the resistance is founded on contingencies using antecedent parental injunction cues and such script messages as, "You are not able to change." The TA model of discriminating Parent-Adult-Child response classes allows for the contingencies controlling resistance behavior to be dealt with fairly systematically. Clients can often relate to the metaphor of a child refusing to move, since it is a familiar scene to most of us. As we have seen before, this PAC imagery can be very helpful in conceptualizing and confronting the contingencies controlling our inability to perform as desired.

The TA use of the contract is pervasive throughout the treatment process. While not as specifically laid out as in Behavior Therapy, it is nonetheless used effectively and with great frequency. There are contracts for attendance, paying fees, behavior during the treatment session, and for homework assignments each week. There is a real attempt to make the contracted behaviors reasonable and possible, taking into account the skill levels of each client. One of the ways TA therapists do this is to insist that clients contract for behavior without qualifications. Therapists will help clients who say, "I will try," make a contract to which they can say, "I will." Contract failures are systematically dealt with so clients can feel good about what they have learned rather than putting themselves down. Covert self-depreciating dialogues about not meeting contract expectations can be behaviorally specified and modified by overtly reenacting this Critical Parent-Child dialogue.

I am not so impressed with the behavioral activity of a redecision contract as I am with the pervasiveness of contracting throughout TA treatment in general. Regardless of how systematically behavior is monitored and shaped, there is ongoing support for forward movement and some degree of accountability as well. In my view, redecision behavior is one of many possible important successive approximations along the road to reaching treatment goals.

Working Toward the Cure

At the intervention stage TA becomes very behaviorally active. Since TA is conceptually well founded in the Laws of Behavior it should increase the probability that the actual treatment techniques will follow suit. And indeed they do.

However, before analyzing therapist intervention behavior, we must dispense with the concept of the *cure*. I have big problems with the cure. It is supposed to occur when clients have decided to abandon their scripts, have the ability to interact game free, occupy the I'm O.K.-You're O.K. life position, and be able to handle their future problems while still feeling good about themselves. Attaining the cure is surely such an idealistic goal; I do not believe any person has ever achieved it. In my opinion, it is misleading and unnecessary. I have seen many clients who, after terminating therapy with the cure, have later returned for more therapy, feeling "not O.K." Were these cases necessarily examples of therapy failure? I think not. Ending therapy with this kind of dependent variable is too simplistic for the kinds of realities that people face in the long run of their lives. Since any kind of behavioral definition of a cure is extremely vague at best, I believe it is more functional to primarily discuss whether presenting problems have been successfully dealt with at the end of therapy. To try to make the success or failure of therapy dependent upon what happens one, two, five, or ten years from termination is unfair not only to any theoretical and practice foundation but to the client as well.

It is impossible for TA and its clients to expect that all new situations can be successfully dealt with based upon what was learned in a therapy experience. Life has a way of presenting extraordinary kinds of stimulus situations so complex there is no way we could be prepared for all of them and still feel good about ourselves. With economic recessions and booms, the ever-present threat of nuclear annihilation, the rapidly changing stability of the primary family, the explosion of knowledge, and just normal crises, it is unlikely that anyone could face all of life's experiences without serious frustration, depression, and periods of real helplessness, therapy or no therapy. But most important, the success of therapy cannot be dependent on variables too far removed in time from the experience itself. As behavioral scientists, we are currently having enough trouble establishing that therapy has any short-term effect beyond placebo and magic. Let us spare ourselves the further burden of making therapy success dependent on events possibly years from termination.

We have already discussed some of the behaviorally active techniques used in TA, particularly in relation to assessment. The double chair, so helpful in the behavioral reenactment of controlling conditions, is also used for behavioral rehearsal and behavior modification. Once a game has been clarified, it is subject to the behavioral chain rules and TA therapists apply them effectively, even if they are not aware of them from the behavioral approach. First, clients are taught to refuse to accept the strokes ending their games. The double chair is an excellent place to practice this extinction behavior, and of course here-and-now interactions provide the same assertive training opportunity. Next, therapists work with clients to find game "stoppers," removing the antecedents that start the chain rolling, Therapists teach clients to be aware of the cues starting games and to perform alternative behaviors. Parental injunctions also are viewed as part of the chain's discriminative stimuli. Helping clients assert themselves while refusing to follow these rules acts as another important stimulus-control technique. Differential reinforcement is used extensively as clients are encouraged to practice working for positive strokes as games are extinguished. You may refer back to the previous TA chapter for examples of how this is done.

TA's unique PAC model provides a behavioral rationale for using rehearsals in the present, past, overt, or covert domains just as in Gestalt, but with a more systematic structure. For example, on the double chair, clients could practice extinguishing the Kick Me game by confronting an actual parent from their past, the symbolic covert Critical Parent response class within themselves, a critical person in their present environment, or if the opportunity presents itself, a here-and-now person in a therapy group—very flexible. Using the same options, alternative behaviors receiving positive stroke reinforcers could also be practiced. Clients could put supportive figures from their past on the other chair to rehearse receiving positive strokes for desired behavior; a covert Nurturing Parent symbol and of course present interactions could do the job as well.

TA therapists also consistently remind clients to modify the way they use language as another support for extinguishing games and learning alternative behaviors.

There are certain Critical Parent words that clients are reminded to avoid. They include *should, must, ought to,* and *have to*. Clients are taught to substitute the word *want* for all these cases. Thus, "you should" becames the statement, "I want you to. . . ." Certain Child phrases are also modified. "I can't" becomes "I won't." This systematic semantic substitution has the remarkable effect of extinguishing parental injunctions, one of the important stimulus controls of games. Perhaps the unmeasurable qualities of this and other TA experiences is clients' realizing that they do not have to follow the rules of childhood or continue working for negative strokes. In any case, the systematic modification of language in therapy is one area that deserves continued empirical attention.

Assertive Training in TA

While many of the techniques we have already discussed have behavioral activity in their own right, I believe that TA ultimately combines them into a unique and effective assertive training procedure. TA integrates Gestalt techniques with the PAC model to personify the past and present in covert and overt dynamic interactions. As we have mentioned, while this personification of symbols is similar to Gestalt, it significantly differs by ending up with structured dialogues between Parent, Adult, and Child response classes. Since these symbols are uniform and familiar, it is somewhat easier to identify how PAC dynamics allow for teaching saying no (or yes), making requests and demands, and the expression of negative and positive feelings. The model is especially helpful in developing these skills with contingencies from the past, using covert behavior and symbols. In this area I believe that TA makes a significant contribution to a behaviorally active practice.

By the very nature of the PAC model with its games, stroking patterns, and payoffs, it becomes clear that assertive skills will be needed to stop the game playing and substitute more appropriate behavior. The ability to express negative feelings often is the beginning of an assertive process to decrease game-playing behavior. Many people also need to learn how to express positive feelings and give "warm fuzzy" strokes, especially to the self. Clients learn to say no to the parental injunctions cuing games as well as to accepting the strokes at the end of them. This often takes the form of learning to make requests and firm demands on those who have been involved in client games. For example, a client could learn to reply to the parental injunction, "You should not cry," with, "Yes, I want to." To those who wish to continue to play games, clients learn to say, "I will not participate and if you wish to maintain a relationship with me I request [or demand] that you tell me what you want and feel."

These same assertive skills can be learned to refuse to accept the negative strokes and messages we covertly give ourselves, and to more effectively give ourselves support. Remember, the Parent-Adult-Child framework is applicable for structuring cognitive as well as overt behavior. Therefore, there is no reason we can't take a problematic way we depreciate ourselves, personify it into the PAC dynamic, and learn to assert ourselves against the Critical Parent response class and express positive and supportive strokes to the Hurting Child.

In the same way, assertive skills can be learned by dealing with people from the past when reenacting games. I, and many TA therapists, have seen clients finally learn to effectively assert themselves in reenactments with past mother or father figures and then apply these skills to parent figures in their present. Similarly, clients have been able to recreate themselves as children, learn to become more effective Nurturing Parents in this child recreation, and again apply all of the supportive and protective assertive skills they learned to themselves in the present.

Since most clients normally conceptualize such assertive behaviors as saying no and making requests to the people who are part of their lives, TA offers an assertive training model that takes advantage of familiar territory. It ultimately boils down to an empirical question of behavioral generalization. I believe people can more easily generalize the learning of assertive skills when the therapeutic symbols used are familiar to the client. Thus, comparing the actual assertive behaviors learned between a symbolic green blob of a feeling, such as in Gestalt, and a Critical Parent, as in TA, I would hypothesize that the assertions learned using a parent figure would generalize more efficiently. It would follow, then, that dealing with the actual people who are part of the problem would be the most effective strategy of all. It is not always possible, of course, to reach everyone involved in problem situations. Additionally, it may be that symbols of any kind have value as approximations to the more potentially threatening stimuli occurring in a client's present interactions. Research could be designed to begin addressing these interesting questions.

Acceptance Training in TA

The reduction of tension in TA therapy obviously occurs, but there is not a systematic model for teaching muscle relaxation. Normal interactional behaviors are used to help people reduce tension, such as physical contact, empathy, active listening, and other support. There is nothing in TA theory that would be hostile to integrating relaxation training techniques into its therapy, and I am sure there are a number of TA therapists who use it since TA and Behavior Therapy have much conceptual compatibility. Certainly, it would enhance the therapy's effectiveness to be able to teach clients' Nurturing Parents such a helpful way for them to further take care of their anxious Children.

Teaching people in TA therapy to cognitively accept the things they cannot change occurs conceptually about the same as it did in Gestalt. Clients are guided into acknowledging their inability to manipulate situations and people, the grief process supported, and then plans made to make sure that the frustrating repeat-attempt chains of behavior are extinguished. However, as we have seen before, a combination of Gestalt techniques, the PAC dynamic structure, and TA's unique labeling system make the process relatively systematic.

TA defines nonfunctional repeat-attempt chains of behavior as a game, with the Child continuously railing against an intractable Parent who refuses to comply with the Child's demands. This dynamic, also called the *endless dialogue*, is maintained by the strokes exchanged in these game transactions, including Kick Me or NIGYYSOB. The frustrating "endless dialogue" is directly maintained, then, by the strokes (reinforcers) the Child receives from the Parent in a game (chain of behaviors). In addition, TA labels these nonfunctional attempts to change things as "rackets," the signal being a recurring negative feeling that does not functionally lead to problem solving.

In practice, when it becomes evident to the therapist that the client is performing an endless dialogue, the game these transactions represent is identified. Using heightening techniques and the double chair similar to Gestalt, the Parent in another person and symbolically in the client eventually makes it clear that there is no way the Child's demands will be met. For example, the therapist could request the Parent to say something like, "You have been trying to get something from me for years and you can keep on trying. It won't do you any good. In fact, I kind of like that you keep coming back for more."

TA guides the client into extinguishing the strokes for endless-dialogue games by directing the client away from transactions with the Critical Parent, often to the vulnerable Child of the Parent. This Child-Child transaction in the context of the grief process culminates in the client's removing the negative strokes maintaining the game. The final approximations in the shaping of acceptance and muscle relaxation are reached as the client's frustrating endless-dialogue game is extinguished and new game-free patterns are positively stroked.

One can get lost, at times, in the dynamics of the Parent-Adult-Child metaphors, but essentially TA's approach to accepting one's sometimes limited ability to manipulate the environment is behaviorally active. Nonfunctional repeat-attempt behavior is extinguished, including the muscle tension associated with frustration; new chains that include relaxation are reinforced.

CONCLUSIONS

In its own rather colloquial way, TA strongly supports the Laws of Operant Behavior. While the payoff may be a bit less behaviorally specific than would be desirable, it still reaffirms the ultimate power of the consequence in predicting the future of a behavior. Other than positive reinforcement, the delineation of different kinds of consequences controlling operant responses is not dealt with in TA, which limits its theoretical and practice breadth to some extent. In addition, there is not a clear place for integrating respondent conditioning into the PAC framework, TA being essentially an operant model of therapy.

Like Gestalt, TA is a "kitchen sink" therapy. You come in for a faucet and end up buying the kitchen sink. If clients terminate before becoming script free, the assumption is that therapy will likely be a temporary Band-Aid for a much larger sore. The question of how much clients need to do and learn to be reasonably ready for therapy termination in terms of those broader behaviors we call *personality changes* or *script redecisions* is light-years from being established empirically. We will just have to continue to use our own best subjective judgments. It is clear, though, that it is very difficult to determine the success of therapy with preconceived theoretical dictates. Therefore, beyond the obvious need to establish some desired change in a therapeutic dependent variable, let us not judge one another harshly if clients terminate without the proverbial kitchen sink, or in TA's case, the script-free "cure."

In the context of what TA does have to offer, there is the potential for integrating some exciting behaviorally active techniques into one's clinical practice. Its attempt to codify chains of behavior; the interesting Parent-Adult-Child response class transaction dynamic; the unique way cognitive and past symbols can be personified into the PAC model for assessment and intervention; its structured model for overt and covert assertive training; and TA's attempt to develop a comprehensive psychology more easily assimilated by its client population—all of these highlight some of what I believe TA has to offer the therapist interested in a behaviorally active practice. TA therapists generally are very concerned with defining what clients do in behaviorally specific terms. This concern, coupled with practice techniques that often utilize the Laws of Operant Behavior, is what gives TA its behaviorally active power and, in my opinion, what makes this therapy as effective as it is.

CHAPTER EIGHT
EGO PSYCHOLOGY
A Behavioral Analysis

INTRODUCTION

Making a behavioral analysis of Ego Psychology is a potentially mammoth task. I could spend the whole book discussing the similarities and differences between the two, and still be left unfinished. What will make the endeavor possible is my approach of separating theory from practice as much as possible. By essentially circumventing and deemphasizing an analysis of the mass that is Freudian theory, I can concentrate my energies on assessing behavioral activity in the actual practice of Ego Psychology. In so doing, I have established the boundaries of a task that can be reasonably accomplished.

I am going to be rather hard on the theory supporting Ego Psychology. From such a massive and comprehensive practice theory we should expect an equally well designed treatment technology. Such is not the case. Of the four major therapies discussed in this book, the guidelines for actual therapist behavior are the least behaviorally specific in Ego Psychology. What is generated from the theory base are general directions for therapists to follow which get translated into diverse clinical behavior. From an empirical point of view, the ability to replicate treatment techniques and procedures becomes extremely difficult.

Still, we will find that much of what Ego Psychology therapists purport to do has some basis in the Behavioral Laws and thus impacts on the antecedents and consequences that control human behavior. And we will find that in its own way, the practice of clinical Ego Psychology has a model for the behavioral reenactment of the past and present so that the contingencies of reinforcement controlling problem behavior can be assessed and new behaviors practiced.

THE TREATMENT PROCESS

The Ego Psychology treatment process was more a summary of therapeutic events, not necessarily occurring in sequential order. These events were:

1. Assessment
2. Ego Strengthening
3. Insight
4. The Corrective Emotional Experience
5. The Transference

As before, we shall proceed through the treatment process looking for behavioral activity, discussing theoretical issues as necessary.

Assessment

We must give some attention to Freudian theory at this point since it is the foundation used for assessing the conditions controlling problem behavior in Ego Psychology practice. So as not to dwell too long in theory, I shall look briefly at only the basic theoretical constructs, emphasizing those which may lead to behaviorally active assessment and practice techniques.

The Ego States.   The center of Ego Psychology starts with the ego, Id, and the superego. Unfortunately, with the way they are described, it is very difficult to find behavioral activity in these concepts. The model as a theoretical construct suggests a totally covert phenomenon, parts of which are never available to conscious awareness. While it might be possible to behaviorally specify what controls our use of the term *ego*, and to a somewhat more limited extent of the term *superego*, there are no reliable behavioral referents for the Id. I laid the groundwork in chapter 6 for the consideration of behavioral activity for unconscious covert responses; I never had any intention of promoting an independent variable that could never be reliably connected with measurable behavior except through inference. Such is the problem when faced with the concept of the Id—a covert instinctual drive, sexual and aggressive in nature, most of which can never be tied to measurable behavior except through interpretation. While it may be possible or even likely that sexual states of deprivation are important in many patterns of behavior, and that deprivation is also associated with anger, I do not find these two "drives" inclusive enough to reasonably explain the basic causes of most common behavior problems.

However, as a behavioral scientist, the central issue that stops me from seriously considering what is, I believe, a rather elegant and intellectually stimulating theoretical construct, is how resistant the ego states are to the behavioral specificity necessary for good empirical examination. In rank order, the Id is most difficult, the superego next, and the ego the easiest of the behaviorally nonspecific lot. Perhaps this is why Ego Psychology developed out of psychoanalysis. At least there is some hope for specifying what therapists observe when the emphasis of treatment is on the ego. Thus, while we may enjoy theorizing about the dynamics between the three ego states for problem behavior, I believe only the construct of the ego has potential for leading to behaviorally active practice. The superego may also fall into this category to the extent that we discuss how rules, attitudes, and values control what we do. I know I commit heresy, but I do not believe it can be demonstrated that the construct of the Id leads to meaningful behaviorally active treatment.

The Defense Mechanism. With a little conceptual manipulation, it is possible to conceive of the defense mechanisms as labels for generalized chains of behavior, similar to TA's games and Gestalt's resistances to contact. Ego Psychology theorists might have problems with this analysis since the defense mechanisms are generally supposed to be unconscious mental mechanisms, the dynamic process protecting the ego from Id impulses. Be that as it may, I contend that therapists who identify defense mechanisms always make that interpretation based on observable behavior. Therefore, what they must be seeing or hearing is some response pattern which cues one of the defense mechanism labels. How therapists theoretically play with mental mechanisms after they are identified may certainly be interesting, but I think not essential to the technology of treatment. As we have seen before, regardless of the source of the concept, labeling chains of behavior can become part of a behaviorally active treatment process. Let's look at some of these defense mechanisms and examine what behavior chains they could represent.

Displacement was defined as the reattachment of a feeling from one object or person to another, an example being when you kick your dog instead of your spouse. It is easy to hypothesize how this pattern could be conditioned, and not unreasonable to suggest that this chain is a common one. The contingency would be conditioned similarly to a retroflective resistance with overt instead of covert aggressive behavior reinforced. In fact, there is a phenomenon in operant punishment that strongly supports the validity of a displacement contingency. One of the possible side effects of being exposed to aversive stimuli is aggressive behavior. Two response classes have been identified: operant aggression and elicited aggression. An organism may attack the source of an aversive stimulus, supposedly trying to make it stop—this is operant aggression. When the subject is aggressive toward objects that have nothing to do with the delivery of the aversive stimuli, it is called *elicited aggression*, such as a rat attacking a rubber toy in its cage instead of the researcher, or a person kicking a dog instead of a spouse.

We have already gone through chain analyses that would be roughly analogous to the *introjection* and *projection* defense mechanisms. In addition, one of the most important defense mechanisms, *repression*, could be viewed using a behavioral analysis of the unconscious, the negative reinforcement of covert responses. As long as you stay with what measurable behaviors are used to control the use of the defense mechanism terms, then it is possible and intellectually challenging to specify the chains of behavior they represent.

I could go through the exercise of behaviorally specifying more chains that the defense mechanisms may represent. It wouldn't be difficult since *denial* and *isolation,* all have fairly obvious referents in analyses we have already done in Gestalt and TA. In addition, the possible contingencies represented in *provocative behavior* are easily worked out using the behavioral training you have already had. I invite you to indulge in these exercises; it will be good practice.

One of the reasons I do not have as much interest in the defense mechanisms as labels for patterns of behavior is that they are not really integrated into the Ego Psychology treatment technology. Thus their behavioral activity is limited. Defense mechanisms may not even be shared with clients since they are usually unconsciously protecting the ego; even when they are identified, the practice of Ego Psychology does not in any way systematically apply the behavior chain rules to extinguish these chains. The concept of labeling generalized behavior patterns was behaviorally active in Gestalt and TA because it lead to relatively systematic therapist attempts to break these response chains. Such is not the case in Ego Psychology. When defense mechanisms are shared with clients, any behavioral activity comes primarily from what they do with that insight. Depending on the client, this can be of considerable significance. But since there may be much variability in how defense mechanisms are identified and utilized with clients, and very little predictability whether particular clients can use that insight, I do not believe that the identification of defense mechanisms adds much to a behaviorally active practice when used in the context of Ego Psychology.

Personality Development.   As part of the assessment process, therapists using Ego Psychology attempt to identify the stage of development where significant fixations have occurred. The oral, anal, Oedipal, latency, and adolescent stages of personality development each represented important problems to be solved for satisfactory social functioning as an adult. You will notice that of the major therapies described in this book, only Ego Psychology attempts to systematically integrate historical stages of development with contemporary client problems. In addition, there is an honest effort to tie the therapeutic process to the behavioral deficits connected with whatever developmental fixations have been identified.

Regardless of how successful Ego Psychology has been with this integration, we should seriously consider the general hypothesis connecting present problems with a systematic assessment of developmental stages. Furthermore, even if we do not like some or all of the Freudian labels used in this hypothesis, it is worthy of our consideration since there is essentially no competition. That mastering important developmental tasks is part of psychological development, there can be no question. The impact of not learning these tasks sufficiently well will of course be felt in adult life and likely be related to problem behavior. In order for a developmental psychology to be systematically tied to present client behavior in a way that supports problem resolution, at least three conditions would need to be satisfied for reasonable empirical investigation:

1. The kinds of problems to be resolved at each stage of development would need to be behaviorally specified;
2. There would need to be at least some minimal agreement among behavioral scientists concerning what these stages are;
3. Treatment techniques for each unresolved developmental problem area would need to be carefully specified so that therapist behavior could be replicated.

Clearly Ego Psychology does not come close to fulfilling all three of these conditions. The descriptions of the problems to be resolved at each stage are too general and nonspecific; the agreement concerning the stages of personality development is still too general; and identified fixations result only in vague and general treatment guidelines for therapists to follow. Yet, for all its problems, we can learn a great deal from Ego Psychology's lonely attempt to tie these important issues together.

Looking beyond the labels Freud put on developmental stages, we can see a variety of important themes emerging that obviously relate to therapy: dependence-independence issues; the ability to love; reciprocity in relationships; our response to limits and controls; sexual identification; competition and cooperation; the identification of our own values and attitudes. If through an assessment process therapists can identify themes that clients agree relate to their presenting problems, then a theory that guides such therapist behavior might have some utility. The value of such labeling would heavily depend on how themes further directed therapists to help clients resolve problems.

During assessment client behavior cues one of these developmental themes for therapists which they then relate to a fixation in childhood. The client as a child was not taught the necessary skills to resolve an important developmental problem or was taught nonfunctional skills. If this were the case, it would certainly become clearer what kinds of new skills clients need to learn in therapy. At the very least, it would suggest what kind of experiential dynamics in the past could be reenacted for subsequent modification of behavior in the present. To the extent this theme development and goal setting is reasonably behaviorally specific and leads to any systematic therapeutic interventions, we might be able to attribute some behavioral activity to the process.

Even though the clarification of goal behaviors in Ego Psychology is rather general, and the interventions to learn the new skills suggested by personality development themes somewhat unsystematic and vague, I believe that we can make a case for some behavioral activity in this aspect of the Ego Psychology assessment process. Identifying the theme of behavioral deficits and suggesting the goals for new skill learning probably guides therapists and some clients to eventually figuring out what specific behaviors need to be learned. We shall see that there is enough behavioral activity in Ego Psychology's four major intervention techniques to make the specifying of such skill deficits useful, to the extent that it occurs.

I have not made a strong case for the behavioral activity in using Ego Psychological personality development theory in the assessment process. But I believe I have suggested enough possibilities that we should continue considering how a systematic approach to developmental psychology could be integrated into a therapeutic process, at least for assessment, to enhance an efficient behaviorally active practice.

Ego Strengthening

When therapists work to strengthen the ego, they are trying to make it more able to handle Id impulses without using debilitating defense mechanisms, thereby freeing psychic energy to use for problem solving. However, I have suggested that the Laws of Behavior will not generally support the Id-ego-superego theoretical construct. On the other hand, I believe I can reasonably establish that *therapist behavior* in relation to ego strengthening follows the Behavioral Laws to some degree, along with insight, the Corrective Emotional Experience, and the transference.

When therapists work to strengthen egos they are obviously looking for the performance of behaviors that control their use of that term. While some of these desired behaviors are idiosyncratic to particular therapists, they usually conform to one or more of the following response classes: the ability to verbalize positive comments about oneself; the ability to take responsibility for one's own behavior; the ability to express positive and negative feelings; the ability to make requests and demands; the ability to say no; the ability to make a reasonable problem-solving plan of action; and the ability to make self-disclosure. And of course if symptomatology decreases, there is the reified inference that ego strengths are increasing. Ego Psychology therapists work to achieve these behavioral goals by helping clients partialize problems, making statements of support, being empathetic, asking directed questions, and active listening, which inclues restating and eye contact. What all of these therapist behaviors boil down to is helping clients define successive approximations to one of the ego strength response classes, and then reinforcing these approximations with whatever interpersonal means are at their disposal. To the extent that this occurs, these therapist behaviors are obviously behaviorally active. The question becomes, however, the efficiency with which behavioral goals are defined, approximations made, and reinforcers utilized.

When the ego-strengthening process is viewed in this light, it may seem pretty inefficient, basically because Ego Psychology therapists generally do not like to suggest to clients what to do. As in Gestalt, therapists are wanting clients to be able to come up with problem resolutions on their own. With this end in mind, it is not likely that the defining of behavioral goals, approximations, and systematic reinforcement plans will be explicated as in Behavior Therapy. Ego Psychology is after bigger game, similar in this respect to Gestalt and TA: the ability for clients to face larger life issues and learn to take responsibility for solving their own problems. Thus, we must ask what structure or systematic set of therapy rules is developed to support clients as they struggle in learning to resolve their own problems.

Essentially the structure and guidelines to support clients in this task are as general and vague as the treatment guidelines for therapists and may represent Ego

Psychology's greatest practice problem. While Gestalt and TA also dictate some non-directive behavior for therapists, they also teach clients a reasonably specific problem-solving method. There is some systematic structure supporting the therapist's request that clients come up with their own answers. Ego Psychology, on the other hand, offers clients much less of this kind of support. What Ego Psychology does offer is a supportive, accepting atmosphere where clients can feel the freedom to be themselves away from the pressures in their environment. While this kind of haven is of course helpful, and perhaps even necessary to successful treatment outcome, I do not believe it is followed up with as systematic a learning process for clients as would be desirable to most efficiently reach the broad goals of Ego Psychology therapy. Thus, when viewed from a behavioral perspective, ego strengthening incurs two basic problems: 1) the specification of goals, approximations, and reinforcement plans are too general and behaviorally nonspecific; and 2) there is not a systematic enough problem-solving process taught to help clients resolve problems for themselves, and possibly, to further integrate their resolutions into broader life issues. This is the first time in our analysis that we have encountered a therapy that has not attempted to systematically direct its practice behavior to at least one or the other of these important therapeutic components.

To the extent that Ego Psychology therapists are directive with clients, they can be very effective. Helping clients partialize their problems by asking directed questions and giving opinions is an excellent way to make short-term goal statements and take advantage of a client's present skill levels. Partialization could even be conceived as developing approximations in a broader shaping plan. And when therapists observe or are told by their clients about a behavior approximating one of the response classes of a strengthened ego, they usually attempt to verbally and nonverbally reinforce it with all the means at their disposal. In fact, because the practice of Ego Psychology is so dependent on the "curative" elements of the therapist-client relationship, therapists are well motivated to develop effective interpersonal reinforcement skills. It would not surprise me to discover empirically that therapists of this persuasion generally demonstrate the most effective strategies in this regard. For example, I have observed Ego Psychology therapists intuitively and systematically structure interpersonal deprivation into the therapist-client relationship using silence. This tack could increase the power of the therapist to interpersonally reinforce desired behavior. In addition, their ability to give attention and differentially reinforce selected response classes through such behaviors as restatement and eye contact is often outstanding. While obviously many therapists acquire these skills, I believe the structure of Ego Psychology practice better encourages the development of interpersonal reinforcement strategies, since so much of the therapy centers around the relationship. This represents a potent force in helping people to change. The personal power of therapists to reinforce and extinguish client behavior, at least in the therapy setting, is of critical importance, and probably central to therapist effectiveness regardless of theoretical orientation.

One other area of ego strengthening needs to be highlighted. Therapists of all persuasions probably try to support clients when they verbalize positive things about themselves and what they do. To Ego Psychology therapists this response class is also important. It represents a covert reinforcement support system that not only helps clients feel better about themselves but allows people to be more independent of the inconsistent mediators of reinforcement in their environment. Since therapists using Ego Psychology theory do not normally deal outside the dynamics of the treatment setting in systematic attempts to actively manipulate the environment, developing clients' covert reinforcement skills is very important. Of course in some cases an "avalanche" or "snowball" effect in the client's life will immediately support a developing behavior pattern. However, any therapy that does not practically or theoretically deal directly wiith environmental systems reinforcing client problem behavior is especially dependent on the power of self-reinforcement, including covert reinforcement. People dealing with relationships that are not easily manipulated, or are even relatively hostile, will need all of the therapist and self-support they can get. While the ability to make positive statements about oneself is not conceptualized as a covert reinforcement skill in Ego Psychology, I believe that the generalization of whatever is learned in treatment is particularly dependent on clients' being able to reinforce themselves, whether it is called ego strengthening or something else.

Insight

The behaviors called *insight* are certainly pervasive. It is a "connecting" experience, bringing past and present awareness to the foreground in efforts to understand and solve problems. Behaviorally, it can be defined as the ability to identify the contingencies controlling our behavior, the antecedents and consequential stimuli.

The approach to gaining insight in the practice of Ego Psychology is often part of a larger shaping procedure which includes the Corrective Emotional Experience as one terminal goal. Insight behavior in this context is often shaped by therapists reinforcing clients for remembering and talking about early-childhood experiences and then relating them to present-day behavior. Since it is my contention that the contingencies controlling current behavior are essentially similar to those occurring in the past, this method for developing insight could be reasonably effective in assessing current controlling conditions.

To the extent that the development of insight leads to some change in behavior, it is certainly behaviorally active. But insight has not been empirically established as a necessary precursor to change. Indeed, the behavioral approach has demonstrated that people can significantly alter their behavior patterns without any historical insight at all. This is particularly true of seriously retarded and psychotic individuals. However, if we consider my behavioral definition of insight and do not insist on the necessity of going back into history, I think everyone would agree that all therapies attempt to help people assess the conditions controlling their behavior before intervention. At the very least this skill is necessary if clients on their own are to be able to effectively deal with new problems cropping up after therapy termination. A behaviorist would probably believe that it is more efficient to discover the contingencies affecting problem behavior by looking at present situations instead of going into the past. I am not so sure. I think that by this time in our analysis of four therapies, we should be open to considering assessment data from historical relationships and experiences as well.

It is difficult to analyze insight solely as a technique of intervention. In chapter 4 describing Ego Psychology, I suggested with my example of a little boy and a hooting owl that insight might be directly connected to the reduction of anxiety as a dependent variable. If this could be systematically demonstrated, it would certainly be a behaviorally active intervention technique. And there are many clients who, after gaining insight, have the skills to successfully manipulate their environment without any further therapy. In these situations, too, one could make a case for behavioral activity. However, most therapists have had many experiences with the type of client who is full of insight but does nothing further with it. In fact, one of the common characteristics of neurosis is just this behavior pattern: the suffering client who can tell you exactly what his or her problem is and why, but is apparently unable to do anything about it. "Professional clients," the ones who go from therapist to therapist over the years, are particularly good at this game.

Therefore, in conclusion, I feel very comfortable in assigning behavioral activity to insight as an assessment technique helping clients identify controlling conditions. It is not clear whether achieving insight has any direct effect on behavior change. It may have an anxiety-reduction effect; there are some people who apparently can use insight immediately with no further therapist intervention. Until we can be more definitive as to the effects of insight, I will have to leave its behavioral activity as intervention in the questionable category.

The Corrective Emotional Experience

By this point, the phenomenon called the *Corrective Emotional Experience*— the CEE from now on—should be familiar territory. It has classical links to Gestalt's unfinished business and TA's moments of redecision and could easily be considered the grandparent of both concepts. In its purest form the CEE is a reexperiencing of an early-childhood scene that has apparently been suppressed. Through a shaping process, including the reinforcement of early memories, insight, and the possible use of a transference, the experiences locked in the past are literally reenacted, at least at the feeling level. There is often a burst of emotion, with clients reexperiencing thoughts and feelings repressed for many years. Ego Psychology theory explains the value of the CEE by postulating the release of needed psychic energy, since the ego is no longer having to use a debilitating defense mechanism to keep repressed feelings under control.

I believe what we are seeing here is another example of how the reenactment of historical contingencies allows for the development of new solutions to current problems. The actual scene where the CEE occurs is an important example of the behavior chains that were conditioned in the past and are active in the present.

Since there is often much energy and emotion connected with these early scenes, representing significant and current nonfunctional patterns of behavior, clients may become more aware of the deprivation states—feelings associated with heightening that experience. As I have suggested before, using early-childhood experiences is a viable way to assess current controlling conditions and develop effective strategies to break dysfunctional chains while conditioning new ones.

In the previous Gestalt and TA chapters I have already established the behavioral activity of such techniques, leading to historical reenactment for assessment and intervention. We need not go through that analysis a third time. However, there are some aspects of the CEE that need special attention. First, Freudian theory suggests that early experiences such as those finally confronted in the CEE are an especially significant part of what is controlling clients' present problems. I would rather view significant past events as symbolic of current and past dysfunctional chains of behavior. Consider, for example, a client who finally becomes aware of the time she was badly abused by her father at the age of five. All of the confusing feelings connected with that experience might surface: fear, anger, love, hate, hurt. Significantly, however, this scene would never have been repressed if there had not been a prior foundation of conditioning demanding that she not be allowed to express her feelings in ways that would functionally get the support she needed. Thus, since that support and protection were apparently not forthcoming at the time, the CEE likely represents the general contingencies reinforcing her acceptance of being hurt then, and probably, now.

Corrective Emotional Experiences do not just happen. They are the culmination of a treatment process which includes therapists reinforcing many behavioral approximations, and developing a supportive and protective professional relationship. While the end product is in essence no different from what we have seen in Gestalt and TA, there is far less structure for telling therapists and clients how to get there. The parameters of what is needed are clearly established in Ego Psychology—just not the particulars. For example, in order to support clients in reaching a meaningful CEE, therapists need to reinforce much more than the verbalizations of childhood memories. They need to concurrently work with clients on strengthening their egos, develop a supportive therapist-client relationship, and provide the atmosphere where clients can freely express what they feel. Without careful behavioral specification, it is not clear how therapists are supposed to behave in the context of all of these guidelines. But regardless of their lack of clarity, I believe these generalizations do encompass the basic parameters for designing behaviorally specific successive approximations of a shaping plan for reenacting past experiences. Many therapists, I believe, intuitively figure this out and thus reinforce client behavior accordingly. The process may not be efficient, but the end point is often reached, nonetheless.

One might suggest that Gestalt and TA took parts of this general map from Ego Psychology, conceptualized it a little differently, and developed more behaviorally specific technical guidelines for therapists to use. Thus, Gestalt discusses protection as the more specific setting of boundaries; the personification of symbols and the double chair make internal dialogues clearer; the concept of unfinished business systematically directs clients into dialogues with the past. TA also uses similar strategies with its PAC model. Both Gestalt and TA also have more specific and systematic techniques for helping clients develop those skills that are part of ego strengthening. Even the end product, the CEE, which finds its equivalent in both Gestalt and TA, is harder to describe behaviorally in Ego Psychology. The CEE itself is often a kind of one-way dialogue, perhaps best described as one half of a double chair. Clients sit in their chairs and talk emotionally to someone in their imagination, either overtly or covertly. Sometimes only the emotional behavior is initially visible and we may find out what covert imagery and dialogues occurred only after the client has calmed down. In Gestalt and TA, it is more common for there to be an observable reenactment of the experience using the double chair, role playing, or the personification of a symbol.

To suggest that Gestalt and TA are paragons of behavioral specificity and systematic practice compared to Ego Psychology is not exactly what I had in mind. All three need extensive work in this regard. Yet, the comparisons are instructive. Gestalt and TA were developed subsequent to Freudian theory. Let us hope psychotherapy is evolving into more clarity of practice and purpose.

While much therapist energy may be utilized in helping clients achieve a true Corrective Emotional Experience, it is by no means the end of the road. Clients may indeed achieve new awareness of their feelings and know what new behavior should follow. But whether or not they have learned those new skills is quite another matter. The actual CEE may represent the first time a new behavior is performed. It will need to be generalized to environmental relationships and receive continuous reinforcement if it is to be established. For example, a client may reach a CEE and for the first time ventilate repressed anger at a parent, subsequently taking a firm stand by establishing what he will and won't tolerate. It is one thing to do this under the protection of therapy; quite another to do it at home and work. Under whatever guise you wish to call it, approximations of these assertive skills will likely have to be made, practiced, and reinforced until a satisfactory terminal goal is reached.

For all of the lack of behavioral specificity and systematic guidance, Ego Psychology therapists do help clients reach CEEs and support their efforts at generalizing new behavior to the environment. I find the process the least easy to follow, the hardest to imagine empirically replicating, and the techniques the least behaviorally specific and systematic. Yet, to the extent that therapists are able to find their way to the CEE and beyond to supporting the development of new behavior chains in the environment, they are likely utilizing a process that is behaviorally active. They are differentially reinforcing and shaping client behavior toward a Corrective Emotional Experience and reinforcing the skills learned there to problem solve in the environment. The CEE itself is an opportunity to heighten and become aware of deprivation states (feelings), assess controlling conditions, and begin practicing the assertive skills essential for successfully manipulating the environment.

The Transference

Transferences are projections by clients onto their therapists, and as such, are not easily subject to a behavioral analysis. As you will recall, there was so much covert behavior occurring in a projection, some of it below the level of awareness, that we could not even rely on verbal report. Yet, I was able to develop a tentative model true to behavioral principles supporting the phenomenon leading to behaviorally active practice. Consider the transference as a specific response class of the broader projection experience. We will not, then, have to reestablish the behavioral foundation of the transference projection, and can instead spend our energies defining and assessing its behavioral activity.

While many therapists consider the transference pervasive in psychotherapy, the behaviors defining the term are like any other—they can be reinforced or extinguished. I believe a behavioral analysis of the phenomenon will suggest there is almost always a tendency for transferences to occur—a therapeutic operant level, if you will—that therapists reinforce or extinguish depending upon their point of view, practice style, and self-awareness.

When clients start therapy, they are putting themselves into a position that can mimic the reinforcement contingencies and behavior chains of childhood. They attribute power to the therapist to impact on them. This is one of the significant basic dynamics of childhood where children feel dependent on parents who are obviously more powerful mediators of reinforcers and punishers. In addition, clients may be initially behaving in ways that are compatible with reestablishing past parent-child dynamics. Depending on their conditioning histories, and how voluntary their therapy participation is, this could include any combination of being vulnerable, indecisive, helpless, anxious; or conversely, hostile, mistrustful, or withdrawn. Thus the initial therapy situation offers the structure to potentially reenact contingencies reminiscent of early parent-child interactions. The therapist takes the role of parent figure; the client's role is childlike.

The final ingredient determining whether transferences can occur involves the expectations clients have of their therapists. Every transference relationship is unique and needs to be behaviorally specified, but there are some generalizations that can be made. If clients expect therapists to perform behaviors similar to what they expected their parents to do, the potential for a transference is there. These expectations might include: giving advice, guidance, feedback, support, knowing answers; or conversely, they might expect to be rejected, mistreated, or ignored. It is these kinds of expectations combined with the clients' structural position that make the transference possible. Using behavioral terminology, if the stimulus control of therapy, including the physical setting and interpersonal dynamics, are similar enough to stimulus situations from one's early conditioning history, there will be the chance for behavioral reenactments of past contingencies using the client-therapist relationship. It is my contention that the dynamics of therapy make the potential for this stimulus-control situation very common.

Since so much of the behavior in the development of a transference projection involves the reinforcement of covert expectations, observing the process is quite difficult. When clients verbalize their expectations, assuming they know them, we at least have one dependent variable documented. But it is often the case that only after some time is it clear how the transference has been conditioned. For example, most clients expect their therapists to help them, and may have specific ideas about how this is to be done. If help is not forthcoming as requested, a transference projection of rejection may be reinforced. For example:

CLIENT: I want you to tell me what to do.
THERAPIST: I don't want to do that, but I will support you in working to come with your own answers.
CLIENT: But I don't know what to do and I need your advice.
THERAPIST: I can't give you advice. What are you feeling right now?
CLIENT: Frustrated!
THERAPIST: I can see that. I imagine it is very frustrating to want advice and not get it. Tell me more about how that is for you.

If this client is one who has a conditioning history of receiving too little support and guidance from parents, then the therapist's stance will likely renew feelings similar to those experienced in childhood. Each time the therapist verbalizes a refusal to give advice, it reinforces any one of a number of projections, including: "You just can't expect anyone to help you"; "You can't trust men [or women, as the case may be] "; "I won't be loved or taken care of." At this point the therapist, perhaps unwittingly, is taking on an archaic parent role with the client's selective perception supporting his or her projection being fulfilled. Thus, with very little effort, therapist behavior can become part of a parent-child chain of behaviors from the client's past.

Certain therapist behavior patterns will reinforce some transferences better than others. For instance, a number of therapists use silence more than others. This behavior could very well reinforce the transference for a client who expects to be rejected. Other therapists have a pattern of giving clients ongoing positive and negative feedback, which might reinforce the projection of a client who expects to be criticized. There are those therapists who prefer to be in a more cerebral teaching role. They might reinforce the projections of clients who expect to have their feelings ignored. Remember, projections are based on learning that occured with primary parent figures. To the extent these contingencies become active in the therapy setting, they are a reenactment of past controlling conditions in the here and now.

There are obviously too many patterns of therapist behavior and client projections to predict the potential for reinforcing transferences when therapy begins. Our inability to adequately specify and label these chains of behavior makes empirical investigation of how transferences are conditioned very difficult at this time. However, I believe that we can build enough of a behavioral foundation, especially with single-organism research designs, to better establish how the process occurs. This, in turn, should give us a better basis to explore the next issues, the identification of the transference after it is conditioned, and then its potential for behavioral activity. For the present, I believe we have hypothetically applied the behavioral approach with enough vigor to suggest: 1) a model for how the stimulus control of the client-therapist relationship can establish cues to reenact contingencies from early childhood, and 2) how therapist behavior might increase the probability that this dynamic would be reinforced.

Identifying a transference uses the same behavioral cues as for any projection. Client over or underreactions and inability to take corrective feedback are two overt clues. Both involve the therapist's interpretive skills since degree of reaction and ability to respond to feedback are basically subjective judgment calls. In addition, if therapists are also caught up in a countertransference, they may not be able to completely trust their own judgment anyway. The best measurable behavior that defines a transference is when clients verbalize an acknowledgment of the dynamic: the therapist reminds them of a past authority or parent figure. With that data, the cat is out of the bag, so to speak, and therapists can carefully explore with their clients how the current relationship is similar to and different from the historical one. Through these discussions, the present interactional behavior that defines the transference can be specified, and actual therapist behavior discriminated from the behavior of the original parent.

It is entirely possible that a relationship can look like a transference but not be labeled as such. *Unless clients verbally acknowledge at some point they are indeed responding to the therapist as if the therapist were someone else, I see no way we can call the relationship a transference.* No matter how sure we are, how classical the apparent transference behavior seems to be, any such labeling must use therapist interpretations and projections and are thus subject to serious question. I have personally observed and been part of professional relationships where I was *sure* the client was involved in a transference. However, if I had a dollar for every client who refused to own up to my projections, I'd be rich. For all my certainty, I could not label the relationship a transference. These personal judgments are much too contaminated with subjective variables to be used in any analysis which is striving for eventual empirical validation. If you will recall, I suggested the same thing in my behavioral analysis of projections. Unless the client eventually owned them, the concept was of no practical use to us.

The professional relationship is of course potentially therapeutic without labeling transferences. But without clients' acknowledgment of their projections onto the therapist, the tie to the past is not available through this route. Ego Psychology therapists might contend that an eventual tie needs to be established to past relationships if the client is to be more permanently "cured." The behavioral approach has demonstrated to some degree that any relationship in the present is, given motivation and opportunity, amenable to modification without going into history. This would of course include any problems incurred between therapists and clients. If clients worked to change interactions with their therapists to the point where newly learned skills generalized and impacted on problem behavior in the environment, this kind of work would certainly be deemed therapeutic. People can learn to express feelings and behave in ways that are quite different from their childhood, without going back into history. History is an option, but not the only option.

However, let us assume, for the purposes of our analysis, a transference has been acknowledged and the client-therapist interactions defining the term for them behaviorally specified. Does this identification lead to behaviorally active practice? Yes, it can. The transference can be a here-and-now reenactment of past contingencies relating to present problems. Clients are faced with the same dilemma as when they were children, but this time as adults they hopefully have more skills with which to problem solve. In addition, as we have discussed previously, reenactments of early contingencies can act to heighten deprivation states (feelings) and provide motivation to change current behavior.

Once a transference has been fully established, a behavioral analysis suggests it is extinction that eventually reduces the client's transference behavior, culminating in a CEE. One of the side effects of extinction is emotional behavior, which helps to explain why clients can get so upset. If you will recall, selective perception and interpretation keep projections going even when confronted with corrective feed-back. For example, consider clients who feel rejected because their therapists use silence. They have selectively attended to one response class which fulfilled their projection. While this one aspect of therapist behavior reinforced the projection, it is not the only behavior being emitted. As time goes on, the reality of the full range of therapist responses, including caring and support, begins getting discriminated and the transference projection starts losing its power. But, the client is still caught up in a behavior chain that has been and still is being intermittently reinforced by rejection. As it becomes clear to the client that the therapist is not simulating Daddy or Mommy, and will not reinforce the chain as was done in the past (and as others still do in the present), we have a classical extinction process underway.

This is not the first time we have seen how cognitive selective perception influences reinforcer effectiveness. It is as evident with the transference as it was with all projections. Here we have a therapist behavior pattern first reinforcing the establishment of the transference projection, and then losing its reinforcing power as the client's selective perception of therapist behavior broadens to include other response classes. Returning to our example will be instructive.

Initially, the client was in a state of deprivation for therapist attention. The silences increased his deprivation and reinforced the development of an already established behavior chain that is cued by insufficient attention from important parent figures—a projection. The continued silences initially acted on a CRF schedule to establish the transference projection between the client and the therapist. By the time transferences are established, or even before, therapists usually pick up on enough behavioral cues to hypothesize that a transference has developed. Assuming that the therapist is performing other behaviors that mean caring and acceptance, the power of silence to reinforce the projection will likely weaken over time as the client attends to other stimuli. This begins the extinction process. Actually, the transference may develop relatively quickly since it is an old chain. The extinction of the projection in the therapeutic setting, on the other hand, should take some time because, 1) the withdrawal of silence as a reinforcer for the projection is going to be inconsistent, based on the client's ability to improve his awareness of the total therapeutic environment, and 2) client projections are still being reinforced outside of therapy.

Clients choose two basic ways to respond to this extinction process: first, some decide to leave therapy, using any one of a number of rationales. The other more common response to the extinction of a transference is for clients to follow the extinction curve, an actual initial increase in the behavior under extinction, and then a return to operant level.

It is conceivable that the height of the extinction curve represents the occurrence of the Corrective Emotional Experience. In any case, the transference can be seen as using a here-and-now relationship to gain entry into the CEE. While the transference is being thus resolved, it is critically important that clients learn new, more functional behavior patterns. Therapists use differential reinforcement as the transference is worked out and these new skills are learned. The "post transference" therapist-client relationship is an excellent ground for applying new reinforcers to build more functional behavior chains. In addition, therapists must be concerned with the generalization of any new learning, since the therapy relationship is relatively safe and may be nothing like those relationships in the environment. This differential reinforcement process in Ego Psychology therapy, which includes the continued reinforcement of whatever behaviors are defined in ego strengthening, is unsystematic and rather vague, but obviously can occur.

The therapeutic application of the transference, as described in Ego Psychology, has certainly created problems for a behavioral analysis. The biggest problem was in defining the response class itself. Gestalt finesses this difficulty by making any client-therapist relationship problem a function of the here and now, thus more easily subject to observable documentation. Ego Psychology, on the other hand, emphasizes the projective transfer to past referents, making behavioral analysis impossible unless clients acknowledge and discuss the dynamic. In addition, general and vague practice guidelines supporting the use of transferences didn't make my task any easier.

To the extent that Ego Psychology therapists are able to find their way to reinforcing transference projections, supporting clients in eventually discriminating the difference between present and past contingencies of reinforcement in relationships, and providing direct and indirect "post CEE" differential reinforcement for the development of functional behavior patterns, they are using behaviorally active techniques. This is especially true if the behaviors specified as problematic in the transference and the CEE are connected to current problem behavior patterns.

Countertransference is used basically as an assessment tool in Ego Psychology, although in Gestalt it was used for direct intervention as well. As an exercise, define the behaviors controlling the use of the term, develop a model for how clients reinforce countertransference behavior in their therapists, and then explain how its identification could lead to behaviorally active assessment and intervention.

Assertive Training in Ego Psychology

It is obvious there was much assertive training going on throughout our analysis of Ego Psychology therapy. First and foremost, many of the behaviors that are part of ego strengthening were assertive skills. We may find fault with the lack of any systematic identification and shaping method, but nonetheless, assertive training is likely occurring as therapists pay selective attention to these response classes.

The Corrective Emotional Experience is another opportunity for clients to learn to say no, express negative and positive feelings, and make demands. When people finally reexperience early-childhood scenes, they are likely performing assertive behaviors that have been at relatively low levels. The CEE is just the beginning of a shaping process that needs plenty of support both in and out of therapy before new assertive skills are established. Assertive training during and after the CEE is similar to what we have already discussed for analogous experiences in Gestalt and TA.

However, assertive training in the context of the transference relationship is unique and deserves special attention. Ego Psychology therapists often do not try to immediately resolve here-and-now problems created between the client and therapist when a transference has developed. This would dilute the effect of extinction and lower the likelihood that a CEE would occur. Working through a transference offers great opportunities for clients to begin practicing important assertive skills on a safer surrogate stimulus before they confront past and present parent figures. For example, practicing getting progressively more angry using a therapist with whom you have a transference may be good preparation for getting angry with past parent figures, which could be a further reasonable approximation to confronting people in the present environment. This opportunity for clients to experientially practice developing assertive skills with their therapists represents the most systematic assertive training we can find in the practice of Ego Psychology. The extinction process naturally leads to a gradual increase of emotional behavior, which will probably provide a relatively systematic increase in the motivation for performing assertive skills with one's therapist. Classically, therapists are supposed to use active listening skills, empathize, and generally keep themselves calm in the face of clients' assertions (within reasonable limits, of course). This therapist response keeps the extinction process going. Referring to our previous example, you'll likely get angrier and angrier with the silent therapist with whom you have a transference as time goes on, and will be more likely to let him or her know how you feel with more and more gusto. And all the while your therapist will accept what you do. Not a bad assertive training model at all!

There is, however, at least one potential problem with this model. As you might have realized by now, therapists are offering themselves up as psychological guinea pigs to be used by some clients as a practice foil for anger, scorn, ridicule, and similar unpleasant interactional stimuli. This may be a wonderful opportunity for clients to practice assertive skills, but it is usually no fun for therapists to have to accept this behavior. As far as the transference is concerned, I do not believe any other psychotherapy asks for more valor from its therapists.

I wish to emphasize one point about the importance of assertive training in the practice of Ego Psychology: earlier I suggested that helping clients learn to reinforce themselves was especially important to Ego Psychology. Since therapists do not normally directly intervene in the environmental systems controlling problem behavior, clients need to be taught two basic self-reinforcing skills. When other people do not naturally reinforce our desired behavior, we have two basic choices to increase the probability the behavior will occur again: 1) we can reinforce ourselves; or 2) we can make a request or demand for others to reinforce us. Thus, it is also extremely important for Ego Psychology therapists to include the ability to make requests and demands as part of whatever other assertive skills they happen to reinforce.

Acceptance Training in Ego Psychology

There are no systematic relaxation training procedures in Ego Psychology therapy. Relaxation probably does occur as a side effect to some interventions. For instance, insight may have the side effect of reducing anxiety; a catharsis likely has a similar effect; some of the assertive skills are incompatible with anxiety; and learning to seek alternative sources of support may also have the same effect. Therapist support, caring, and empathy also lead at times to muscle relaxation.

Ego Psychology's route to learning acceptance goes through the Corrective Emotional Experience. Insight and the use of the transference may facilitate reaching the CEE, but it is where past scenes are being reexperienced at the feeling level that the clients begin their real acceptance work. Essentially the process is the same as we saw in Gestalt and TA. With less systematic guidance, Ego Psychology theory does give therapists a general map for the development of acceptance. Ego strengthening and the CEE make the ego strong enough to face the reality of what cannot be changed, and give permission for the grief process to proceed. Afterward, the ego will have even more strength to problem solve, developing more functional alternative methods of coping.

A behavioral analysis of what happens suggests that clients finally acknowledge their inability to change what has happened in the past, which also simulates the present contingencies controlling nonfunctional repeat-attempt behavior. Therapists help clients through the grief process which supports extinction of their nonacceptance behavior, and often manage to find their way to reinforcing new, more functional behavior patterns that mean acceptance and muscle relaxation. Ego Psychology's approach to gaining acceptance is basically behaviorally active, being similar in nature to Gestalt and TA's strategy. However, the process is much more vague, leaving it to therapists and clients alike to interpret what specific behaviors are required to extinguish frustrating repeat-attempt chains of behavior. In addition, there is very little clarity concerning what specific behaviors are needed to replace nonacceptance patterns and how to reinforce and maintain them in the natural environment when they do occur.

CONCLUSIONS

The behavioral analysis of Ego Psychology was curiously different from that of the other therapies. The theory seemed more abstract and difficult to connect with observable practice behavior; there was not the same emphasis for teaching clients a systematic problem-solving process; the guidelines for therapist behavior seemed less clear. But more than these issues, I believe what made this chapter different from the others was that the behavioral activity hypothesized in Ego Psychology practice could not be matched with at least some similarly strong hypotheses concerning a behavioral foundation for its theory base. While it was not the main purpose of this book to look for how psychotherapy theories could be supported by the Behavioral Laws, major parts of Gestalt and TA theories were often behaviorally compatible with their respective behaviorally active practices. Such was not the case with Ego Psychology. The ego, Id, superego model, with its psychic energy and defense mechanisms, did not easily lend itself to this kind of integration.

On the other hand, once we defined the therapist behavior behind the treatment concepts, there were many places where it was likely that therapist procedures and techniques were behaviorally active. For example, the CEE was essentially similar to its behaviorally active counterparts in Gestalt and TA, and the assertive training model in the transference relationship seemed potentially productive.

Although my behavioral analysis has not been altogether kind to Ego Psychology theory or practice, it still plays an important role in contemporary psychotherapy, and thus should be taken seriously. I believe, however, the relatively vague and general guidelines for therapist behavior will continue to create difficulty for any analysis of Ego Psychology practice, regardless of how it is done.

CHAPTER NINE
THE INTEGRATION

After describing and analyzing four therapies, it is now time to consider what constitutes the most behaviorally active treatment strategies, taking into account each theory. It is not the purpose here to develop a new, unified field theory of psychotherapy; that task is beyond the scope of our present discussion. Rather it is my belief that therapists will continue to utilize whatever basic psychological belief system that is compatible with their present philosophy of life, and practice accordingly. My hope is that through analyses such as we conducting here, professionals will consider expanding the scope of their practice behavior to include techniques from other therapies, even those that are philosophically incompatible, using more scientifically founded rationales. The question is not so much whether you agree with my assumptions, analyses, or conclusions. The matters we are considering are complex enough, and the field diverse enough, that any kind of integrative analyses would generate serious disagreements. What is important is for the conclusions arrived at here to stimulate your struggling with the problem. It is our collective wisdom over time that will lead to the most functional integration of psychotherapy.

TREATMENT PROCESSES

It should not be surprising that the four psychotherapies have some similar treatment processes (*see* Figure 9-1). Whatever else therapists do they must come to a reasonable hypothesis concerning the etiology of a client's problem (assessment) and then attempt to help the client resolve it (intervention). Assessment involves the eventual identification of therapeutic dependent variables. Intervention is the independent variable of treatment and is supposed to directly affect client outcome. Even though assessment initially precedes intervention, both therapist behaviors are ongoing throughout the therapy experience as more information becomes available. Since therapist assessment and intervention behaviors are so important to each therapy, it seems reasonable to discuss the integration of practice separately for each of these two major therapeutic endeavors. You will notice, however, that some of the techniques therapists use to do assessment are the same as those used in intervention.

THERAPIST ASSESSMENT BEHAVIOR

Motivation and Feelings

When all is said and done, *motivation* is similarly defined in three of the four therapies, Ego Psychology being the odd therapy out (*see* Table 9-1). Clients are motivated to perform depending on the state of deprivation for a reinforcer, stroke, or need for contact. I have demonstrated that all of these are essentially describing

FIGURE 9-1 Four Psychotherapy Treatment Processes

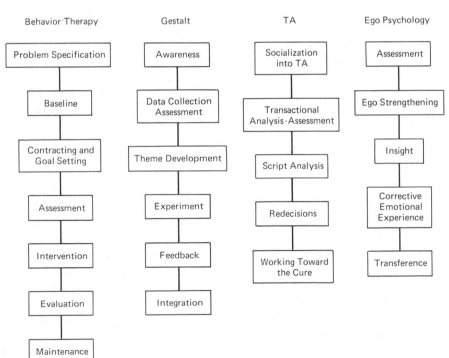

TABLE 9-1   A Comparison of Three Basic Psychological Concepts Across Four Therapies

DEFINITIONS

TERM	GESTALT	TRANS-ACTIONAL ANALYSIS	EGO PSYCHOLOGY	BEHAVIOR THERAPY
Motivation	unfinished business, need for contact	stroke deprivation	satisfying Id drives (pleasure principle), need fulfillment	states of deprivation for reinforcing stimuli
Assessment of controlling conditions	Awareness Cycle	transactional and script analyses	personality development fixations, defense mechanisms	functional analysis of antecedent and consequence stimuli
Identified patterns of problem behavior subject to modification	resistance to contact	games	defense mechanisms	chains of behavior

the same phenomena and are associated with observable behavior, which is absolutely necessary if the concept is to be used in a behaviorally active assessment. Regardless of respective theoretical dictates, these definitions affirm operant control of behavior, and the possibility of manipulating deprivation states to affect motivation. It is remarkable that three such apparently different approaches to psychotherapy define such a basic concept so similarly.

I like the behavioral definition better because it more specifically takes into account all possible stimuli from which there could be a state of deprivation. TA and Gestalt tend to emphasize attentional consequences, and thus have not developed a comprehensive technology using artificial reinforcers. However, Gestalt's Awareness Cycle is very useful in behaviorally breaking down the steps occurring in deprivation, and TA's idea of lumping all kinds of attention into one concept, the stroke, may make it easier to understand the motivational properties of deprivation for negative attention. Ego Psychology's view of motivation is not compatible with a behaviorally active assessment. Assessing motivational stimuli using unobservable variables requires too much interpretation to make the process useful. Gestalt's unfinished business, while an interesting metaphor, was behaviorally defined as a chain affected by states of deprivation and reinforcers like any other pattern of behavior, and thus is not primarily a foundation concept.

Probably the most common assessment question in psychotherapy is, "What are you feeling?" It has been my contention that the answer is an indication of clients' current states of deprivation and suggests for what reinforcers they are motivated to work. Insofar as feeling states are assessed with the idea of connecting feelings to the behavior chains of which they are a part, and identifying deprivation states, I believe they are a very important source of data for a behaviorally active assessment. Seen in this context, behaviorists should be more comfortable in utilizing such a response class; in the other three therapies this conceptualization should make it clearer why identifying feelings can be helpful.

Assessing motivation in terms of deprivation is quite compatible for TA and Behavior Therapists, and relatively easy for Gestalt therapists since the concept is already a part of the Awareness Cycle. Ego Psychology therapists, on the other hand, will have a more difficult time applying the concept. I contend, however, that any psychotherapists who attend to what they do with clients, instead of what they think, will be able to observe motivation in terms of what their clients are deprived of. For those of you who must remain wedded to the Id, do so. But please tell me what clients specifically need from their environment and for what they are willing to work.

Resistance

Resistance is diversely defined between the four therapies. While Gestalt and TA's definitions are essentially similar, Ego Psychology again suggests a hypothetical construct that requires interpretation of observable behavior. Behavior Therapy really doesn't discuss the issue at all, except in terms of reinforcement. I believe assessing resistance can be a valuable and behaviorally active therapist behavior. The Gestalt and TA definition make the concept observable and useful in determining the contingencies controlling a client's inability to perform as desired. In addition, I like the idea from Gestalt, and implied in TA, that resistance is always ultimately a reaction to an environmental request, and can be viewed as a client's attempt to set up a protective assertive boundary to real or perceived threatening cues.

It is true that people are resistant to change when there is no viable reinforcer for which they are willing to work. But assessing the conditions controlling the statement, "No, I won't meet the request that I change my behavior," and identifying the perceived threats for the projected behavior change, just makes good sense. It is similar to the issue I raised during the discussion on assertive training in chapter 1. You can surely teach people to be assertive, but unless you help them deal with the consequences of that assertion, they could be in big trouble. In the same way, you can help clients overcome their refusal to perform by helping them find a reinforcer for which they are willing to work, but if the perceived threat for new behavior patterns is real, they will not be prepared for the consequences.

I see no reason behaviorists should not feel comfortable in using resistance when it is defined behaviorally. In fact I would recommend it. Ego Psychology therapists might have some trouble in assessing resistance in this way, but in my opinion the definition is behaviorally active and can be effectively utilized with clients regardless of one's theoretical beliefs.

Defining Patterns of Behavior Problems

For all the apparent differences between these four therapies, it is amazing that they have developed such similar models for identifying problematic behavior patterns (*see* Table 9-1). The labels used are surely quite different—behavior chains, resistances to contact, games, and defense mechanisms—but they all attempt to generally describe similar phenomena. The way the behavioral approach defines patterns uniquely for each situation is obviously the most behaviorally specific. Looking at patterns as behavior chains also allows us to fundamentally understand how chain members are linked to one another and how chains are conditioned and broken.

However, the chain-labeling systems suggested by Gestalt, TA, and Ego Psychology are worthy of our consideration for a behaviorally active assessment. It is not possible at this time to establish which generalized chains are the most viable, but rather than ignore the problem, I believe we should carefully use the idea. Behaviorally specific chains should be identified with clients, and metaphors used to label them. I am less concerned with which labels are used from what theoretical orientation than I am with the behavioral specificity used to arrive at the labels, and then how they are used during intervention. I believe the identification and labeling of key patterns of problem behavior is a cornerstone for all behaviorally active assessments.

Assessment of Controlling Conditions

This point in assessment is at the very heart of the theoretical orientations of the four therapies. Each of them has somewhat different explanations concerning why people behave as they do (*see* Table 9-1), and therapist assessment behavior reflects these belief systems to some extent. However, since it is very important to Behavior Therapy, Gestalt, TA, and Ego Psychology to assess patterns of behavior, we can look more at how rather than why therapists perform this task. There will come a point, though, when we have to face the fact that the ultimate controlling conditions for client problems must include the Laws of Operant and Respondent Behavior. Operant behavior will not occur unless it is reinforced. While we can make direct use of this phenomenon as in Behavior Therapy, we have also seen throughout our analyses how antecedents and consequences are manipulated without directly identifying them. Regardless of how behavior patterns are identified in assessment, and later used for intervention, it has been my contention that the Laws of Behavior are operating no matter what belief system is used to explain why people behave as they do.

A Behavior Therapist looks for controlling conditions by conducting functional analyses of a number of problem situations—asking questions about what happens before, during, and after. These situations are then synthesized into a behavior chain, which is really an hypothesis concerning not only what behavior constitutes the chain but also what antecedents and reinforcers control its performance. TA therapists are actually behaving similarly, identifying games by doing transactional analyses, which are eventually synthesized into a script. In Gestalt, therapists ask clients what they want to do, using the Awareness Cycle as a guide to look for where and how clients stop themselves. While a pattern of stopping oneself can be identified at any point in the Cycle, the most clearly prelabeled patterns are the resistances to contact. Those therapists who follow Ego Psychology look for behavior patterns that can be interpreted as defense mechanisms. Behavior that suggests unresolved problems in personality development also aids in this task.

I am not in a position to recommend which assessment strategy for identifying controlling conditions is the best. My own bias is with the behavioral approach since it works to directly assess those antecedent and consequential stimuli controlling behavior. What I believe is essential is that therapists come out of assessment with a working hypothesis of behaviorally specific patterns of behavior and that this hypothesis be shared with clients, if possible. Depending on one's theory base, it is clear that the way problems are defined will be instrumental in what chains are identified. I feel I have demonstrated reasonably well that each of the four therapies identifies patterns of behavior that can be connected with client's presenting problems, and furthermore, can lead to behaviorally active interventions.

Once a hypothesis has been established connecting a behaviorally specified pattern of behavior to a client's problem, then that hypothesis can be tested when intervention takes place. It is my contention that every pattern of behavior, whether it is called a behavior chain, resistance to contact, game, script, or defense mechanism, is ultimately controlled by its antecedents and consequences. When intervention takes place, the pattern will be modified according to the chain rules. If the established assessment hypothesis was functionally related to the client's problem, behavior will change, hopefully for the better.

The key, in my mind, to doing an effective behaviorally active assessment of controlling conditions is 1) a pattern be identified that can be described using observable behavior; 2) an hypothesis be established, using whatever theory base you wish, connecting the pattern to client problem behavior which is then shared with the client; and 3) the hypothesis be tested by manipulating antecedent and consequential stimuli, under whatever guise, and monitoring whether client behavior changes.

The Unconscious

Now that I have suggested the basic boundaries for a behaviorally active assessment, we should look at what behaviors subject to therapist observation should be included for the best chain hypothesis. For instance, is it advisable to include covert behaviors not in the awareness of the client in a behavior chain hypothesis? Three of the four therapies, Behavior Therapy excluded, deal in one way or the other with the concept of *the unconscious*. Where Ego Psychology stands on the matter is clear. Covert behavior outside of our awareness unquestionably does occur at two levels: that which is not usually available to awareness—unconscious behavior; and that which is potentially available to awareness—subconscious behavior. Both are supposed to be very important factors in the control of behavior. Gestalt deals with the concept in a different way. It acknowledges a reality of covert behavior below the level of awareness but suggests that there are always observable referents in the body. Gestalt therapists ask clients to connect these body cues to covert behavior and are not supposed to impose their projections upon clients. TA also helps clients deal with behavior initially below the level of awareness, and definitely includes it in its script concept. However, it is only when parential injunctions and script messages become observable that they are finally included in the behavior chain hypothesis. And, of course, Behavior Therapy generally ignores the issue.

While a behavioral analysis of the unconscious suggested its potential viability, it is the Gestalt approach that I believe offers the most promise for the inclusion of covert behavior below the level of awareness into behavior chains. Ego Psychology's use of the concept requires too much interpretation, and while TA theoretically approaches the issue more concretely, in practice it utilizes many of the same techniques as Gestalt.

Systematically requesting clients to be aware of their observable physiological and cognitive behavior gives us an operational way of allowing behavior below the level of awareness to be verbalized and potentially made part of a behavior chain hypothesis. Unless covert behavior can reliably be made public, I see no way it could be included in a behaviorally active assessment.

Domains for Behaviorally Active Assessments

Throughout the analysis of the four therapies there have been recurring themes discussing the behavioral activity of past versus present, and observable versus cognitive (covert) issues: what is the value of assessing the past for current behavior problems; can cognitive and physiological behavior be reliably integrated into intervention and outcome treatment variables? Traditionally, Behavior Therapy's stance has generally been that observable behavior was most useful for assessment and modification, although this has changed somewhat in recent years with the advent of Cognitive Behavior Therapy. Gestalt is viewed even more in the present as the "here and now" therapy but has also always allowed for covert and past behavior to be included. TA looks at past relationships and present dynamics, and with the integration of Gestalt into its practice, would probably be considered working in the present and past with both overt and covert behaviors. Ego Psychology has traditionally been seen as a therapy working in the past. I think such categorizations do not accurately reflect how these psychotherapies are actually practiced, and I invite you to examine Table 9-2, A Behaviorally Active Assessment Matrix.

There is no question that behavior directly observed by therapists in the present is the best source of data for developing hypotheses concerning controlling conditions. However, it should be clear by now that it is possible to bring covert and past behaviors into the present therapy experience for assessment and intervention purposes. I have also suggested that the way we treat ourselves covertly, and the contingencies controlling past behavior, are essentially the same as those controlling our current behavior problems. As long as cognitive and past behavior can be made observable in the present, then the four quadrants of the Assessment Matrix (Table 9-2) are all potentially useful for a behaviorally active assessment.

TABLE 9-2 A Behaviorally Active Assessment Matrix

	PRESENT	PAST
Overt (observable) Behavior	observable and verbal behavior occurring either in the here and now or in the present environment	observable and verbal behavior that occurred in the past which can be described and reenacted
Covert (cognitive, physiological) Behavior	covert behavior, including thoughts, imagery dreams, and physiological responses occurring in the here and now or present environment that can be described and reenacted	thoughts, dreams, imagery, or physiological responses from the past which can be remembered, described, and reenacted

For example, in the Present-Overt quadrant of the Assessment Matrix, interpersonal dynamics between group members or between client and therapist allow for direct assessment analyses. Descriptions of problem incidents in the present environment from clients and relevant others can also be used, although if these reports are suspect, actual on-site observations or assessment in another matrix quadrant should be considered. In the Present-Covert quadrant, Gestalt brings cognitive and physiological behavior alive by personifying symbols to label internal events and reenacting them dynamically in the double chair. Normally unobservable interactions involving any part of the body or abstract idea can become observable in this way. TA uses the same technique to structure the behavioral reenactments of internal dialogues. Behavior from the Past-Overt quadrant is brought into the present by using similar Gestalt and TA techniques. In addition, when a transference is acknowledged, as in Ego Psychology, it is an observable example of the reinforcement contingencies from a past as well as present relationship. The Corrective Emotional Experience, also from Ego Psychology, is another example of a here-and-now reenactment of past contingencies. The Past-Covert quadrant is assessed similarly to behavior in the Present-Covert quadrant using symbols and behavioral reenactment; Gestalt's dreamwork and polarities are two specific examples.

Thus a behaviorally active assessment can include combinations of the past and present and observable and cognitive/physiological behavior, depending on a therapist's ability to structure the appropriate behavioral reenactments in the therapy session. When covert behavior and events from the past are viewed in this way, I heartily recommend that therapists utilize all four domains of assessment information represented in the Assessment Matrix. This will come more easily to those practicing Gestalt and TA. Ego Psychology therapists will resist assessing the controlling conditions of present behavior because of that theory's theoretical dictates; many Behavior Therapists also cannot easily look to assessing past behavior or covert dynamics.

However, if you can accept the following two assumptions, which I feel I have reasonably well established, then it should be possible to integrate the assessment of controlling conditions into any of the four quadrants of the Assessment Matrix, regardless of what theory you generally follow: 1) it is possible to structure behavioral reenactments using symbols, metaphors, or people from the past, such as in Gestalt and TA, that reasonably represent historical interpersonal dynamics and/ or covert chains of behavior; and 2) these reenactments essentially represent the same kind of contingencies that control clients' present problem behavior. I believe that by bringing past and covert events into the therapy experience to be observed just like here-and-now interactions, we greatly widen our scope for the behaviorally active assessment of controlling conditions. In the next section I will further suggest that the same strategies widen the scope for behaviorally active interventions as well.

INTERVENTION

The Symbolic Control of Behavior

While the use of symbols is integrated only into the practice of Gestalt and TA, of our four therapies, the techniques associated with the concept merit serious consideration for behaviorally active interventions. The ability to transform a part of the body or an abstract idea into an observable dynamic interaction representing a problematic chain of behaviors offers a remarkable means of intervening therapeutically. The double-chair technique is probably the most common example of this. Gestalt and TA personify symbols in three major response classes: imagery and abstract ideas; parts of the body; and people from the present or past. Once the symbols are personified and the problematic patterns identified, these behavior chains are subject to the wide variety of behaviorally active stimulus control and differential reinforcement techniques that each therapy offers. Personified symbols can be used over and over again in reenactments to practice new behaviors as approximations for the eventual generalization of learning from the therapy setting to the client's natural environment. In addition, I believe the personification of symbols is behaviorally active for modifying the covert behavior chains tied to overt problem behavior, providing a dynamic means of tying covert and overt behavior together in the therapeutic setting before attempting new skills in a potentially more unsupportive environment.

The Behavior Chain

Once a behavior chain hypothesis has been made connecting a pattern of behavior to a client's problem, using whatever theory base you wish, the ultimate efficiency and success of intervention will include two important factors: what techniques are used, and the point on the chain where the intervention is applied.

Each of the four therapies intervenes at characteristic points on behavior chains (*see* Figure 9-2). Gestalt and Ego Psychology typically attempt to affect the reinforcing consequences occurring at the end of a chain; Behavior Therapy and TA have conceptual models for modifying behavior at both ends. As you will recall, interventions occurring at the beginning of chains were attempting stimulus or antecedent control, while those occurring at the end were trying for consequence control.

For example, a client has an overeating problem and an assessment suggests the pattern of behavior in Figure 9-3 as hypothetically controlling the behavior. Behavior Therapy calls the pattern a *behavior chain* and attempts to help the client stop the chain before it starts, using stimulus-control techniques. It could also act to extinguish the chain at the end by making sure the negative attention was withdrawn while reinforcing more appropriate eating behavior (differential reinforcement). One of the standard behavioral diets and relaxation training could provide stimulus control by structuring the eating experience and breaking the power of the cues to set off snacking behavior. Teaching the client to demand a cessation of negative comments through assertive training would be one of many ways to extinguish this chain's reinforcers. Cognitive Behavior Therapists might also attempt interventions at the covert level (dotted line in Figure 9-3).

Gestalt would call this behavior pattern a *retroflection*: doing to yourself what you would rather do to others. Undoing the retroflection might include using the double chair to direct negative statements to the client's spouse demanding the criticisms stop, among other requests. This intervention is basically directed at the overt and covert reinforcers occurring at the end of the chain. TA's label for this pattern could be a Kick Me game, which is really a smaller segment of a broader script pattern. Actually, for all of the therapies, this pattern could be conceived as only one part of a more complex chain, and the interventions suggested here are by no means comprehensive; but they are instructive. In any case, TA therapists typically try to help people find the stoppers to games, which is a form of stimulus control, and teach them to refuse to accept negative strokes and work for game-free positive strokes instead, a general differential reinforcement strategy for consequence control. Ego Psychology therapists might suggest this overeating involves a displacement defense mechanism, an example of kicking oneself instead of someone more threatening. Treatment would include ego strengthening, raising a person's

FIGURE 9-2 Characteristic Intervention Points on Behavior Chains

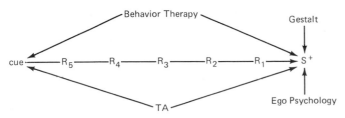

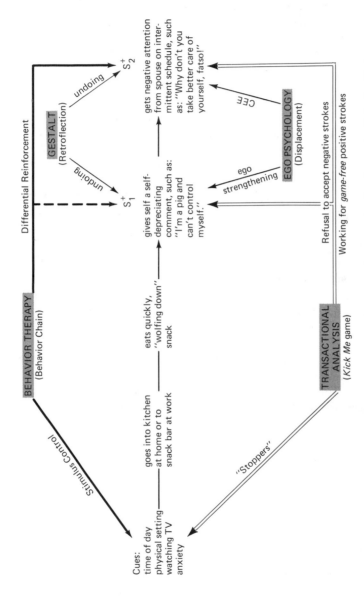

FIGURE 9-3 Examples of Intervention Points and Possible Treatment Strategies for One Overeating Behavior Chain

self-esteem, which would mean a decrease in self-depreciation, and eventually a corrective emotional experience, or the reexperiencing of early-childhood scenes related to the problem area. While of course much more is involved, these types of interventions in Ego Psychology basically affect behavior chains at their end points.

The implications of these respective intervention strategies are important. Following the behavior chain rules, if only the consequences of a chain are affected by an intervention, the cues setting off the chain will still have some power. In the case of our overeater, he will be sitting in front of the television watching an anxiety-producing program, and may suddenly find himself in the kitchen looking for food. Even though he may be learning to effectively extinguish the consequences ultimately controlling this chain, once the chain starts, it tends to go to completion (chain rule 3). Thus our client will be under tremendous pressure to stop a powerful behavior chain after it has started and before it gets to the eating stage, potentially setting himself up for an immediate self-depreciating reinforcer if he fails. Interventions dealing only with consequences tend to neglect the powerful conditioned effects that antecedent cues have over our behavior. Clients are thus more vulnerable to "regression,' or the return of problem behavior to preintervention levels. On the other hand, if our client had begun controlling the cues setting off the overeating chain by learning to relax as the only intervention, for instance he would be left in a state of deprivation for important consequences. His motivation to work for a "kick' would thus be increased and he might find a new behavior to earn himself one—symptom substitution.

No psychotherapy has a license on effectively covering both ends of problem chains of behavior. Even though Behavior Therapy and TA conceptually attend to antecedents and consequences, therapists do not always do so. It has been my experience that therapists of all persuasions tend to emphasize intervention strategies at one end of behavior chains or the other When these types of singular strategies are successful it is likely because of a natural "avalanche" or "snowball" effect or because the greater power of competing reinforcers for newly developing behavior overcomes those controlling problematic behavior.

Of course, the point of intervention in chains is only half the story. The interventions themselves must be effective as well or behavior will not permanently change and be maintained. However, Ego Psychology and Gestalt therapists leave themselves a little more vulnerable to stimulus-control problems since their theory bases do not conceptually guide them into interventions with antecedent stimuli. And while TA does deal with beginning chain behavior to some extent, it is fairly rudimentary compared to the vast systematic stimulus-control technology developed in the behavioral approach.

In general, I believe that more carefully attending to the therapeutic issues raised at both ends of behavior chains can be easily integrated into the practice of psychotherapy. Any theoretical incompatibilities raised about considering chain intervention points, especially in Gestalt and Ego Psychology, are outweighed, in my opinion, by the significant behavioral activity of such an integration. Regardless of the therapeutic techniques utilized from whatever theoretical base, I recommend considering the following guidelines to make intervention more effective: 1) make sure that behavior patterns are identified during assessment in such a way that antecedent and consequence conditions are clear; 2) consider at what point in the chain interventions are targeted for; 3) always work to help clients concurrently develop new, more functional chains of behavior as dysfunctional ones are being extinguished—this involves differential reinforcement and shaping; 4) remembering the chain rules, if the intervention strategy is aimed at only one end of the chain, at least be cognizant of the therapeutic issues raised by neglecting the other end—have a rationale for believing that intervening at one end will take care of the conditioning at the other end as well; and 5) when "symptom substitution" or "regression" occurs, consider the chain intervention point as a potential problem in addition to all of the other independent variables we consider when treatment is not effective.

Utilizing Resistance and Feelings

While each of the four therapies faces *resistance* during intervention in different ways, Gestalt has made its operational definition of the term the very center of its intervention strategy. The technique of heightening those behaviors defined as resistance, as well as feeling behaviors, make chains more amendable to modification by clarifying them and often markedly increases clients' motivation to change. TA eventually helps clients confront its definition of resistance, the "don't change" script message adopted by the Child, at the redecision phase of treatment. Whenever the Child says, "I can't do it," it is changed to an, "I won't do it." This strategy essentially heightens resistance similar to Gestalt, but the emphasis is more on integrating it into the Parent-Adult-Child dynamic structure. Resistance in Ego Psychology, involving the defense mechanisms, is indirectly handled by ego strengthening and reducing environmental threats to the ego. And as mentioned previously, Behavior Therapy doesn't really have a standard operational definition for the term. When clients do not change their behaviors, it is because there is no reinforcer available for which they are willing to work. The therapist's job, then, is to help them find one.

Behavior Therapy's response to resistance is fundamentally the most correct. TA's approach also appears functional—not too dissimular from Gestalt since Gestalt techniques are infused in its practice base. Ego Psychology, as we have seen before, reifies resistance to the point it makes operational definitions for therapist behavior very vague. In addition, all of these therapies reach for client feeelings, Behavior Therapy probably less than the others. But it is Gestalt that I believe utilizes the power of resistance and feelings in ways that should be seriously considered for integration into behaviorally active interventions. The technique is clearly useful for assessment, but heightening also allows clients to develop assertive skills and manipulate motivation as well.

First, the Gestalt definition of resistance suggests a reciprocal reinforcement contingency between the therapist and client. This is, of course, a clear advantage for the modification of resistance behaviors. Second, Gestalt assumes that resistance is essentially a healthy organismic response to perceived or real threats from the environment, and is thus a necessary protective mechanism to be respected. A client's ability to say no is an existing assertive skill of powerful proportions, one that can be utilized to develop other assertive behaviors. By heightening resistance behaviors, clients are able to acknowledge and practice the assertive skills they do have, feel their own power so to speak, and make better decisions about qualifying the resistance contingencies under which they are operating.

The same heightening technique is extremely useful in exaggerating feelings to the point that clients become more aware of their states of deprivation. Since resistance is always at least partly a function of the muscles controlling motor behavior, heightening the feelings associated with tense muscles, using symbols, for instance, can greatly increase motivation. Thus the Gestalt technique of heightening can have dual effects: 1) the assertive skills involved in the refusal to perform are clarified and practiced; and 2) feelings, representing deprivation states, are exaggerated to the point where a client's motivation to work for alternative reinforcers is enhanced.

TA already integrates much of the heightening technique into its practice. Using the kind of analysis I have conducted here, I see no reason that Behavior Therapists shouldn't be comfortable in integrating the heightening of resistance and feelings into their practices, too. The technique seems eminently founded in the Laws of Behavior, is reasonably behaviorally specific, and offers clear advantages for both assessment and intervention. Ego Psychology therapists may have more trouble using the heightening technique if they dwell on an interpretive theory of resistance. In my opinion, heightening resistances and feelings is very behaviorally active and well worth the effort for integrating into one's clinical practice, whatever the theory base.

The Transference and Countertransference

There is no question in my mind that the behaviors defining the transference and countertransference relationship have a place in a behaviorally active practice. Three of the four therapies already use the dynamic in one form or another, Behavior Therapy excluded. Clearly, the relationship between therapists and clients is a dynamic source of here-and-now behavior amenable to modification, simulating some of the contingencies controlling clients' problems in the environment. As a potential stage for behavioral reenactments, rehearsals, modeling, and assertive training, in preparation for facing relationships outside of therapy, I find it difficult and unnecessary to ignore.

Granted, I have suggested that we cannot label problems between clients and therapists a transference unless the client acknowledges the dynamic. But let us finesse that issue by simply saying that any difficulty occurring in the therapeutic realtionship is a potential simulation of environmental controlling conditions. If clients can be taught to effectively manipulate therapeutic relationships to their satisfaction, then it may be possible to support them in applying this newly learned behavior to the people with whom they live and work. It's fine, too, when clients acknowledge a transference projection. Prior relationships can be brought into the therapy setting to be worked on in simulation, such as with the double chair or the Corrective Emotional Experience. Frankly, it is only Behavior Therapists who may have to accept that transference relationships, or any problems between client and therapists for that matter, have value in the eventual modification of environmental behavior. I believe I have sufficiently established the behavioral activity of the phenomenon, no matter what you wish to call it. Behaviorists should feel comfortable in utilizing the therapeutic relationship as a focus for initial interventions in a broader shaping plan that will eventually include the environment.

The use of the countertransference for intervention follows the same logic as does the transference with, of course, the tables turned. What is good for the goose is good for the gander. Therapist projections and overreactions with clients can also be a good basis for behaviorally active interventions if they are handled rationally. Gestalt suggested a reasonable model for doing this, and to the extent that therapists have good self-support and some comfort with this approach, it could be useful.

The etiology of the transference and countertransference has value in explaining why therapists and clients project expectations onto each other, and thus guides the direction of client reenactments to their proper source. However, I feel that rather than trying to figure out whose projections are at the root of a problematical therapist-client relationship, it is better to simply acknowledge that something is wrong and proceed from there. Many normal raltionships have projective elements as part of their dynamics and people just have to attempt to work out their problems anyway. Sometimes I think it is better to teach people what it functionally means to take responsibility for their role in any interaction than to assign labels which automatically imply whose projections are at fault. It always takes at least two people in any relationship to create problems, and both have a role in their maintenance.

Domains for Behaviorally Active Interventions

In Table 9-2, four quadrants of behavior were displayed that represented domains for a behaviorally active assessment. Intervention, too, can be divided into areas along similar dimensions where therapists apply techniques to modify chains of behavior. Figure 9-4 is such a representation. Behavioral reenactments can bring the contingencies controlling feelings and observable behavior from the past (past-overt, past-covert) and the present covert here-and-now cognitive behavior patterns into the therapy setting for potential intervention. Observable behavior actually occurring during therapy, which I have defined as the here and now, is of course amenable to observation and modification. The most important dependent variable of treatment, however, must be monitored in the environment. No matter how well people have performed in therapy, unless newly learned skills generalize to the situations from whence clients have come, we must consider that interventions have failed.

I have heard many prominent therapists suggest the most important learning occurring in therapy is in the utilization of the here and now. Others have stated that

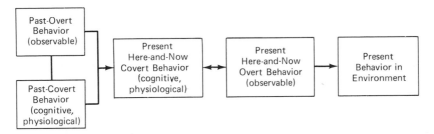

FIGURE 9-4 **Domains of Intervention**

a "cleansing" of the past is the most important element. While I can see a grain of truth in each stance, I must fundamentally disagree. The most critical learning for clients in therapy occurs when they attempt to perform newly learned behaviors in their natural environment.

In my opinion, the generalization of treatment will ultimately represent the greatest challenge facing the practice of psychotherapy. No matter how effective interventions are to change here-and-now behavior, it is what happens when clients leave the therapy room that counts. The ideal model of treatment would be for therapists to be in the environment with clients and their major mediators of reinforcement, having gained enough trust and power to make assessments and guide interventions in the actual situations where problems occur. Therapists who work with couples and families often try to simulate the stimulus control of real life by asking everyone in close association with the identified client to come for therapy. Group therapy also simulates larger social systems to some extent, and it is not uncommon for therapists to attempt behavior modification directly in vivo, so to speak, such as in classroom settings.

For all practical purposes, though, it is not possible or efficient for psychotherapists to step out of the office for normal outpatient problems. And frequently, relevant mediators of reinforcement can't or won't come with the client for treatment. Under these conditions, the logical outcome of a behavioral analysis of treatment would be, then, for therapists to practice according to the following guidelines: 1) attempt to make the therapeutic situation in the office simulate the environment as much as possible using behavioral reenactments for assessment and behavior rehearsals during intervention; and 2) design and structure environmental interventions to increase the probability behavior learned in the here-and-now therapy setting will generalize and be supported in the environment.

Figure 9-4 is thus a schematic representation of what must happen for therapeutic interventions to be effective, starting with therapists who help clients reenact past-overt and past-covert behavior, which for present purposes I will consider interactive. Therapists who delve into past relationships, reenacting them for modification in the here and now, must make sure newly learned patterns of behavior will generalize to present covert cognitive here-and-now behavior, which must then be translated into the overt observable demonstration of new skills with the therapist and whoever else is present.

For example, consider a shy client who has reenacted a past family scene where she was constantly critized and practiced effectively confronting important introjects or parental injunctions, including the parent figures who taught them. These newly learned assertive skills could then generalize to her present-covert thinking and imagery behavior. An indication of this generalization would be evident in the new kinds of positive messages the client now gave herself, which could be seen by the way she generally talked about herself or by personifying the relevant symbols in a double chair. Next, the way she covertly treated herself would have to be further demonstrated in new overt behavior in the here and now. An example of this step might be the client's confronting her therapist when she felt she wasn't getting the support she deserved. And, of course, whether cognitive or overt behavior needs to come first is like the chicken and the egg issue. The observable demonstration of behavior could conceivably occur before a congruent cognitive skill has also been developed. At this point, the therapist and client have had to concern themselves with the generalization of behavior from the symbolic past to the here and now; but the job is still far from complete. The newly established behavior chain, finally developed, reinforced, and maintained in the artificial support system of therapy, is still relatively vulnerable to extinction outside of therapy. Subjecting it to an unpredictable and sometimes hostile environment often represents a challenge of considerable proportions. And yet this is the important task facing therapists and clients. The same general process of generalization must occur no matter from what intervention domain therapists start. Generalization of learning remains a central concern.

Each of the four therapies emphasizes treatment in some of these intervention domains more than others (*see* Figure 9-5), and thus faces unique problems of generalization from one domain to the next. In addition, limiting or essentially omitting intervention activity in one or more domains creates other problems as well. For example, Figure 9-5 suggests Ego Psychology therapists who use the transference and Corrective Emotional Experience emphasize the learning that takes place when the past is reenacted. Ego strengthening is more concerned with self-esteem and the kinds of verbal reports people make about their behavior. Ego strengthening also relates to the overt demonstration of more effective functioning in the here-and-now therapy setting. Present behavior in the environment is of course very important to Ego Psychology therapists, but generally their technology only allows them to indirectly affect those important variables. Thus, Ego Psychology is stronger in dealing with the past reenactments for assessment and modification, but weaker in directly generalizing new learning into the here and now. It is downright deficient in having a technology for supporting clients in generalizing behavior from the therapy setting to the environment.

Gestalt, on the other hand, emphasizes the here and now for intervention activity. Yet it still has the technology for bringing the past to life for modification, and then generalizing it to the here and now. Where Gestalt is really left hanging is in its systematic ability to support clients in generalizing behavior to their natural environment.

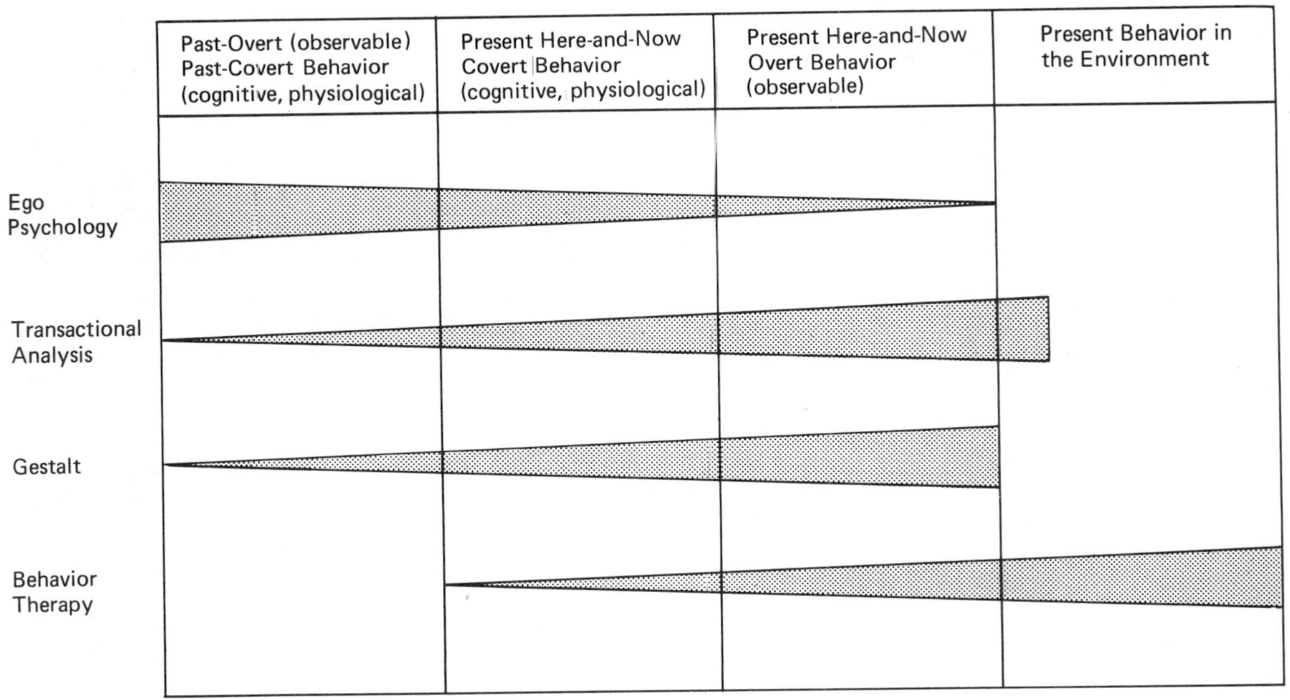

FIGURE 9-5 Emphases of Therapist Intervention Activity across Four Therapies

TA has the technology to intervene in the past and generalize the acquired learning to the here and now by combining its Parent-Adult-Child model with such techniques as the Gestalt double chair. The major emphasis of intervention activity is still ultimately on the transactions occurring in the present. In addition, TA has some limited support for clients in the environment, basically through its contracting technology.

The only therapy that has developed a comprehensive technology for directly supporting clients in developing and maintaining behavior in the enviroment is Behavior Therapy. With all the advantages this emphasis may bring, I believe behaviorists miss out on many behaviorally active interventions in their lack of technology for the other three domains, especially in past relationships and present-covert areas. And frankly, although there are behavioral interventions designed for the present-overt and covert domains, such as assertive training and systematic desensitization, respectively, the therapy misses many of the important dynamic simulations of environmental contingencies other therapies take for granted.

In general, Gestalt, Ego Psychology, and TA need to very much attend to the comprehensive technology Behavior Therapy has developed for direct intervention in the environment. On the other hand, behaviorists could benefit from using behaviorally active interventions from past events and present-covert domains, and even in making the here-and-now therapy session more dynamic.

Assertive Training

As you will recall, I suggested at the beginning of our integration journey that assertive training was one of the integrative formats by which we could compare the diverse treatment procedures of Gestalt, TA, and Ego Psychology. I believe my suggestion weathered the journey quite well. As one of the logical outcomes of all four therapies' behaviorally active interventions, we saw assertive training cloaked in very creative clothing.

Gestalt's major treatment technique, the heightening of resistance, was essentially the affirmation and further development of client's ability to say no. In fact, even at the conceptual level of the Awareness Cycle, resistances to contact with another person were defined as a major problem to eventually be resolved. Since taking responsibility for making contact always involves some assertive behavior, it should come as no surprise that assertive training was such an integral part of Gestalt therapy.

In my opinion, one of the great gifts Gestalt has given to the technology of assertive training is the personfication of symbols and the double chair. These two techniques have opened up new vistas for the assessment and modification of assertive behavior. Using double-chair reenactments, scenes from the past and complex covert symbols are made observable so that assertive skills can be learned and practiced as an approximation to dealing with the here and now, and then the environment.

Examples of how the double chair worked in assertive training abounded. For instance, at least two of the resistances to contact, introjection and retroflection, were labeled chains of behavior. The double chair allowed introjects to be confronted by using the abstract idea, the actual person from the past who taught the rule, the symbolic part of oneself that dictated the introject, or even a person in the present who was supporting it. Undoing a retroflection required directing negative feelings to someone else. Again, the double chair allowed the development of this assertive behavior in a wide variety of ways.

Boundary setting, another important task in Gestalt therapy, was directly related to assertive training. Helping people develop their ability to discriminate and share the differences between themselves was an exercise in expressing negative and positive feelings, the ability to say no, and making demands.

Transactional Analysis has also developed a unique and creative way of teaching assertive skills to clients using a combination of the Parent-Adult-Child transactions and Gestalt's double chair. Parental injunctions were confronted similarly to introjects, but this time with the metaphors of the Child confronting the Parent. Game transactions were also played out with the clients learning to say no to negative strokes while demanding positive ones.

The structured PAC interaction in double chairs represented a significant advance for covert assertive training, in my opinion. The model allowed the development of self-reinforcement and self-support, and the expression of positive feelings to the self in observable dialogues that were relatively clear and easily replicated.

A behavioral analysis of the practice of Ego Psychology suggested assertive training occurring in three areas: the Corrective Emotional Experience, ego strengthening, and the transference. As in its counterparts in Gestalt and TA, the CEE supported the initial development of assertive skills not presently evident in a client's behavioral repetoire. Ego strengthening, too, was concerned with the reinforcement of assertive behavior, although not as clearly as I would have wished. The transference relationship, as it is uniquely developed in Ego Psychology practice, was a fertile learning ground for the relatively systematic shaping of assertive skills, especially the ability to express positive or negative feelings and to say no or yes.

It is my recommendation at this point that behaviorists and Ego Psychology therapists consider integrating the use of symbols and the double chair into assertive training procedures. In addition, the Parent-Adult-Child model for covert assertive training should be seriously considered as well. Gestalt, TA, and Ego Psychology should take advantage of Behavior Therapy's much more systematic procedures for teaching assertive behavior. It would also be helpful for Gestalt and TA to more clearly specify assertive skills with clients and connect intervention procedures with the assertive behaviors they are supposed to produce.

Acceptance Training

I believe my contention that true acceptance ultimately required the ability to reduce muscle tension and relax successfully stood the test throughout the behavioral analysis. And it seemed to be a reasonably good fundamental foundation from which to view broader issues. However, it quickly became clear that the road to acceptance was generally not through systematic relaxation training as in Behavior Therapy. In fact, only Gestalt utilized any similar strategy, and that in conjunction with a more dynamic approach.

While Gestalt, TA, and Ego Psychology described their dynamic pathways to acceptance using very diverse descriptions and terminology, a behavioral analysis of all these approaches boiled down to the same basic strategy: 1) helping clients acknowledge their inability to manipulate situations and people now and in the forseeable future; and 2) helping clients structure their environment so that frustrating repeat-attempt behavior chains would be extinguished, and new, more functional acceptance behaviors reinforced. All of the strategies supported the grief process integrally related to the effects of extinction, and the resulting peace and relaxation that comes with true acceptance. As we have seen throughout our analysis, reenactments of the past and covert behavior were instrumental in bringing about acceptance. Gestalt and TA used symbols, metaphors, and the double chair; Ego Psychology used the reenactment occurring in the Corrective Emotional Experience. Behavior Therapy, on the other hand, used systematic desensitization or relaxation training alone to directly teach muscle relaxation in the face of anxiety-producing stimuli.

It is my opinion that the best approach for teaching clients acceptance behaviors would be represented by an integration of approaches from Behavior Therapy, Gestalt, and TA. I would take the behavioral description of the process, using the Laws of Behavior, and systematic relaxation training, and combine them with the more dynamic strategies from Gestalt and TA. I see nothing incompatible about teaching people to control their muscle tension while reenacting scenes representing the contingencies controlling frustrating nonfunctional repeat-attempt chains of behavior. Gestalt makes some limited attempts to do this, but could use the technology from Behavior Therapy to good advantage. TA already incorporates the idea that reinforcement contingencies control nonacceptance behavior.

Of course, a specific treatment procedure needs to be worked out concerning how this integration would take place, but I imagine it would include relaxation training and possibly a more dynamic form of systematic desensitization; the personification of symbols and the double chair; heightening techniques; and some of the dynamics of the Parent, Adult, and Child. Combining relaxation training with the ability to differentially reinforce acceptance behaviors represents a true integration of respondent and operant techniques. Since the ultimate control of all behavior probably involves the principles of respondent and operant conditioning, the development of therapeutic strategies utilizing treatment techniques from both domains just makes good sense.

A Summary of Behaviorally Active Interventions

Table 9-3 is a listing of what I considered behaviorally active interventions. These judgments were based on the analyses of how each intervention respected the Laws of Respondent and Operant Conditioning and incorporated at least some of

TABLE 9-3 A Summary of Behaviorally Active Interventions from Four Therapies

BEHAVIOR THERAPY	GESTALT	TRANSACTIONAL ANALYSIS	EGO PSYCHOLOGY
Contingency contracting	Personification of	Double Chair	Ego Strengthing
Reinforcement	Symbols	Contracting	Insight
Extinction	Double Chair	"Stoppers"	Transference
Punishment	Heightening	Positive Stroking	Corrective Emo-
Shaping	Resistances	Withdrawal of	tional Exper-
Modeling	Heightening	Negative Strokes	ence
Behavioral Rehearsal	Feelings	Language Manipu-	
Assertive Training	Dreamwork	lation	
Relaxation Training	Polarities	Transaction and	
Systematic Desensitization	Resistance to contact	game Manipula-	
Stimulus Control Procedures	Manipulations	tions	
Artificial Reinforcement			
Systems			
Behavior Chain			
Manipulations			

the eight basic behaviorally active elements: reinforcement, extinction, punishment, shaping, chaining, stimulus control, modeling, and behavioral rehearsal. Some of these treatment labels seemed to be techniques, and some, more complex procedures. We found them frequently related, either by their being used in conjunction with one another, or one the part of another.

What can we say, looking at the interventions together at one time? First, it was very difficult in many cases to distinguished between concepts and what therapists actually did to bring their respectives theories to life. Clearly, psychotherapy needs to more carefully delineate the difference between what therapists think and what they do, in very behaviorally specific terms. Second, there already seems to be significant integration of therapist intervention behaviors, especially between Gestalt and TA, and to some extent Ego Psychology as well. TA has incorporated many important Gestalt techniques into its practice, and one shouldn't be surprised to symbolically see a Parent nurturing a Child in Gestalt. Transference, insight, and behavioral reenactments also seemed to be used in one way or another throughout therapy.

In summary, I believe I was able to establish my original contentions. It could be demonstrated that many of the major interventions from Gestalt, TA, and Ego Psychology utilized the basic behaviorally active elements and followed the Laws of Behavior, and were thus viable, even preferable in some cases, for the modification of behavior. The behavioral approach turned out to be a reasonably good therapeutic Rosetta Stone for developing an integrative foundation across four apparently diverse therapies.

The question of which interventions therapists choose to integrate into their work will be based on many factors, including their experience, training, theoretical biases, and a sincere desire to provide the most effective therapy for their clients.

Clearly, I have my own subjective preferences, which by now you should have ascertained. It is probably not possible to make all behaviorally active interventions interchangeable between theory bases. However, I believe that I have laid a reasonable foundation for therapists to attempt to integrate many more of these techniques and procedures into their practices, no matter with which theory-related philosopy of human behavior they are comfortable. In many cases, I feel integration is imperative, such as in defining practice and outcome in behaviorally specific terms, and identifying interventions that support clients' attempts to generalize behavior from the office to the environment. It is evident to me that Behavior Therapy, Gestalt, TA, and Ego Psychology therapists have important behaviorally active assessment and intervention behaviors to share with one another that fill the serious gaps each therapy leaves in its theory and practice base. Let us proceed to integrate the practice of psychotherapy with due caution, always striving for empirically founded integrative foundations; but let us proceed.

APPENDIX

B.A.S.E.S. Behaviorally Active Screening Exercise Strategies

For those of you with some interest in examining the potential behavioral activity of your practice interventions, especially therapists who have had very little if any behavioral training, I would suggest two possible strategies: 1) the AB single organism experimental design; and 2) the retroactive after-the-fact clinical design.

The AB single organism design implies that you have a predetermined hypothesis of what will happen before you do it. You have some measure of client behavior levels before the intervention—that is, the "A" of the AB. You take a measure of what the behavior level is after intervention—the "B." Unless you are doing research, it is not necessary that you actually count specific behaviors, but you should have clear overt behavioral indicators of what happened before and after. Even in the best of circumstances, you cannot be too sure that your intervention influenced a change in client behavior. There are too many placebo effects in psychotherapy. But at least by documenting your hypothesis concerning controlling conditions and what you plan to do before the fact, you are better able to infer a causal relationship between intervention and outcome.

The second strategy for assessing the behavioral activity of intervention is the clinical retroactive design. This is used after the fact by reviewing as carefully as possible what you did in light of what happened. It is commonly used during supervision in trying to understand what caused client behavior changes when the original intervention hypothesis was apparently not borne out or something inexplicable happened.

One or both of these intervention assessment strategies need to be applied to therapist behavior in each treatment session and for the whole therapeutic experience. In addition, attention needs to be paid to connecting what actually happened in therapy to how the client behaves in the environment. I have listed a series of exercises you might consider for each of these three areas, regardless of which intervention assessment strategy you use. They are certainly not exhaustive but are designed to help you make causal connections between what you did that was behaviorally active, and what happened. In addition, these exercises should support you in experimenting with integrating behaviorally active interventions from one of the therapies I have described in this book into the kind of therapy you normally do.

I. For Each Session.

1. Describe what happened and what you did during the session using behaviorally specific terms. Imagine you are a video tape player. In fact, if one is available, you should consider using it. The ability to describe events using behaviorally specific terms is a skill whose difficulty should not be minimized.
2. If you noticed any significant behavior change in either you or the client during the session that departed from what you consider your normal interactional pattern with that client, emphasize a behaviorally specific before, during, and after analysis around that period.
3. Assuming no verbal or overt behavior changed during the session that was different from the normal pattern, try to put the interactions into contingency form and assess what you might be doing to reinforce ongoing client behavior.
4. If behavior did change either in a desired or undesirable direction, describe what the antecedent conditions were, such as requests or some relationship dynamic, and then what you did to reinforce, punish, or attempt to extinguish the behavior after it occurred.
5. Try to put intervention labels on what you did no matter from what therapy they originate. At the very least you should be able to use labels from the behavior approach. Assess the degree to which your interpretation of what affected client behavior conforms to the Laws of Behavior.
6. If possible, summarize the previous five issues with your client toward the end of the session. It never fails to amaze me how clients and therapists reciprocally interpret each other's behavior differently.

II. For the Whole Therapy Experience:

Actually, the next part of the behaviorally active screening exercise can be done at any time after the initial series of therapy sessions are over.

1. Describe what the client is doing now during the therapy sessions that is different from previous sessions. What behavior have you been performing that reinforced this new behavior and extinguished the old behavior pattern?
2. Identify the steps, approximations, the client went through to reach the present level of responding and specifically what you did to reinforce each approximation.

3. Attempt to put a label on the procedure you used, no matter from what therapy. Does your interpretation of what you did conform to the Laws of Behavior?

4. Share your conclusions with your client, if possible.

III. For the Environment:

1. Identify what client behaviors are changing in the environment. Be very behaviorally specific.

2. By what process do you find out about environmental changes? Can you trust client verbal reports? This is an important issue across all therapies. It is not always so much a question of trust as it is one of interpretation.

3. Assuming behavior is changing in the environment, describe in behaviorally specific terms what the client learned in therapy that would increase the probability he or she would be reinforced by others for new behavior patterns. Then describe what you did to either structure that this would happen or how you taught the skills to the client so that he could do it for himself.

4. Label the procedure you used and assess whether or not it conforms to the Laws of Behavior.

The guidelines I have suggested here are essentially those I used to do the behavioral analyses in this book. They should give you a good start in assessing the behavioral activity of the interventions you presently use in your clinical practice and in integrating new ones.

BIBLIOGRAPHY AND REFERENCES

AYLLON, T. and N. AYRIN, *The Token Economy*. New York: Appleton-Century-Crofts, 1968.

BANDURA, A. *Principles of Behavior Modification*. New York: Holt, Rinehart, and Winston, 1969.

BARNES, G. (ed.). *TA After Berne: Teachings of Three TA Schools*. New York: Harper's College Press, 1977.

BERNE, E. *Games People Play*. New York: Random House, 1964.

———. *Transactional Analysis in Psychotherapy*. New York: Grove Press, 1961.

BLANCK, G., and R. BLANCK, *Ego Psychology: Theory and Practice*. New York: Columbia University Press, 1974.

BROWN, M., and S. WOLLAMS, *TA: The Total Handbook of Transactional Analysis*. Englewood Cliffs, N.J.: Prentice-Hall, 1979.

DOLLARD, J., and N. MILLER, *Personality and Psychotherapy*. New York: McGraw-Hill, 1950.

FAGAN, J., and I. L. SHEPHERD, (eds.). *Gestalt Therapy Now*. New York: Harper & Row, 1970.

FRANKEL, A. J. "Beyond the Simple Functional Analysis—The Chain: A Family Therapy Case Study." *Behavior Therapy*. 1975, 6, 254-260.

FREUD, S. *An Outline of Psycho-Analysis*. (revised and translated by J. Strachey). New York: W. W. Norton & Co., Inc., 1969.

———. *The Ego and the Id*. (revised by J. Strachey). New York: W. W. Norton & Co., Inc., 1962.

GOLDSTEIN, A. P., K. HELLER, and L. B. SECHREST, *Psychotherapy and the Psychology of Behavior Change*. New York: John Wiley, 1966.

GOULDING, R. L., and M. M. GOULDING, *Power Is in the Patient*. San Francisco: TA Press, 1979.

HARRIS, T. A. *I'm OK–You're OK*. New York: Harper & Row, 1969.

HARTMANN, H. *Ego Psychology and the Problem of Adaptation*. New York: International University Press, 1958.

——. *Essays on Ego Psychology*. New York: International University Press, 1964.

HATCHER, C., and P. HIMELSTEIN, (eds.). *The Handbook of Gestalt Theory*. New York: Jason Aronson, 1976.

HOLLIS, F. *Casework—A Psychosocial Therapy*. New York: Random House, 1972.

JAMES, M., and D. JONGEWARD, *Born to Win*. Reading Mass.: Addison-Wesley, 1971.

JOSSELYN, I. *Psychosocial Development of Children*. New York: Family Service Association of American, 1977.

KARPMAN, S. B. "Fairy Tales and Script Drama Analysis." *Transactional Analysis Bulletin*, April 1968, VII, 26, 39-43.

KEMPLER, W. *Principles of Gestalt Family Therapy*. Salt Lake City: Desert Press, 1974.

LAZARUS, A. A. *Behavior Therapy and Beyond*. New York: McGraw-Hall, 1971.

——. *Multi-Modal Behavior Therapy*. New York: Springer Publishing Co., 1976.

MAHONEY, M. J. *Cognition and Behavior Modification*. Cambridge, Mass.: Ballinger, 1974.

MEICHENBAUM, D. H. *Cognitive Behavior Modification: An Integrative Approach*. New York: Plenum, 1977.

MILLENSON, J. R. *Principles of Behavior Analysis*. New York: Macmillan, 1967.

PARAD, H. J., and R. R. MILLER, (eds.). *Ego Oriented Casework*. New York: Family Service Association of America, 1963.

PERLMAN, H. H. *Social Casework—A Problem-Solving Process*. Chicago: University of Chicago Press, 1957.

PERLS, F. S. *Ego Hunger and Aggression*. New York: Vintage Books, 1969.

——. *Gestalt Therapy Verbatim*. New York: Bantam, 1969.

POLANSKY, N. A. *Ego Psychology and Communication: Theory for the Interview*. New York: Atherton, 1971.

POLSTER, E., and P. POLSTER, *Gestalt Therapy Integrated*. New York: Brunner/Mazel, 1973.

SCHIFF, J. I., and B. DAY, *All My Children*. New York: Jove Publications, 1977.

SCHWARTZ, A., and I. GOLDIAMOND, *Social Casework—A Behavior Approach*. New York: Columbia University Press, 1975.

SHAFFER, J. B. P., and M. D. GALINSKY, *Models of Group Therapy and Sensitivity Training*. Englewood Cliffs, N.J.: Prentice-Hall, 1974.

SHEPARD, M. *Fritz*. Sagaponack, N.Y.: Second Chance Press, 1980.

SIMKIN, J. S. *Gestalt Theory Mini-Lectures*. Millbrae, Calif.: Celestial Arts Publishing Co., 1976.

SKINNER, B. F. *Beyond Freedom and Dignity*. New York: Knopf, 1971.

——. *Contingencies of Reinforcement*. New York: Appleton-Century-Crofts, 1969.

——. *Verbal Behavior*. New York: Appleton-Century-Crofts, 1957.

——. *Walden Two*. New York: Macmillan, 1962 (c1948).

SLOAN, R. B. *et al. Psychotherapy Versus Behavior Therapy*. Cambridge, Mass.: Harvard University Press, 1975.

SMITH, E. W. L. (ed.) *The Growing Edge of Gestalt Therapy*. New York: Brunner/Mazel, 1976.

STEERE, D. A. *Bodily Expressions in Psychotherapy*. New York: Brunner/Mazel, 1983.

STEINER, C. *Scripts People Live: TA of Life Scripts*. New York: Grove Press, 1974.

SUNDEL, M., and S. S. SUNDEL, *Behavior Modification in the Human Services.* New York: John Wiley, 1982.

THARP, R. G., and R. J. WETZEL, *Behavior Modification in the Natural Environment.* New York: Academic Press, 1969.

ULLMAN, L. P., and L. KRASNER, *A Psychological Approach to Abnormal Behavior.* Englewood Cliffs, N.J.: Prentice-Hall, 1969.

WACHTEL, P. *Psychoanalysis and Behavior Therapy : Toward an Integration.* New York: Basic Books, 1977.

WANN, T. W. (ed.). *Behaviorism and Phenomenology.* Chicago: University of Chicago Press, 1964.

WATSON, D. L., and R. G. THARP, *Self-Directed Behavior.* Monterey, Calif.: Brooks/Cole, 1972.

WENRICH, W. W., H. H. DAWLEY, and D. A. GENERAL, *Self-Directed Systematic Desensitization.* Kalamazoo, Mich.: Behavior delia, 1976.

WHALEY, D. L., and R. W. MALOTT, *Elementary Principles of Behavior.* New York: Appleton-Century-Crofts, 1971.

WOLPE, J. *The Practice of Behavior Therapy.* Elmsford, N.Y.: Pergamon Press, 1969.

YALOM, I. D. *The Theory and Practice of Group Psychotherapy.* New York: Basic Books, 1975.

ZINKER, J. *Creative Process in Gestalt Therapy.* New York: Brunner/Mazel, 1977.

INDEX

Self-image/self-esteem, 33, 118, 149, 182, 219
Self-reinforcement, 39, 195, 206, 227
Self-support, 49, 78, 168-69, 170, 177, 194, 222, 227
Sexual nonperformance, 8
Shadow side, 74
Shaping, 227, 229
  in Behavior Therapy, 133
  definition, 19
  in Ego Psychology, 196-97, 198, 199, 205
  in Gestalt, 151
  problems in shaping, 21
  procedure, 19, 21
  in TA, 182, 187
Single organism research designs, 134
Skinner, B. F., 6, 41, 128
Smoking, 8
Snowball-Avalanche effect, 26, 195, 219
Socialization into TA, 98, 173, 174
Stimulous control, 217, 219, 220, 223, 229
  in Behavior Therapy, 133
  definition, 26
  in Ego Psychology, 201, 202
  in TA, 184
Stoppers, 93, 185
Strokes, 175-76, 184, 187, 227
  negative, 86, 180, 186, 219
  positive, 86, 183, 219
Subconscious, 138, 214
Subliminal stimuli, 139
Successive approximation, 19-21, 134, 150, 152, 186, 187, 194, 195, 198, 199
Suicide, 60
Superego, 107, 193, 207
  analysis, 190
  definition, 107
Suppression, 197
Symbols, 164, 166, 169-71, 176, 180, 185-86, 188, 197, 198, 216, 217, 222, 223, 224

Symbols (cont.)
  analysis, 144-47
Sympathy, 151
Symptom substitution, 160, 220
  definition, 126
Systematic desensitization, 130, 169, 221, 223
  procedure, 7

Termination, 39, 74, 102, 125
Theme development, 70, 141, 143, 193
Time-out from reinforcement, 14
Time structuring, 87-88, 175-76
Transaction:
  analysis, 176-178
  complementary, 86, 177
  crossed, 87
  definition, 86
Transactional analysis, 86, 92, 98, 173, 174, 213
Transference, 39, 75, 103, 125, 126,
  analysis, 168, 199-205

Unconditioned response, 6
Unconditioned stimuli, 6
Unconscious, 106, 108, 164, 190, 191
  analysis, 138
  definition, 138
Unfinished business, 76, 131, 142, 151, 169, 171, 197, 198, 210
  analysis, 137
  definition, 43

Verbal Therapies, 127
Visceral feedback, 152

Warm fuzzies, 85, 186
Weight loss, 8

Yoga, 169